AMIENS

DAWN OF VICTORY

JAMES MCWILLIAMS
and R. JAMES STEEL

DUNDURN PRESS
TORONTO · OXFORD

Design: Jennifer Scott
Printer: Webcom

Canadian Cataloguing in Publication Data

McWilliams, James L.
    Amiens: dawn of victory

Includes bibliographical references and index.
ISBN 1-55002-342-X

1. Amiens, Battle of, 1918. I. Steel, R. J. II. Title.

D545.A56M32 2000   940.4'35   C00-931876-3

1   2   3   4   5   05   04   03   02   01

THE CANADA COUNCIL | LE CONSEIL DES ARTS
FOR THE ARTS | DU CANADA
SINCE 1957 | DEPUIS 1957

Canada

ONTARIO ARTS COUNCIL
CONSEIL DES ARTS DE L'ONTARIO

We acknowledge the support of the *Canada Council for the Arts* and the *Ontario Arts Council* for our publishing program. We also acknowledge the financial support of the *Government of Canada* through the *Book Publishing Industry Development Program, The Association for the Export of Canadian Books,* and the *Government of Ontario* through the *Ontario Book Publishers Tax Credit* program.

All photographs courtesy of National Archives of Canada.

Care has been taken to trace the ownership of copyright material used in this book. The author and the publisher welcome any information enabling them to rectify any references or credit in subsequent editions.

                                                              J. Kirk Howard, President

Printed and bound in Canada.⊛
Printed on recycled paper.

www.dundurn.com

Dundurn Press
8 Market Street
Suite 200
Toronto, Ontario, Canada
M5E 1M6

Dundurn Press
73 Lime Walk
Headington, Oxford,
England
OX3 7AD

Dundurn Press
2250 Military Road
Tonawanda NY
U.S.A. 14150

TABLE OF CONTENTS

PRELUDE
The Domart Bridge

Corporal Harry Brice of the Canadian Engineers lay flat on the Domart Bridge as machine-gun bullets whined inches above him in the darkness. Evidently the German sentry had traversed the gun slightly, for the bullets began sparking off the brick parapets on each side of him. Brice had had a premonition and feared these screaming ricochets more than the regular bursts that droned above him. It was midnight, Saturday, August 3, 1918, and Harry Brice felt very far from his beloved Saskatchewan. The Domart Bridge he hugged crossed the marshy River Luce a few miles east of Amiens on the Western Front.

A lot had happened since Brice and his comrades were withdrawn from the Canadian line near Arras two days ago. The seven-man squad had been specially trained "to be used anywhere for anything." Every man could handle a variety of German weapons or dismantle a booby trap, and they even carried their own Lewis machine gun with them. Nevertheless, when they had been ordered to remove all badges and identification and sent off to a railway station in rear of the line they, had all been taken by surprise.

At the station they had watched a troop train pull out with a Canadian infantry battalion heading north — "to Ypres" — that was the scuttlebutt now spreading like wildfire through the Canadian Corps. Consequently, the seven sappers had felt somewhat nonplussed when they were given a special code number and quietly bundled onto a train heading *south* — away from Ypres. Just as mysteriously they had next been taken from the train to Fourth Army Headquarters where their own officers materialized and handed Brice a packet of sealed orders. Those orders were the reason why Corporal Harry Brice and two sappers now lay on the Domart Bridge in no man's land a few inches beneath a stream of German machine-gun bullets.

The gun ceased firing. It was obviously fixed there for night firing and some sentry had been ordered to loose off the occasional burst while patrolling his beat, so things should be quiet for the next few minutes. Brice and his men set to work with picks digging a shallow trench across the old brick bridge. They were looking for the detonator wire for a series of charges secreted someplace on the bridge. The picks sent occasional sparks flying — and worse — shattered the silence of the night. Brice stopped the work and sent one of the men back to the swamp that surrounded the bridge. Soon the man returned with a pail full of thick, sloppy mud. This they spread over their working surface. Now the sounds were muffled, and no longer did the tell-tale sparks dart out with each blow. The backbreaking work continued through the early morning hours under intermittent machine-gun fire. At three o'clock when the dispatch rider appeared at their "bivvy" back in a cellar in Domart, Brice was able to give him his first written report to take back — the first charge had been located and removed.

Stealthily, as light began to streak the eastern sky, Corporal Brice returned alone to his hideout under the mysterious bridge. Sheltered by four-foot bulrushes, he had to lie on his back in the mud studying its structure. As darkness gave way to a pale, watery daylight, Brice scanned the floor and underpinnings from one end to another. Except for a spot on the northern side where five bricks were missing, the whole looked secure. Snipers were active in the area so his return journey had to be made along a two-foot wide path the sappers had cleared through the bulrushes.

Brice's squad had discovered the name of their village only by accident, but where Domart was they didn't know. The charge they had discovered was French, suggesting that this bridge was in the French portion of the front. Therefore they must be well south of Arras. But the outpost they had relieved had been held by Australians — which only deepened the mystery. Why were they here, all alone in the middle of no man's land?

The sealed orders gave Brice's squad four tasks: (1) remove three charges on the bridge — no mention was made of the type of charges to look for, let alone their locations; (2) examine the bridge for structural defects; (3) find a suitable place to conceal the building material that would be sent up to reinforce the bridge; and (4) submit a report at 03:00 every morning by means of a dispatch rider who would be sent for that purpose.

PRELUDE

Reading between the lines of their sealed orders, Harry Brice reasoned that the Allies planned to use this bridge to cross the Luce, marshy and almost thirty feet wide at this point. Trucks or artillery would need a bridge to cross the river, and the Domart Bridge was ideal — sturdy and wide. The problem was that the Germans had ranged in on the vital crossing, and if one of their shells set off even one of the French charges the bridge would be destroyed. For that reason this special squad had been given the job of secretly removing the charges — at least that's how Brice had reasoned it.

On succeeding nights their work progressed. Sunday night the large stack of thirty-foot iron rails and hardwood planks arrived for members of the squad to hide. This material, regularly employed by the Canadian Corps to make their famous "corduroy roads," was soon hidden in a swampy area covered with long marsh grass. Over each pile they laid camouflage nets — chicken-wire woven with strips of coloured cloth.

The same night Brice and two sappers located and removed the second charge. On Monday night they ran into much heavier machine-gun fire on the bridge. Some new sentry on the German side was firing the gun at irregular intervals. Although there were no serious casualties, Harry was hit on the shoulder by a ricochet. His premonition had come true. He was lucky, and crawled back from the bridge with only a painful bruise, but the squad had failed to find the third charge. On the following night, despite his wound and the sentry across the river, Brice and his men discovered and removed the third charge. Their task was completed!

Consequently, on Wednesday night Corporal Brice and his squad stood-to as a Lewis-gun crew guarding their precious bridge. They were just about out of supplies and realized that their long isolation was soon to end. "It's going to happen one of these mornings," Harry assured his men. "There's going to be a big breakthrough here. You can tell by what's going on. You've seen all the stuff hidden there — all those ammunition stores and those guns camouflaged."

Now shortly before dawn on Thursday, the sappers noted an unusual sound that penetrated the white fog blanketing the low-lying areas. "We heard one of our aeroplanes going backwards and forwards as if he was lost," Brice recalled years later. "Something's going on here boys, something's — Listen!" As the droning of the plane receded northward another more ominous sound could be detected. It came from close behind them on the Amiens-Roye Road — the muffled roar of engines slowly turning over mingled with a subdued clanking. Brice was sure he knew what it meant, but he jumped to his feet and followed the parapet of the road back through the dense fog that shrouded everything. In a few moments he could distinguish a threatening silhouette — a tank. Behind it in the fog an endless file of the monsters disappeared in the mist. It was moments before dawn on the eighth of August, 1918 — the Dawn of Victory.

PART I

THE MAIN OFFENSIVE CAMPAIGN

"The 1st July 1919[1] should be taken as the date by which all preparations are to be completed for the opening of the main offensive campaign."
Chief of the Imperial General Staff,
Sir Henry Wilson, 25 July, 1918
"British Military Policy 1918-19"
(Memorandum issued by the Imperial General Staff)[2]

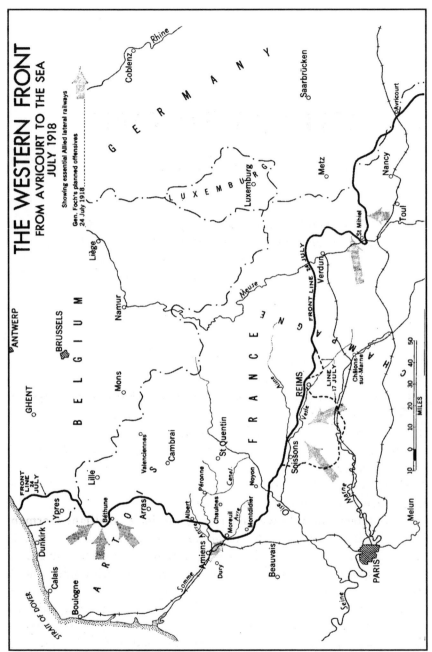

THE WESTERN FRONT
FROM AVRICOURT TO THE SEA
JULY 1918

Showing essential Allied lateral railways

Gen. Foch's planned offensives
24 July 1918.

From Col. G.W.L. *Nicholson, Canadian Expeditionary Force 1914-1919*. Ottawa, Queen's Printer, 1962, p. 387.
Courtesy of Minister of Public Works and Government Services, Canada

CHAPTER ONE

THE PLAN

"The main thing is to always have a plan; if it is not the best plan, it is, at least better than no plan at all."
Lieutenant-General John Monash
commanding the Australian Corps[3]

Would the dawn of victory never come? By 1918, four hideous years of darkness had brought neither side the longed-for success. Casualties on both sides had mounted astronomically while the horrors of war seemed to multiply with every new development. The tide had appeared to turn on several occasions when one side or the other had achieved a victory that its press had immediately trumpeted as "decisive." Yet nothing seemed to come of these successes; each had become merely an ebb or a flow in the tides of war.

The latest example was a series of tactically brilliant German offensives that ultimately failed to produce any strategic result. On the morning of March 21 the Germans achieved an absolutely stunning surprise against the unsuspecting British Third and Fifth armies with a stupendous bombardment that wiped out entire battalions within moments. German "storm troopers" then advanced into the stricken sectors, not in the usual waves, but in small parties using infiltration tactics. Aided as they were by the incredible good luck of a dense fog, these new tactics of penetration achieved results beyond the wildest dreams of their devisors. Second-line battalions were overrun before they even knew the attack had commenced.

> The front crumbled like plaster; each probe loosened a little more for its neighbours; soon the Germans achieved the cherished aim of so many attacks of the war — they reached the gunline. On 21 March the British Fifth Army lost 383 guns; by midnight on the 22nd the Third Army had lost 150. The British line was breached; the Germans poured through. It was no longer a question of assault; it was pursuit.[4]

Nevertheless, the final results were disappointing. The toughness of the surviving British troops proved astonishing as they continued to resist in the most hopeless circumstances, while the poorly fed German infantry, entering a land of plenty, succumbed to the temptation of looting and failed to pursue effectively. Indeed, there was no real provision for pursuit on the part of the German High Command. They possessed no tank force worthy of the name, and had no cavalry ready to exploit their breakthrough.

Between March and July, four similar hammer-blows drove other portions of the Allied line back many miles but with equally barren strategic results. The offensives produced stalemate rather than checkmate.

As July and the fourth anniversary of the war loomed closer, the Allies too found themselves in serious difficulties. Morale had slipped at home. Certainly, if less dynamic leaders than Clemenceau and Lloyd George had been in charge, it was quite possible that neither France nor Britain would have found the strength to go on. For many citizens the problem had become whether it would be possible to hang on long enough for the United States to save the situation. The "Yanks" could not reach their peak before the summer of 1920, so the end seemed terribly far off. The most recent evaluation by the new Chief of the Imperial General Staff, Sir Henry Wilson, projected July 1, **1919**, as the date when preparations for the "main offensive campaign" should be completed. Only by this date did he anticipate that a great enough numerical superiority would be assembled to ensure success. Wilson considered himself an optimist, for he advised, "it would be unwise to defer the attempt to gain a decisive victory until 1920."[5]

The stunning German successes had forced the Allies to at last name a supreme commander to co-ordinate not only their actions but their dwindling reserves. This suggestion had come from Sir Douglas Haig, the Commander-in-Chief of all British Empire troops on the Western Front. His nominee was Ferdinand Foch, a French general with an unconquerable will to win. Foch had often proven to be impractical and unrealistic despite the stirring orders he issued, and he often talked in vague parables rather than coming to grips with troublesome facts. Nevertheless, his spirit and optimism were what was needed in those grim days. A veteran of the Franco-Prussian War of 1870-71, Foch was best known for having been a Professor of Strategy at the *Ecôle de Guerre* before the war. Here his emphasis on *élan* over material had imprinted itself upon an entire generation. After the war had broken out in 1914 — as Foch had predicted it would — he rose through the ranks to become Generalissimo on March 26, 1918, owing responsibility directly to both the French and the British governments, and eventually to the United States government. His direct subordinates were General Henri Pétain, Commander-in-Chief of the French Army, General John J. "Black Jack" Pershing of the American Expeditionary Force, and Haig, commanding the British forces.

Sir Douglas Haig was of an entirely different mould. This Scots cavalryman was almost colourless and seemed devoid of emotion. He had first seen action in Kitchener's Nile Expedition and later won praise for his many roles during the Boer War. Despite rising rapidly through the ranks, he was not highly respected by his peers. Brigadier-General Sir James Edmonds, the British Official Historian, later said of Haig, "He really was above the — or rather below the average in stupidity."[285] Haig's famous comment in a minute to the War Council on April 14, 1915, gives insight into his mind-set: "The machine-gun is a much over-rated weapon, and two per battalion is more than sufficient." Enormous casualties had been the chief product of Haig's tenure as Commander-in-Chief. Tragic disasters such as The Somme and Passchendaele will forever be linked with him, as were missed opportunities like Vimy Ridge and Cambrai. After three years of his strategy of attrition — best described as "reciprocal slaughter" — few of his soldiers felt confidence in their Commander-in-Chief.

The summer of 1918 was a desperate one for the Allies. Their "united front" was much less united than it appeared to the public. The political leaders of both nations, each with his own plan to achieve victory, were continually embroiled in petty bickering. Their diaries reveal distrust and back-biting at every level and upon every subject. The military leadership was no less acrimonious, and every failure caused a search for scapegoats. Both commanders-in-chief were on shaky ground. Although Lloyd George's famous description of Haig as "brilliant — to the top of his boots" came after the war, it illustrated his contempt for the man commanding his nation's troops. General Henri-Philippe Pétain, Commander-in-Chief of the French Army, despite his great victory on the Marne that July, watched with apprehension as his replacement, General Guillaumat, was brought from the

Army of the Orient to wait in the wings. The "united front" was a constantly bickering, perpetually nervous collection of generals and politicians, each alternately watching his back or taking a swipe at his colleagues while absorbing the blows of their common enemy.

In later years there was some controversy over who first proposed the operation that became known as the Battle of Amiens. Foch, the Supreme Commander; Haig, the British Commander; Rawlinson, commanding the Fourth Army; and Monash, the Australian Corps Commander — all have taken credit for the scheme. It is probable that the truth will never be known because the sequence of events is not clear.

On May 16 Haig had received from Foch a request to prepare plans for a big offensive. Sir Douglas agreed to the request but stressed the need for secrecy. The next day Haig visited Rawlinson and gave him orders to investigate the possibility of attacking Villers-Bretonneux to the east of Amiens. These early discussions were to involve British forces in a supporting role co-operating with the French First Army in its planned thrust through Montdidier. By May 26 orders were issued to prepare this operation for mid-June, but the very next day the long-expected German offensive broke upon the French in Champagne. The Amiens plan was consequently brushed aside and almost forgotten in the tide of disasters that engulfed the French Army.

While the French fought on to stem Ludendorff's offensive, an Australian and two British generals were independently looking at altered versions of the aborted operation. The Australian was John Monash, a former consulting engineer from Melbourne, but now the Lieutenant-General commanding the Australian Corps. Born of German-Jewish parents and brought up in West Melbourne, Monash had through sheer ability and unbounded determination propelled himself over adversity to success in civil life. Then came the war, and Monash arrived in Gallipoli early in 1915 commanding the 4th Infantry Brigade. Now a little over three years later, he had been appointed Corps Commander. "M [Monash] is a most thorough and capable commander who thinks out every detail of any operation and leaves nothing to chance," wrote Haig in his diary on July 1.[6] This was praise indeed from Sir Douglas, who two years earlier had written of the Australians, "Some of their divisional Generals are so ignorant and (like many Colonials) so conceited, that they cannot be trusted to work out unaided the plans of attack."[7] Since then several new Australian divisional generals had also been appointed, which may have relieved Haig somewhat.

John Monash's years of business experience had convinced him "to deal with every task and every situation on the basis of simple business propositions, differing in no way from the problems of civil life, except that they are governed by special technique. The main thing is to always to have a plan, if it is not the best plan, it is, at least better than no plan at all."[8] He believed that it was not the infantryman's job to struggle against enormous odds. Instead, every mechanical resource was to be employed to enable the infantry "to advance with as little impediment as possible, to be relieved as far as possible of the obligation to fight their way forward, to march resolutely, regardless of the din and tumult of battle, to the appointed goal, and there to hold and defend the territory gained; and to gather, in the form of prisoners, guns and stores, the fruits of victory."[9] Monash's theory was considered radical — almost heretical — by the majority of cavalry generals who had risen to command on the Western Front and who still believed the infantry's role was to slog through hell to breach the enemy line, thus enabling the cavalry to sweep on to a glorious victory.

Monash had on July 4 put his theories to the test in a brilliantly conceived small-scale attack at Hamel. Using both Australian and American troops, he had won a resounding victory with small losses. At General Rawlinson's insistence the Australians had employed British tank forces extensively with spectacular results. Now Monash was anxious to try the same thing again but on a much larger scale and with much deeper penetration.

Sometime after Hamel, Monash met with Rawlinson and pressed his ideas, boldly stating that on a two-divisional front the Australians could advance up to five miles. "'Couldn't you go farther?' asked Rawlinson. 'If you gave me safe support on my right flank,' was the reply. Rawlinson suggested several corps for this purpose, but Monash shook his head until the army commander mentioned 'the Canadians.' 'Monash leapt at this suggestion.'"[10]

Meanwhile Rawlinson had also been considering a revival of the proposed mid-June offensive. It is not certain how far these plans had progressed before his meeting with Monash, but it is known that around the same time he also met with Haig at Beaurepaire. Apparently Haig too had been pondering a similar operation although Rawlinson broached the subject first. The latter outlined a plan whereby his Fourth Army, keeping its arrangements secret, would thrust south of the River Luce and break through to the Old Outer Defence Line of Amiens — if Haig would give him the Canadian Corps. Haig liked the idea and ordered Rawlinson to continue work on the plan. However, he placed two serious conditions on the plan: one had to do with the idea of extending the British front south of the River Luce. This he could agree to only if it were temporary. Secondly, Haig did not intend to take the offensive until the German reserves — over twenty divisions under Crown Prince Rupprecht — had been drawn away to some other sector.

Previous to this meeting, Haig had received on July 12 another proposal from Foch, still eager to launch his long-cherished offensive. The latter suggested a British offensive in Flanders between Rebecq and Festubert. But Sir Douglas had been thinking along the same lines as his subordinate, Rawlinson. Consequently, on July 17 he turned down the Supreme Commander's proposal and advanced the following project:

> The operation which to my mind is of the greatest importance, and which I suggest to you should be carried out as early as possible, is to advance the allied front east and south-east of Amiens so as to disentangle that town and the railway line. This can be carried out by a combined French and British operation, the French attacking south of Moreuil and the British north of the River Luce.[11]

The next day was July 18, the date of the French counterattack on the Marne. Because of their remarkable success the situation had altered drastically by the time Foch replied to Haig on July 20. He urged Haig to seize the opportunity to hit the Germans, "without delay against the parts of the front that are simply held by troops of occupation." The Generalissimo suggested several possible offensives, stressing the Amiens plan as one that could be profitable. Foch also mentioned that General Eugene Debeney of the First French Army had been working on a plan of his own, and suggested that Debeney and Rawlinson should confer at once. Haig did not immediately follow up the last recommendation but delayed action until he met with Foch on the 24th.

There followed a series of conferences that developed the scheme to its final form. The first was called by Rawlinson, the commander of the British Fourth Army, which occupied the Amiens sector. Sir Henry Rawlinson was an old hand. He had served with Lord Roberts in India and with Kitchener in the Sudan. During the Boer War he had been present at the Siege of Ladysmith and later commanded a mobile column. Throughout World War I he had served in various exalted positions until being given command of the shattered Fifth Army after the March disasters. A new commander and his staff — which carried with it a new name — would erase unhappy memories, it was hoped, so the Fifth was rebuilt by Rawlinson and renamed the Fourth Army. Although Rawlinson had earned from his peers the nickname, "Rawly the Fox," Haig, in a letter to Lady Haig, referred to him as "a humbug."

To Rawlinson's conference of July 21 came two strangely contrasting corps commanders — Monash, the Australian, and Currie, the Canadian. Both were rank amateurs in terms of experience. John Monash, as has been mentioned, began the war as a successful consulting engineer and scholar. Arthur Currie, unfortunately, had not shone in civilian life. Born in the small town of Napperton, Ontario he went west to Vancouver where he was, in order, a school teacher, an insurance salesman, and a real estate broker. His military career commenced in 1897 at the bottom rung, as a gunner in the local militia. Twenty years later Arthur Currie earned command of the Canadian Corps.

Monash was natty enough to pass for a regular British officer. The Australian even sported the requisite moustache. But Arthur Currie could never for one moment have been mistaken for a regular British officer. Very tall, wide in the beam, with his Sam Browne belt worn high over his paunch, he was certainly no clothes horse. His long, knock-kneed legs had not been designed to show off breeks and riding boots, and Scots undoubtedly stared aghast when he wore the kilt of his old militia regiment, the 50th Gordon Highlanders of Canada. His jowly, morose face, devoid of the standard moustache, loomed above a thick neck. On top sat a flattened cap a shade too small for the large head. There was nothing theatrical about Arthur Currie; he was just another grim-faced Canadian, but his men worshipped him and never once doubted his ability to lead them to victory and to protect them from useless casualties.

There was a total of nine men at the July 21 conference. Rawlinson brought his three senior staff officers, while Currie and Monash were each accompanied by one member of their own staffs. Also in attendance was Lieutenant J.F.C. Fuller from Tank Corps Headquarters, for the tanks were to play a major role in the proposed Amiens offensive.

The French had achieved startling success three days earlier on the Marne by using a swarm of 324 tanks in their surprise counter-stroke. Fuller now suggested that the number of tank battalions recommended in the new plan be increased by 50 percent. As a result it was agreed that twelve battalions, rather than eight, would be employed at Amiens. This meant that every British tank brigade except the 1st, which was at that time being converted from Mark IVs to the new Mark Vs, would be thrown into the offensive. This decision was a gamble, for if anything went wrong, the Allies' great ace-in-the-hole would be seriously depleted if not destroyed. Even a successful attack launched as a stunning surprise was costly when it came to tanks. The French in the last three days had lost a total of 184 heavy tanks — 57 percent of their total. A disaster to the British tank force would almost eliminate the heavy tank from a role in the war at the very time that it had finally been accepted by infantry commanders as the key to eventual victory.

Consequently, secrecy and deception were felt to be vital to success. So many operations in the past had been robbed of success by wagging tongues or by preparations made all too obviously. Now the fate of the British Tank Corps and of the Allies' two finest infantry corps lay in the balance. Consequently, it was agreed that the greatest secrecy had to surround every conference, and had to extend to each preparation no matter how monumental. No one who did not absolutely have to know would be told of the operation until the last moment. Even those who would eventually make the detailed plans or carry out the actual assault had to be kept in the dark. It was on this note that the conference broke up.

The July 24 meeting was momentous. To it came Foch the Supreme Commander, as well as Haig, Pétain, and Pershing. The Supreme Commander seemed optimistic — possibly overly so — when he said that he envisioned final victory as early as mid-1919, and requested the three commanders-in-chief to forecast their strengths for April 1, 1919. Foch went on to propose an offensive in two stages. First: relieve threatened communication centres and remove enemy salients. Second: assume the offensive along the whole front by a series of attacks at various points, thereby wearing down the Germans' power of resistance.

In order to carry out the first phase, three offensives were agreed upon: (1) The French counter-offensives already begun on July 18 would be pressed home. (2) The Amiens offensive would free the Paris-Amiens railway. (3) The First American Army — whose formation had been agreed upon only that day — would attack the Saint Mihiel salient. This attack would have to be held in abeyance until the First American Army could be assembled.[12]

Further conferences at various levels were held almost daily to develop the plan to a workable state. On July 26 at Sarcus, Foch met with Haig, Rawlinson, and General Eugene Debeney, commanding the French First Army. Debeney had been thinking of a relatively small attack, but Foch would have none of that, and it was decided that the French First Army would now be included in Haig's plan on the southern flank. The date for the attack was also fixed as August 10. On July 27 general boundaries and objectives were set for the first day of the offensive. The next day brought two further developments — Foch placed Debeney's French First Army under Haig's command, and the date for the offensive was advanced two days to Thursday, August 8. For the Canadian Corps this meant enormous complications to an already difficult task. At that moment Currie's men were holding the line near Arras, thirty miles north of their proposed jumping-off line. The Corps, still unaware of what was afoot, was required to move over thirty miles in complete secrecy, and prepare for a major attack employing new tactics — all within ten days.

On July 29, the British XVII Corps was ordered to relieve the Canadians. The relief was to be completed by daybreak of August 2, giving the Canadian Corps a mere six days to carry out its tasks. For the first time divisional commanders were informed of the operation and of their roles in it, but were cautioned not to discuss this information with subordinates. That same day, deception plans were completed. "It would be given out freely that the Canadian Corps was moving to the Ypres front, where the Second Army expected a German attack," wrote Currie.[13]

That day Haig sent his final orders to his two army commanders, Rawlinson and Debeney, and the first troop movements commenced. The die was cast. In nine days the Battle of Amiens would be launched. It was a magnificent gamble. The future would show if the plan and the men were equal to the task.

CHAPTER TWO
THE CONJURER'S BOX

"So all the old tricks are coming out of the conjurer's box. I have seen it too often before — the Somme, Messines, Ypres, Cambrai — to be fully confident of a great success on this occasion. But one thing is sure: if we take the knock this time after Ludendorff has shown us how it is done, we may as well give up."

From the diary of "an inconspicuous and youthful British liaison officer" with the French 42nd Division — (Cyril Falls)

Detailed planning for the offensive now got under way. In outline the plan was simple: a sudden surprise attack against the bulge east of Amiens to free the Paris-to-Amiens rail line from German interference. Amiens was a major rail centre and this action would enable the Allies to enjoy transportation facilities that would be necessary for the big offensives planned for 1919 and 1920. The British Fourth Army under Rawlinson would command the assault force. The Canadian Corps and the Australian Corps were to provide the main punch. On the Australians' left, north of the River Somme, the British III Corps would make a modest advance to protect the Aussies' left flank. On the right of the Canadians and south of the Amiens-Roye Road, the French First Army would advance after the Canadians' assault. The French would first employ their XXXI Corps on the Canadian right, with the IX, X, and XXXV corps advancing in succession to their right as far south as Montdidier.

After breaking through the German defences, the Canadians and Australians were to advance to their first objective — the so-called "Old Amiens Defence Line," the British position during the 1916 Battle of the

Somme. Without pausing they were to continue to the second objective — the old German rear line. For this phase cavalry and medium tanks would be available.

To carry out this ambitious scheme the Allies would employ 29 infantry divisions against the enemy's 25. In reserve along the whole front, but available in an emergency, Foch had 77 more divisions: 38 French, 21 British, 10 American, 5 Belgian, 2 Italian, and 1 Portuguese. Of these distant reserves only half were battleworthy and reasonably fresh.

In addition to this narrow margin in infantry, Haig's combined command could call upon six cavalry divisions whereas the enemy had long since disbanded theirs. It was not known how many artillery pieces the Germans could employ, but certainly the Allies could achieve a preponderance by bringing in the artillery support from divisions disbanded or being reconstituted elsewhere. Eventually the French were able to amass 1,606 guns and the British 2,034 — an awesome weight of firepower.

The "sledge-hammer force" of the attack would be provided by the Tank Corps. Amiens would see the largest concentration of tanks ever assembled to that date — 324 heavy tanks and 96 medium tanks on the British sector plus 72 light tanks on the French. Supporting these would be 120 supply tanks and 22 gun-carrier tanks — a total of 634 tanks.[14]

The Allies would have a tremendous *initial* advantage in air power — 625 British plus 1,104 French aircraft against an estimated 365 German. However, the Germans had many more readily available in nearby Champagne where they had been employed lavishly since mid-July.

Clearly the Allies' margin of superiority was very small. Aside from tanks — of which the entire German Army had but 40 (15 German-made and 25 captured Allied tanks) — the Allies' only real superiority was in the quality of the troops, for the Canadians and Australians were rated by friend and foe alike as the finest shock troops in the world. Consequently, the Allies' hopes of success lay in surprise.

Almost all of the attack zone near Amiens was ideal for mobile warfare. From the Avre River in the south to the Somme in the north the terrain was relatively flat — like a billiard table in the French zone, though less so on the British side. There, two rivers, the Somme and the Luce, meandered through the countryside creating steep banks and broad loops. The Luce was little more than knee-deep, and at its widest point less than thirty feet across. The difficulty lay in negotiating its deep valley with its two-hundred-yard wide belt of woods. The Luce's many surrounding swamps and tributary valleys would also provide assistance to the defenders. The Canadians would attack opposite this area.

THE MAIN OFFENSIVE CAMPAIGN:
THE CONJURER'S BOX

Farther north the Australians had flatter countryside to cross with few natural obstacles. However, on their left flank the River Somme twisted westward providing several problems. In most of its bends the high bank lay on the north, the side that would have to be taken by the British III Corps. If the "Tommies" fell behind in this difficult country, the Germans would be left overlooking the Australian left flank. The many spurs and re-entrants on both sides of the Somme made this sector unsuitable for tanks, so the British infantry would have to carry the ball themselves.

The Fourth Army's artillery was given two initial tasks. Of the 2,034 guns, one-third was to form a creeping barrage at zero hour. The rate of advancement varied according to circumstances, but moved at an average rate of one hundred yards every three and a half minutes. At the same moment, the main force of the guns — almost 1,400 strong — was to hit all known enemy gun emplacements at zero hour. This was to be one of the largest counter-battery operations ever attempted, and it required meticulous planning. The guns would have to fire without registration (i.e. firing shots before-hand to range-in on a target); therefore all firing would have to be done by maps. To make up for possible errors on the part of individual batteries the counter-battery barrage on each target would be carried out by guns of several batteries. Thus each battery of heavy guns would be firing on several targets at once when the barrage opened up.

Camouflaging such an array of guns and ammunition was a major problem. The Canadian heavy artillery alone required 91,000 rounds, which had to be distributed and stored close to each gun, yet all of this had to be hidden from the enemy aircraft that were certain to scan the area. Lieutenant-Colonel A.G.L. McNaughton was so confident of his fire-power that no attempt was to be made to hide the flash of his guns because he felt the enemy would be powerless to retaliate after the initial barrage.

The use of massed tanks was the unique feature of the Amiens offensive. This tactic had been dramatically successful at Cambrai in the previous November. In fact, the success was so startling that the British High Command was unprepared to seize the opportunity presented by the tanks. The recent, more modest battle of Hamel had once again shown what tank-infantry co-operation could achieve, and it was intended that the offensive at Amiens would dwarf this achievement. Certainly the number of tanks available was without precedent.

The variety of tanks was also novel. The so-called "fighting tanks" were mostly twenty-nine-ton Mark Vs. These were the most recent of a line of "heavies" first developed by the British in 1915. They were classified as "males" (armed with two six-pounders and four machine guns) or "females" (six machine guns). These monsters were over twenty-six feet in length and males were 13 1/2 feet across, females 10 1/2. Several features of the Mark V gave it great advantages over its predecessors — it had one driver rather than the four required in previous models; it travelled as fast as 4.6 miles per hour; it had a radius of action up to forty-five miles; and it was more manoeuvrable. There were, however, two serious problems, even by 1918 standards. Ventilation in the Mark Vs was very poor, and crews suffered severely from fumes and carbon-monoxide poisoning — sometimes to the point of suffering temporary insanity or being rendered unconscious. Secondly, visibility for the eight-man crew was limited. The commander had a periscope that was generally put out of action quite early by small-arms fire; otherwise there were only several minute slits in the visor plates. These facts made the crew almost entirely dependent upon maps, compass, and preliminary ground reconnaissance.

Communication was another unsolved problem: within the tank it was by voice-tube; from without it was by means of a bell that could be pulled from the outside. If the tank commander needed to send a message he had only two primitive methods: a collapsible semaphore on the superstructure that was usually shot off early in the action, or carrier pigeons.

An adaptation designated Mark V* ("Mark five star") had recently appeared. It was simply a Mark V made longer by six feet (i.e. 32 feet, 5 inches in length). The reason for this modification was to increase the vehicle's trench-crossing capability. However, another novel use was to be made of the longer tank for the Amiens offensive. Each Mark V* would carry, besides its crew of eight, two 3-men Lewis-gun sections, one 5-man Vickers machine gun crew, one infantry officer, and one scout — a total of thirteen passengers. The idea was to transport these men to the final objective. There they would dig in and hold on until the main infantry force came up. To make up these extra Lewis-gun crews each battalion was to contribute a number of its best men. The heavy Vickers machine guns were to be manned by regular crews from the Machine Gun Corps.

The Whippet medium tanks were also to be used in a novel manner. They would be unleashed with the cavalry to exploit the enemy's rear after the initial breakthrough. The Whippet — a misnomer, if ever there was one — was a recent development, its main feature being mobility. It had a top speed of 8.3 miles per hour, a radius of action of eighty miles, and weighed fourteen tons. Its three-man crew manned four machine guns mounted in a fixed turret. This gave the Whippet an even higher silhouette than the massive Mark V, for it towered nine feet above the ground.

There were two other specialty tanks available. One was the "supply tank." This was the old Mark IV converted to carry supplies forward where wheeled, soft-skinned vehicles could not venture. Sledges had been designed to be dragged on a cable by these supply tanks. At Hamel four supply tanks had delivered almost twenty-five tons of material to within a few hundred yards of the final objective only thirty minutes after it had been taken. This task, which would normally have employed two full-strength infantry battalions, had been accomplished without a casualty by twenty men. Great things were expected of the supply tanks at Amiens.

The fourth tank variety was the forerunner of the self-propelled gun. It was the "gun-carrier tank," capable of delivering or firing from the tank a sixty-pounder or a six-inch howitzer. However, the two gun-carrier companies had already devolved into ordinary supply companies and their promise had never been exploited.

The French First Army would not employ the same overwhelming tank force mustered by the British. Pétain had already committed his main tank force on July 18, so the only tanks available for Amiens were seventy-two light Renaults. These superb little two-man tanks were destined to be used by the armies of many countries till 1940. The seven-ton Renault had excellent cross-country abilities and mounted a traversing turret equipped with either a 37 mm cannon or a machine gun. The plan was to use these lightweights to the maximum of their six miles per hour as weapons of pursuit after the breakthrough had been achieved.

By the summer of 1918 warfare had become a very complicated art requiring enormous administrative arrangements. Whereas noncombatants in the British Army in 1914 had made up only 16.63 percent of the total manpower, they now comprised 32.27 percent. The Fourth Army's twenty-three-page memorandum on "Administrative Arrangements" included such diverse topics as railways and printing, supplies of lubricants and a host of medical facilities, gun-parks and traffic-control, evacuation and feeding of civilians in captured areas, and sadly, grave registrations. Prisoner-of-war "cages" were to be provided, and an optimistic note crept into the memorandum with mention of an "overflow cage."

This immense and intricate machine made up of small cogs could very easily be stalled, or worse, smashed by administrative monkey wrenches. Two wrenches that always threatened to fall into the works were the Australian takeover of the French positions, and the movement of the Canadian Corps from Arras to Amiens. Both were exacerbated by the fact that the administrative officers concerned were not let in on the secret till July 29 — just ten days before the offensive. Their task was herculean. As Currie pointed out:

> The nearest Army dump from which we could draw ammunition was so far away that lorries could not make more than one trip a day. The advanced refilling points had not been selected, and dumping of ammunition at these points did not really begin until August 3. There was a great shortage of lorries, a considerable number of the heavy Artillery Brigades [*sic* Brigades'] arriving only two or three days before the attack. When the lorries of these Brigades became available, there was not sufficient petrol to keep all of them in operation.
>
> In addition, all forward traffic was restricted to two main channels, the Amiens-Roye Road and the Amiens-Villers-Bretonneux Road. The congestion on the latter was increased by reason of its being used in common with the Australian Corps.
>
> There were no dumps of trench ammunition in the area, and, notwithstanding all efforts made by our Administrative Branches in that direction, the supply of small arms ammunition and bombs was not quite adequate. As a matter of fact, some Units, failing to obtain British hand-grenades in time, used French grenades gathered at the French dumps.
>
> The lack of adequate preparations to receive the large number of horses resulting from the great concentration of Artillery caused endless columns of horses to block the roads in the vicinity of the watering points."[15]

The transportation problem alone was enormous, and complicated further by the need for total secrecy. British railway troops and railway construction troops (two-thirds of whom were Canadian) kept 158 trains moving daily by using nine hundred mainline engines and 571 kilometres of British controlled line. By August 7, 302,785 soldiers had been moved in secrecy by these railway troops.

THE MAIN OFFENSIVE CAMPAIGN:
THE CONJURER'S BOX

Another factor usually taken for granted was detailed trench maps of the sector. On July 29 the Field Survey Battalion, Royal Engineers, was given the task of producing over 200,000 trench maps of the area, locating all enemy batteries, and fixing firing position and ranges for 128 British, Canadian, and Australian batteries moving into the sector. By August 8 they had finished the job and had also produced 119,300 enlargements, and 4,500 mosaics pieced together from several photos. These were distributed as far down the chain of command as section commanders. Unfortunately, the supply was a rather mixed selection, some dated as recently as August 4, 1918, with others, dated 1916, being almost antiques. The most recent "barrage maps" went to the artillery and to senior commanders. These were described as "excellent" by those concerned. The older ones were sparse in detail and of course, years out of date. They appear to have ended up in the hands of the soldiers in the field.

The plan of attack required the 4th Australian Division to take over a French section of the line. Rawlinson's original scheme had the Canadians taking over the sector from Monument Wood just south of Villers-Bretonneux to the Amiens-Roye Road several days prior to the attack. Haig realized that this would end any chance of surprise, for the Germans considered the Canadians to be the Allies' top assault troops. Various ways to overcome this glaring flaw were discussed before it was decided to temporarily extend the Australian sector southward. The Germans and the Allied troops themselves would by this means be convinced that their role was to remain defensive, and no one would expect an attack from a force that had been stretched even thinner. As a result, on July 29, the men of the 4th Australian Division had their dreams of a long rest shattered when they were ordered to take over the area between Villers-Bretonneux and the Amiens-Roye Road during the nights of August 1 and 2.

The decision to employ the Canadians and the Australians was vital to the success of the operation. Both corps were experienced and extremely battleworthy. Many British and French units had by this time been battered and diluted by men less fit, both physically and emotionally, than had earlier been the case. Morale had slipped, and Allied troops in general had become cautious as a result of four years of slaughter during which the veterans had seen thousands of their comrades' lives thrown away uselessly. The Americans, new to the front, had the 1914-style *élan*, but were totally lacking in experience. The Aussies, or "Diggers" as they called themselves, and "Canucks" still had much of that dash from another era, *and* they were thoroughly experienced.

A friendly rivalry existed between the troops of the two dominions. Certainly they were dissimilar in almost every way. The Aussies were the darlings of the press and received constant publicity. Their wide-brimmed slouch hats seemed to typify their flamboyant style, and made for eye-catching photos. Beneath their "Digger hats" were bronzed, rugged men possessed in battle by a fierce joy and a readiness to take risks. They were crafty and clever and had an eye for the ground and for their foes' weaknesses. To the rigidly disciplined British troops, the men from "down under" seemed incredibly individualistic and contemptuous of authority. "They were unlike any of our own divisions," recalled P.J. Campbell M.C., a former mathematics scholar now a lieutenant in the Army-Brigade, Royal Field Artillery. "I was not attracted by them. They were noisy and swaggering, they did not march along the road, they just walked, they seemed to be without any kind of discipline."[16] The number of Australian soldiers in prison at any time was nine times that of the other British Empire troops.[17] The Australians were not liable to get the death penalty for any criminal offence as were most other troops, and Field Marshal Haig, for one, thought that this accounted for their high rate of crime.

Although they received much less publicity, the Canadian Corps had proven to be popular wherever they served. Unlike the Australians, whose style had never changed, the Canucks had undergone a gradual metamorphosis. In 1914 and 1915 they had been looked upon as virtually undisciplined. The most famous story was that of a Canadian colonel addressing his battalion: "See here, boys," he had ordered, "an English general is coming around. Stand up straight in line, and quit spitting — and for Christ's sake don't call me 'Alf'!"[18] These young colonels who had led from the front had become brigadiers, and divisional commanders — those who were not killed — and they were generally popular with their men. But early in the war the Canadians had voluntarily exchanged their total democracy for an iron discipline. Nevertheless, this rigorous regime was not permanent; Canadians kept discipline in perspective. It would be difficult to imagine anyone other than a Canadian describing his regimental sergeant-major in the words used by a trouble-prone private of the 46th South Saskatchewans: "Bill Jones, our R.S.M., was a hell of a good pal. On parade he was real strict and gave his orders so clear it was like music. With him you could drill for hours and never make a mistake, 'cause everyone wanted to do his best. 'Course, at night Bill was one of the boys, and he would buy you a beer or give you a hell of a good poke — whichever you had comin'."

THE MAIN OFFENSIVE CAMPAIGN:
The Conjurer's Box

Canadians treated the war as a rotten job that had to be done. They had become deadly serious about the task and approached the enemy grimly with no display of enthusiasm. Their stubbornness and dogged refusal to give in had become proverbial, for they had never lost a gun, had never failed to take an objective, and had never permanently lost an inch of ground. For these reasons they were looked upon with awe by their allies.

Their determination to punish the enemy had recently been jacked even higher by an atrocity that had taken place on June 27. On that night, a Canadian hospital ship, the *Llandovery Castle*, was torpedoed by U-86 and sunk on a return voyage to Britain. *Kapitanleutnant* Patzig, after ascertaining from the ship's captain that the *Llandovery Castle* carried only medical personnel, then rammed all the lifeboats except one, which managed to escape in the dark. Two-hundred and thirty-four died that night including fourteen nurses. The Canadian reaction was typified by Brigadier George Tuxford, a former homesteader from Moose Jaw, Saskatchewan: "Amongst those murdered were two Moose Jaw nurses, Sister Fraser and Sister Gallagher. I gave instructions to the Brigade that the battle cry on the 8th of August should be 'Llandovery Castle,' and that that cry should be the last to ring in the ears of the Hun as the bayonet was driven home."

The strength of the two dominion corps were almost equal, but the Australians had their 53,000 men distributed among five divisions. These were not all at full strength, for enlistment at home had declined to the point where less than half the necessary replacements were being recruited. As a result, the 4th Australian Division had been forced to reduce its twelve battalions to ten. This followed the earlier lead of the British Army, which had been reorganized on a system of brigades consisting of three battalions in place of the old four-battalion format. The Australian battalions were also very tired. They had received little respite during their long tour of duty, and men had begun absenting themselves without leave and in several cases even deserting.

This depletion in numbers and the drop in morale was behind the visit to London of the Australian Prime Minister. William Hughes was at this time determined to impose restrictions on the use of the Australians. As most everyone expected the war to last till 1920, Hughes was alarmed lest Australia's dwindling forces leave her in an inferior position when peace talks eventually began.

The Canadian Corps had been organized on a different plan. The War Office in London had recommended that the Canadians reduce their establishment in line with the British reorganization. If this had been done and the available reserves employed, the result would have been *two*

Canadian corps each of three divisions. However, the Canadians preferred to retain one powerful corps of four divisions backed by ample reserves, and the British government's wishes were rejected. By the summer of 1918 all Canadian battalions were at least one hundred men over-strength, thereby carrying with them their own reserves for immediate use.

Not only had the Canadian infantry been reinforced, the auxiliary arms had also been greatly strengthened. For instance, the Canadian Engineers now included a special motor transport unit to "go anywhere and do anything" — constructive or destructive. When the 5th Division had been broken up before seeing action its artillery was dispatched to France as a complete unit to augment the Corps.

The Canucks had developed machine-gun tactics to a higher degree than had their allies. The Canadian Machine Gun Corps was organized in battalions with the battery as the tactical unit.

Under their colourful commander, Brigadier-General Raymond Brutinel, they had developed into a distinctive arm with tactics of their own and a position somewhere between artillery and infantry. In addition, two Motor Machine-Gun Brigades had been formed complete with a maintenance section. The 1st had been organized by Brutinel himself in 1914 using truck bodies bought in the United States by a special subscription provided by patriotic Canadians. The trucks were partially covered with plating supplied by Bethlehem Steel, and several machine guns were mounted for firing over the trucks' low sides.

Like his trucks, Brutinel was all-Canadian even though foreign-born. A former frontiersman who had roamed the Northwest, he had made his millions and was residing in Montreal when the war broke out. Although a French citizen and reserve officer, he obtained permission to join the Canadian Expeditionary Force.

The other batteries had been raised by self-made millionaires — the Borden Battery, named after the Prime Minister, the Eaton Battery, raised by the department-store magnate, and the Yukon Battery, raised by "Klondike Joe" Boyle, the gold-miner. These unique units struggled through years of bureaucratic disdain to become an eccentric but hard-hitting fighting formation under the dynamic Brutinel. They pictured themselves in a "hell for leather" role.

Even the Canadian Transport Service was superior to the British by 1918. Because of the latter's man-power problems, Category B men were employed as drivers and on occasion the system began to break down due to the men's lack of physical stamina. Currie, however, refused to replace his Category A drivers because he felt they had to be men of the highest calibre. The results showed in the Corps' ability to supply itself regardless of fatigue, enemy action, or weather conditions. Canadians almost never went hungry or ran out of ammunition.

Despite the unquestioned fighting qualities of his two dominion corps, Field Marshal Haig was, for the most part, exasperated by them. He did praise the Australians for splitting up their corps at his request during the German offensives of the spring, but he never forgave the Canadians for resisting his attempts to break them up. Many senior officers shared Haig's resentment, and the Canadian Corps was derisively labeled "Foch's Pets." On July 19, Haig's feelings surfaced when he was visited by Major-General Mewburn, the Canadian Minister of Militia whom he dismissed as "second-rate." Haig constantly referred to Mewburn as "Newburn," which could not have helped their relationship. The latter pointed out that the Canadian government was displeased that the Corps was not at that moment together under their own corps commander. At that, Haig had exploded. "During all this severe fighting, the Canadian Corps has not once been engaged. Why? Because the Canadian Government only wishes it to be engaged as a Corps."[19]

Haig did not wholly approve of the Australians either. In fact, he even compared them unfavourably to the Canadians. "I spent some time today, 23 February, 1918, with the Canadians. They are really fine disciplined soldiers now and so smart and clean. I am sorry to say that the Australians are not nearly so efficient." This he blamed on General Birdwood, their English commanding officer at the time whom he accused of "making himself as popular as possible." Haig continued; "We have had to separate the Australians into Convalescent Camps of their own, because they were giving so much trouble when along with our men and put such revolutionary ideas into their heads."[20]

The Australians' northern flank was to be protected by Lieutenant-General Sir Richard Butler's III Corps. The plan was for the British troops to keep pace with the Australian advance on the south side of the Somme by moving over the high ground on the north bank. The Corps' objective was more modest than either the Australians' or Canadians'; it was simply to go as far as the Australians' second objective and there to form a flank facing north towards Morlancourt. The terrain there was the most difficult that would be encountered during the Amiens offensive. Numerous ravines ran down into the Somme valley, and each was thickly wooded, yet the flat areas in between were totally devoid of cover. This meant ideal ground for the Germans' machine-gun defences. To make matters worse, the whole area rose in a gradual glacis-like slope for about five thousand yards. Thus the "summit" gave splendid observation over the battleground in all directions, including the south, where the Australians could be taken in flank.

III Corps' four divisions were weary. All had suffered severely in the March retreat and had been in the line ever since. The 58th London Division alone lost 3,530 men at Villers-Bretonneux in two days that April. Their replacements were mostly conscripts, and their officers and NCO's inexperienced. When they heard of the move to take over a section of the French line, they reacted pessimistically. Instead of believing that the French troops were being withdrawn to attack, the cynical veterans among them suspected a French collapse. Four years of inept leadership had destroyed the flower of Britain's youth, and those who remained viewed their fates as sealed. Yet in the words of C.E. Montague, "they still worked away with a sullen ardour that no muddling or sloth in high places could wholly damp down."[21]

The terrible effects of the March 21st disaster lingered — particularly in those who had been part of the shattered Fifth Army that day. Every survivor felt himself personally responsible and still carried a secret burden of guilt and shame. "The realization of the magnitude of our defeat came over me and overcame me. This was the most catastrophic defeat that Britain had ever suffered, and it seemed to me that I was partly responsible for the disaster," recalled the young Artillery Lieutenant, P.J. Campbell M.C.[22]

> The Retreat was over, but the memory of defeat remained, and we waited anxiously for the beginning of the second round, knowing that one victory would not be enough for the enemy; he had to destroy us if he was to win the war. All through the months that followed we were waiting. Every night, as I got into my sleeping bag, I was aware that I might be wakened in the morning by a fierce bombardment, the preliminary to the next German attack, and that would mean it was about to start again.[23]

Montague, the English correspondent, recognized with bitterness the cost of British social conditions and British generalship. He bitterly contrasted dominion troops with his own beloved "Tommies" of 1918.

You had already seen them meet on roads in the rear: battalions of colourless, stunted, half-toothless lads from hot, humid Lancashire mills; battalions of slow, staring faces, gargoyles out of the tragical-comical-historical-pastoral edifice of modern English rural life; Dominion battalions of men startlingly taller, stronger, handsomer, prouder, firmer in nerve, better schooled, more boldly interested in life, quicker to take means to an end and to parry and counter any new blow of circumstance, men who had learned already to look at our men with the half-curious, half-pitying look of a higher, happier caste at a lower.[24]

Now despite their battered morale, their exhaustion, and their numerical weakness, III Corps was going to go to the attack on August 8. Due to the difficult terrain and the subsidiary nature of their role, these men would receive scant help from the tanks. Only twenty-two Mark Vs and twelve supply tanks were to take part in their assault.

The southern flank of the Canadian Corps was to be protected by the French First Army, which would advance forty-five minutes after the Canucks. "After the spring losses, we in turn had companies almost entirely re-formed out of 1918 *bluets,* who had never been under fire and for whom we felt real tenderness," wrote Georges Gaudry, a veteran of the 57th Infantry Regiment. "The eyes of our conscripts were big as saucers. They watched our smallest gestures with absolute trust; they took in every word as devoted and obedient footsoldiers, intent on victory. They saw us as old hands at battle, accustomed to its surprises, conditioned to act in combat as are colliers in a mine, sailors in a storm."[25]

In contrast, a French staff officer, in conversation with Sir Douglas Haig, lamented the poor resistance shown by the French Army. "The French Infantry is now inferior to the German," he confessed. When Haig protested that only some units were poor because of a lack of training and discipline, the staff officer replied, "Pétain ought to have shot 2,000 instead of only 30 when so many mutinied this time last year. The situation of the French Army was very grave then, and required severe measures to remove the canker. Instead of training, the men were given 'leave' and 'repose.'"[26]

Nevertheless, since their recent victory on the Marne, the French infantry had shown more poise and confidence. But this victory had been primarily due to the use of large numbers of heavy tanks, and that force had been almost destroyed in the victory. French infantry commanders now constantly requested tanks to support their operations, but it would be some time before French heavy tank forces could be used in any strength again. In the forthcoming Amiens operations the French infantry would once again go "over the top" alone. The unasked question lurked in the minds of everyone: "How will they fare without tanks?"

An issue being pondered by many was the best way to use air-power in the coming offensive. Fighter tactics had been changed by the increased numbers available, and the solitary hunter was now a rare sight. Large formations flew as units, sometimes "stacked" several layers deep for mutual protection. The great aces were nearly all gone by the summer of 1918. Billy Bishop had been returned to duties in Canada; James McCudden, Mick Mannock, and Albert Ball had all died. And of course, the most famous ace of them all — "The Red Baron," Manfred von Richthofen — had been shot down only months earlier. René Fonck was one of the few aces left in a world of teamwork and massed flights. Even the old titles had gone; in April the Royal Flying Corps and the Royal Naval Air Service had been united to form a separate service, the Royal Air Force. It included men from every corner of the Empire — although the Canadians had taken a major part, with 13,000 now serving with the RAF. In fact, arrangements had been completed on July 8 to establish the "Canadian Air Force."

But numbers had not changed the British disdain for caution nor their contempt of odds. "The English ... absolutely challenged us to battle and never refused fighting," von Richthofen wrote. "Frequently the daring of the latter can only be described as stupidity. In their eyes it may be pluck and bravery."[27] The Germans, on the other hand, always calculated the odds before deciding to fight. Therefore they seldom took needless chances and only attacked when the odds were in their favour. The most successful of all exponents of this strategy was the Red Baron himself; many of his eighty kills were against inferior aircraft caught at a disadvantage.

Of course, tactics are always dominated by the quality of the equipment employed. In this the German aviators enjoyed an enormous advantage. Throughout the war their fighters were technically superior to those of either of the Allies. The major factors in 1918 were armament, air-speed, rate of climb, manoeuvrability, and ceiling. In nearly all of these the German D VII biplane outperformed any of its Allied counterparts, and when it came to reconnaissance planes — those used for photography and artillery liaison — the Allies were immeasurably weaker. The French ace, Guynemer, observed, "If the Germans had used such machines I would have guaranteed to shoot down one a day."[28] Certainly by far the highest Allied air casualties were incurred by these poor-quality craft crewed by men of extraordinary valour. As the offensive at Amiens drew closer more and more of these slow and clumsy machines would have to be sacrificed to obtain the information necessary for success. On the other hand, German reconnaissance planes had to be kept away from the Allied build-up at all costs.

Another type of warplane had been developed by 1918. This was the bomber. The Germans had pioneered bombing from the air, but by late July most of the long-range bombing raids were being carried out against them. Large planes had been developed on both sides to carry out these operations both by day and by night. Rest camps, supply dumps, rail yards, and aerodromes were the usual targets. In all cases the material damage inflicted was not very significant, but the effect upon morale was considerable, particularly when results were magnified anywhere from two to ten times by the press.

During the recent French counter-offensive on the Marne the Germans had held an enormous superiority in air power. Airplanes bearing the black cross had soared over the battleground almost at will, but despite this, the Germans had been soundly defeated. The planned offensive at Amiens was expected to reverse this preponderance in air power, at least in the initial stage. What was the best way to make use of this extension of military power? It had already been arranged that villages fortified by the enemy and beyond the range of Allied field artillery would be screened by smoke delivered by the RAF. Strafing ground targets would be carried out although it was of minor value in material terms and posed unwarranted risks for both pilots and planes. Nevertheless, it could produce a great impact on the morale of the ground troops of both sides. Those being strafed were constantly distracted from their main task, and the increasing despair and feelings of impotency often resulted in panic. For friendly infantry there was the wonderful realization that somewhere above a powerful friend knew, cared, and protected.

Air co-operation with tanks was comparatively new. On July 1, No. 8 Squadron RAF under Major T.L. Leigh-Mallory had been attached to the Tank Corps for experiments along this line. The officers of the two arms exchanged places to gain experience, understanding, and camaraderie. Attempts at wireless communications between the two had proven fruitless so a system of disk signals was worked out for the forthcoming battle. Phosphorus bombs with contact fuses were to be dropped at pre-arranged times to cover the advance of the tanks.

But Allied air power was to be used for more than strafing and tank support. On August 1, Major-General J.M. Salmond submitted proposals for the RAF's role in the upcoming battle. In broad outline the plan included several measures to assist the deception before the battle, then at daybreak on August 8 day-bombers with fighter support were to attack German aerodromes opposite the Fourth Army. The fighters were to stand by to operate against German air strength. Finally, evening bombing attacks against enemy railway centres such as Peronne and Chaulnes would be undertaken. By the eve of the offensive British air strength was expected to reach eight hundred airplanes. One fighter squadron was detailed to support each corps (Australian, Canadian, III, Tank Corps, and Cavalry) plus one to drop supplies and ammunition. The bombers and seven fighter squadrons were assigned to the Fourth Army to be used according to Salmond's plan. For the first time ever, the fliers would be provided with an overall picture in advance of the offensive. It was hoped that this would give each airman a better understanding of what he would see, and of the value of his actions and reports.

The French First Army would also be strongly supported by planes. General Debeney had requested an air division, which was duly moved to his sector to support his own fighting group of 180 planes. As a result, the French air strength should have totaled 1,104 aircraft. On the first day, however, only a small proportion of this force would be employed. This combined air force, it was estimated, would outnumber the Germans almost six to one. Intelligence felt that it would take the enemy several days to bring in squadrons from other fronts, thus leaving the Allies with a heavy balance in their favour for the crucial opening day.

The Amiens offensive was based, as Captain Basil Liddell-Hart put it, upon "a subtle compound of many deceptive factors."[29] In the past, surprise had been treated as incidental in planning offensives. The Allied generals had apparently felt that this universally accepted rule of strategy was adequately observed by simply keeping the date of an attack secret. The Amiens offensive would be protected by more sophisticated stratagems.

Two phases of deception were involved. The first involved concealing the giant build-up of troops, artillery, supplies, and transport from the enemy. Secondly, there would be an attempt to distract the Germans' attention to some distant sector. Both tasks presented almost

insurmountable obstacles. For example, the required tank build-up —
how could the 562 tanks in the British sector be hidden from the enemy?
Moreover, each tank required a large and readily accessible supply of fuel
and ammunition. Tanks were huge, cumbersome, and difficult to hide.
They left deep and obvious trails, and their roaring and clanking could be
heard for great distances.

There was not too much that could be done to hide the presence of the
tanks except to leave their arrival to the last possible moment. However, the
enemy could be tricked into finding tanks in the wrong places, so
deception was tried. Several tanks, therefore, were shown on the road near
Vimy at Notre Dame de Lorette and it was hoped that the Germans would
conclude they were going north. A second, more promising scheme was a
faked concentration of tanks near St. Pol, only eighteen miles from Arras
where the Canadian Corps was still situated. Plenty of noise, long streamers
of dust on the roads, and a glimpse or two of several old tanks would, it
was hoped, do the trick. But most convincing of all was the increased radio
activity on the tanks' wavelength. Intelligence knew that the Germans were
aware of the tanks' radio procedure, and this flurry of activity would
convince them of an impending attack east of Arras in conjunction with
the Canadian Corps.

To make this conspiracy of secrecy effective, the obvious first step was
to enlist the enthusiastic support of all ranks. Consequently, every
soldier's pay book had a notice pasted into it. It warned, "KEEP YOUR
MOUTH SHUT," and stressed the necessity for secrecy. It then dealt
with a subject seldom discussed:

> If you should ever have the misfortune to be taken
> prisoner, don't give the enemy any information beyond
> your rank and name. In answer to all other questions
> you need only say, "I cannot answer". He cannot compel
> you to give any other information. He may use threats.
> He will respect you if your courage, patriotism, and self-
> control do not fail. Every word you say may cause the
> death of one of your comrades.

"The pamphlets of course caused some amusement by their
originality," noted the War Diary of the 5th (Western Cavalry) Battalion,
C.E.F., "but the sound sense of the advice was thoroughly appreciated by
everyone, and undoubtedly had the effect it was intended for, and the
answer given to queries on the road from various individuals as to the

identity of the unit, were very humorous, ranging from the Bengal Lancers to the Chinese Labour Corps, but never the correct required answer."

In the pursuit of secrecy preliminary conferences were held in different locations, and all knowledge of the offensive was withheld from those involved till the last possible moment. Even divisional commanders were not informed till July 31 — eight days before the attack. Outside of Fourth Army hardly anyone knew of the plans; even the War Cabinet of His Majesty's Government was kept in the dark.

In the area around Amiens all clues had to be concealed from friend and foe alike. For instance, a build-up of six hundred rounds of ammunition per gun was explained away in Australian divisional orders as due to expected wet weather and "the reduced artillery on the corps front." To explain the Australian takeover of the French section of the line to those who had to know, Rawlinson sent the following memorandum:

> The French, owing to casualties in the Soisson offensive, have shortened their line, and the British have side-slipped south. The Canadians are taking the place of the XXII Corps — which went south — in support of the junction between the French and the British.

The presence of Canadian officers reconnoitring their assault zone had to be explained away as well. Brigadier-General Blamey, John Monash's right-hand man and chief of staff, therefore issued a memorandum that parties of them would be spectators at practices to be carried out with tanks at Vaux-en-Amienois in the last days of July. Several, like the Canadian artillery specialists, General E.W.B. Morrison and Lieutenant-Colonel A.G.L. "Andy" McNaughton, remained in the area dressed as Australians.

To prevent the enemy from noting the huge build-up of supplies, various methods were adopted. Transports, their wheels wrapped in rope, now moved only during the hours of darkness, over roads covered with cut straw. The deserted streets of Amiens were covered with sand to deaden the sounds of both cavalry and tanks. Throughout the daylight hours Allied aircraft patrolled, attempting to spot any signs that an enemy might also detect. This too had to be done in such a way as not to arouse suspicion. The true magnitude of these seemingly minor measures can best be judged when one considers that 230 special trains had to be employed to bring up these supplies. Another sixty would transport troops.

For the Canadians the task of deception was complicated. To move an entire corps from one zone to another over thirty miles away and to attack immediately once there was a monumental operation; but to accomplish this without letting the enemy, their own Allies, or even the troops involved know it was happening seemed beyond hope. Added to the problem was the challenge of diverting the Germans' attention elsewhere.

To achieve these aims Arthur Currie staged a conference on July 22, which was attended by his divisional commanders. Here they were told that the Canadian Corps was to prepare to attack Orange Hill in their own sector near Arras. Currie issued real orders, complete with the time and date of the attack. "It was stated that Tanks would be available for the operations," Currie reported, "and it was therefore essential that all ranks familiarize themselves with the combined tactics of Infantry and Tanks. I explained that demonstrations had been arranged with the Australians and that it was my wish that the greatest possible number of officers should witness them."[30]

"I was a young officer sitting at the back of the room with nothing to say, but watching it all and knowing it was all bunk," recalled "Andy" McNaughton years later. McNaughton, the son of a prairie storekeeper in Wolseley, a speck on the broad Saskatchewan plains, had, in civil life, become a physics professor at McGill University. Now he was the Canadian Corps Counter-Battery Officer.

> I was one of the three or four who had to be in on the real show but I had to attend this conference also; otherwise people would ask questions about the counter-battery fire and there would be no one to answer them. It was one of the most amazing experiences of my life. I don't know another commander who could have carried the thing off as Currie did — the reality that he put into it.
>
> General Macdonnell, who had the 1st Division, got all worked up because another division had more tanks than he had and there was a ten-minute battle over the allocation of tanks. In the end there were tears in the old boy's eyes — he was really upset because he had the best chance to use tanks, and tanks were what he wanted. After a while General Currie said, "I'll have a staff officer phone Army and we'll see if we can get some more tanks for you. The ones we have are all allotted, but we might just get two or three more if that will satisfy you, General." An officer was sent out, ostensibly to make the request, and after a decent interval he came back and

whispered something into Currie's ear. Currie announced that he'd got one or two — he would have overdone it if he'd promised more — and peace descended upon the multitude.[31]

The next step was to draw the enemy's eyes away from both Amiens and Arras (from which the Canadian Corps would be withdrawn). Friend and foe alike had to be deceived into believing that the Canadians were going north to the Ypres Salient to spearhead a major offensive against Kemmel Hill. For the Canadians themselves it became a question of which was for real, Orange Hill or Kemmel Hill?

On July 29 the XVII Corps was ordered to relieve the Canadians during the nights of July 31 to August 2. This order plainly stated that the Canadian Corps was to prepare to move north to join the British Second Army around the Ypres Salient. To make this deception realistic to everyone involved, Currie dispatched the 27th (City of Winnipeg) Battalion, the 4th Canadian Mounted Rifles, and some medical and signal units to the Salient. The signalers were to supply a flow of dummy wireless traffic to deceive the enemy. The infantry (representing two different divisions) would be put on display as it were. The troops themselves were bewildered. The War Diary of the 4th CMR (in a less formal style than is usual in these documents) reported the reaction of the "poor bloody infantry":

> July 28. We had just issued instructions for a repeat order of our 500-man working party when the chill voice of Beer Emma over the wheezy phone advised of the working party being canceled. "You will move by train tomorrow, where I know not, when I know not." ... The evening was spent in preparation, anticipation and invention of rumors. First it was south we were bound, then rearward, then north, and finally to Russia. About 10 p.m. we were informed that our destination was Arneke and that we were to be moved by strategic train. Well, what was to become of us? What is a strategic train, and how can a train show strategy?...
>
> July 29. The G.O.C. Division and the G.O.C. Brigade were there to wish us bon voyage. The remainder of our Brigade stayed behind; in fact, as far as we know, the Canadian Corps and the whole of the dependable military world. (How we despise ourselves!)

No, there is no brigade operation order attached. We move on pink signal, faith and forms. No one knew to whom we belonged, but no doubt some kind staff officer would claim us at our destination.

The train did better than most troop trains in France. We travelled via St. Pol Aire and St. Omer and reached Arneke about midnight. The R.T.O. — a very meek, pious, dyspeptic-looking, spectacled youth — detrained us with the assistance of a still more promising one-pipped Town Major. We were told that we were in X Corps and that we would be billeted.

July 30. A very promising map, in two colours, a list of billets as long as your arm, and the freedom of the area were presented to the C.O. We were to move in the morning and the Town Major knew of a good field and a kind farmer, and we carried on to the field. We found a real hospitable farmer, who got out of bed, turned over his barn to the officers and tucked everyone away splendidly.

The first of the Canadians had arrived in the Salient.

Belgian Headquarters was so surprised that they sent an indignant message to British Headquarters to the effect that common courtesy alone should have suggested that the Belgians be notified of the popular Canadians' arrival to enable them to make arrangements for their reception.

To the delight of those in on the deception, the newspaper correspondents who hovered about Corps Headquarters were also completely taken in. Roland Hill described how he was caught — hook, line, and sinker:

> "If you want to get a good billet for the show," said Brigadier Webber to the writer, "slip up to Second Army Headquarters and get your booking in." It seemed a quite friendly tip, and the correspondent went up to a little village near St. Omer that he knew of old.
>
> "How did you get on to the move?" asked the staff officer of Second Army Intelligence, and he answered it was just a private tip. After credentials were shown, the officer opened up a map with the billeting areas reserved for Canadian divisions and the correspondent chose one near Cassel which was picked for Canadian Corps

Headquarters. In confidential mood he added that two advance battalions and some artillery and transport had already arrived. To prove his bona fides the correspondent mentioned the numbers of the battalions. Never did transport and battalions make such a noise and so freely let their movements be known as did these camouflage units back among old friends in the *estaminets* behind the Ypres salient.[32]

While the 27th and 4th CMR were thus being paraded in full view, the RAF was also swinging into the deception. Squadrons in the Second Army area were ordered to show increased activity around the Salient till August 6. More aerodromes were occupied, and sorties made continually to draw the attention of the German Air Service.

Meanwhile back a Duisans the divisional commanders had been informed of their true destination on Monday, July 29. They had, however, been instructed not to discuss the operation with any of their subordinates. The next day Canadian Corps Headquarters apparently vanished into thin air, and the first troops began leaving the Arras sector. The move was incredibly complicated; forty-eight infantry battalions and the thousands of ancillary troops that supported them, moved by every form of conveyance — trucks, buses, trains, and of course, "shank's pony." All began by heading north, but by nightfall they found themselves moving southwards. The 19th (Central Ontario) Battalion was fortunate enough to travel by train. Joe O'Neill recalled that

> We got on the train and of course in the morning when
> we woke up we were away down on the Somme. And all
> of these boys, especially the oldtimers, they looked out the
> windows and they saw the name on a station and, oh, if
> you could have heard their real old soldier stuff about the
> blankety blank staff that got us on the wrong trains and
> shot us south when we should have been going north![33]

Others less fortunate marched the long nights through the gently rolling, tree-shrouded hills of Picardy. But eventually all units found themselves heading southwards. Even at this stage deceptive orders were issued. These advised that the Canadians were going into General Headquarters Reserve to *support* either the French First Army or the British Fourth. The need for secrecy complicated the move by forcing the Corps to avoid the normal, direct routes. Hours of darkness were short in August, and troops had to be marched hard and without their unit transport sections in order to reach their destinations before daylight revealed them on the roads. During the march each battalion received orders to dispatch certain chosen men to attend "tank school," whatever that was. So a small group of bewildered soldiers were whisked away from each battalion, no one knew where. There was of course, no "tank school"; these detachments were to make up the Lewis-gun crews to be taken forward by the Mark V* tanks.

Just how secretive the operation was is well illustrated by the adventure of Lieutenant-Colonel "Turkey" Ross of the 28th (Northwest) Battalion. Ross, a Regina lawyer, had been in England for several days of leave. On July 30, by sheer luck, he ran into his medical officer (MO), who had just arrived on leave himself. The latter informed "Turkey" that the 28th was about to be moved somewhere. Ross, who had served with his beloved "Nor'westers" since the 28th had first been raised, decided to rejoin them regardless of his leave. The next day he landed in France. To avoid being dispatched all over France, Ross went direct to General Headquarters to find his old friend, Brigadier J.F.L. Embury, the original commanding officer of the 28th. Ross knew Embury would be able to locate his battalion, and he was not disappointed. But Ross was surprised to discover that his old friend would not divulge the 28th's whereabouts, though he would arrange to have Ross transported there. So next morning "Turkey" Ross found himself in a General Headquarters staff car heading out of Paris along a road he had never before travelled. Eventually he arrived in a town with a few Canadians about. Another staff car from the 2nd Canadian Division whisked him away to a village named Saisseval. There the Colonel found his men safe and well, but, like him, wondering why they had been smuggled to this remote village.

Meanwhile in the Ypres Salient, Roland Hill, the correspondent, had become alarmed. It seemed that everyone in Flanders knew that the Canadians were coming there to launch "a big push." Hill decided to return to Duisans and inform the corps staff that the secret was out. But on his arrival the bewildered correspondent discovered that "Foch's Pets" had vanished. The headquarters of the British corps now in occupation could only tell him, "They have gone to Ypres." Hill was completely baffled — but were the Germans?

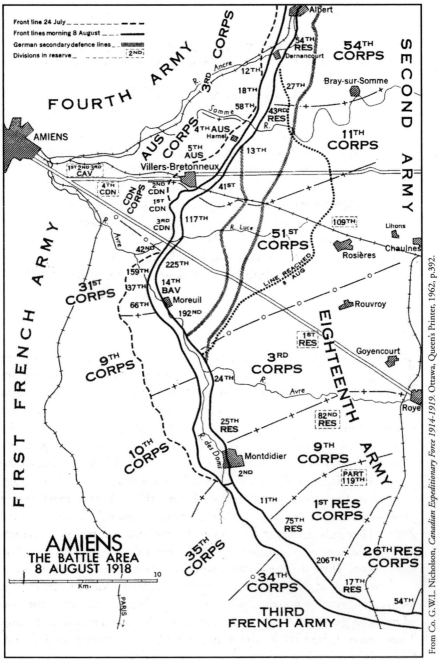

Front line 24 July _ _ _ _ _ _ _
Front lines morning 8 August _ _ _ _
German secondary defence lines_ _ |||||||||||||||||||||
Divisions in reserve_ _ _ _ _ _ _ _ [2ND]

SECOND ARMY

Albert

54TH
RES

54TH
CORPS

Dernancourt

FOURTH ARMY

3RD CORPS

R. Ancre

12TH

27TH

Bray-sur-Somme

18TH

AUS CORPS

R. Somme

58TH

43RD
RES

11TH
CORPS

4TH AUS
Hamel

AMIENS

5TH
AUS

13TH

Villers-Bretonneux

1ST 2ND 3RD
CAV

CDN CORPS

4TH
CDN

2ND
CDN

41ST

1ST
CDN

109TH

Lihons

3RD
CDN

117TH

R. Luce

51ST
CORPS

Chaulnes

R. Avre

42ND

Rosières

31ST
CORPS

159TH

225TH

LINE REACHED 8 AUG

137TH

14TH
BAV

Moreuil

Rouvroy

66TH

192ND

1ST
RES

9TH
CORPS

Goyencourt

3RD
CORPS

EIGHTEENTH ARMY

24TH

R. Avre

Roye

FIRST FRENCH ARMY

25TH
RES

82ND
RES

10TH
CORPS

R. des Doms

Montdidier

9TH
CORPS

2ND

PART
119TH

11TH

1ST RES
CORPS

75TH
RES

26TH RES
CORPS

AMIENS
THE BATTLE AREA
8 AUGUST 1918

10

35TH
CORPS

206TH

17TH
RES

Km.

34TH
CORPS

54TH

PARIS →

THIRD
FRENCH ARMY

From Co. G.W.L. Nicholson, *Canadian Expeditionary Force 1914-1919*. Ottawa, Queen's Printer, 1962, p.392.
Courtesy of Minister of Public Works and Government Services, Canada.

CHAPTER THREE
A RIVER OF MEN

"The weather was lovely, and we marched through each night in step, in harmony, to our unknown destination, to our destinies — whatever the God of Battle and Death's indifferent hand had in store for us. It was a river of men — young, happy, and confident in our record that whatever we had to do, no other outfit would do it better."
Lieutenant E.D. Macdonald,
46th (South Saskatchewan) Battalion, CEF

On the night of July 28/29, while the 4th CMRs and the 27th Battalion were packing for their trip northwards to Ypres, the 5th Australian Division seized the crest of Brick Beacon Ridge. This minor prominence south of Morlancourt had caused considerable inconvenience to the "Diggers," so before they turned it over to the "Tommies" they resolved, as a farewell gesture, to eliminate the problem. This involved a full-scale infantry assault by the 29th Victorians, 32nd South Australians, and 53rd New South Wales battalions. They surged forward in their usual battle frenzy. "I don't think there is much use in preaching mercy to my men," wrote Lieutenant-Colonel McArthur of the 29th. "They fight to kill if the enemy shows resistance, but are extremely kind to prisoners when captured."[34] Of the latter there were 128, including four officers. These the Aussies feted with chocolate, biscuits, and hot cocoa.

The attacking waves received a mixed reception. Many Germans ran forward begging to be made prisoner. Others fought bitterly to the last, while some gathered sheep-like in their dugouts and refused to come out. These were killed by hand-grenades when all coaxing had failed. Certainly those taken prisoner were very demoralized, given the course the war had taken. Despite this fact, casualties were almost equal, but the

Diggers had taken Brick Beacon Ridge. Ironically, their success carried with it the seeds of disaster.

Canadian Corps Headquarters had arrived at Molliens-Vidame, known to the Canucks as "Molly-be-Damned." This village, a dozen miles west of Amiens now lay swamped in a sea of canvas tents that buzzed with staff officers twenty-four hours every day. The gigantic Currie was in his element here, and his exhausted aides would leave him pouring over reports at two in the morning, then hear at breakfast that he had been in the field at six.

The most secret aspects of the work at Molly-be-Damned were carried on by three clerks who lived and worked in a tent by themselves. "Living like Trappist monks," they slaved day and night copying operations orders for the big day. Everyone near the tent was bursting with questions but the three remained silent as totem poles.

As the date for the offensive drew closer, the whirlwind of preparations rose to a higher pitch. On July 30 the British III Corps completed its takeover from the 5th Australian Division. The weary 58th (London) Division occupied the north bank of the Somme including the crest of Brick Beacon Ridge. The same day heavy artillery units began to arrive, including those of two defunct infantry divisions — the 25th (being reconstituted in England) and the 5th Canadian (broken up for reinforcements). As a cover story it was noised about that this was part of the "first stage in the rearrangement of the artillery."[35]

During the next night the first tanks began to arrive in the rear areas of the Fourth Army sector. Six battalions were disembarking at four different rail centres and their supplies had already begun to pour in.

Throughout the last few days the French Air Service had been assembling its *escadrilles* for the offensive. The great ace, Captain René Fonck, celebrated his return by shooting down his 57th victim over Hangard Wood on August 1 at eleven o'clock. The weather was good for flying, with clear visibility for miles, but few German planes ventured over no man's land. Nevertheless, Rawlinson ordered his own planes up to check the Allied lines for any signs that might betray the offensive. That same night the 4th Australian Division began its relief of the 37th and 74th French divisions south of Villers-Bretonneux.

FRIDAY, AUGUST 2

The next morning brought the Allied high command some worrying intelligence. A German prisoner taken on the Ancre River to the north revealed for the first time that the German forces in the sector opposite the centre of III Corps had withdrawn during the night, abandoning Dernancourt, Albert, and Aveluy Wood. Patrols were immediately sent out, but no enemy could be found. Where had they gone? Had the enemy got wind of the impending offensive? Was this a manoeuvre to avoid it?

There was some good news, however — the meteorological forecast: rainy weather had settled in that day and appeared certain to remain for several days. Also, it was believed that the Germans had discovered that the Australians had taken over from the French south of Villers-Bretonneux. The Diggers were not at all secretive by nature, and they were soon roaming the area searching for building materials to improve the primitive shelters they had inherited. While the French had occupied this zone nothing had moved; now the area seemed alive with these happy-go-lucky warriors. Indeed, some of the 49th Queenslanders had discovered a dump of rifle grenades and spent the day potting at "Fritz." It was prayed that OHL ("*Oberste Heeresleitung*," the German High Command) would draw the desired conclusions.

It was also on August 2 that the first Canadian infantry began to arrive. For most, those nights on the roads of Picardy were ones they would remember for the rest of their lives whether fate decreed it to be a matter of days or decades. "It was a warm night and the stars looked like diamonds set in a dome of velvet," wrote Jerred Mansfield, a former game warden, farm labourer, section-hand, and fisherman from Ontario. Now the "Jack of all trades" was a private in Transport Section of the 3rd Canadian Machine Gun Battalion. As a member of Transport he enjoyed the march from the back of a horse.

> The only sound beside the clap clap of the horses' feet on the hard surface of the road, were the clink of chains and the creak of the harness. The occasional loud rumble of distant artillery could be heard, and looking back over our shoulders, we could see the reflections of the star shells as they rose in full brilliancy, fell, and died out. Sometimes, the hum of the aeroplanes could be heard overhead, coming and going, and they were not always our machines. About once an hour, a halt was called and everyone pulled off to the side of the road for a few minutes. Cigarettes would glow like fire-flies all down the line, and the men would form into groups and talk in low tones, until the order came to "mount up" again. Columns

of motor trucks, with their lights dimmed, passed us at different times and also a few swiftly moving touring-cars, filled with officers. Sometimes, we grew drowsy and leaned over and slept in the saddle. As soon as it was light in the east, we came to a halt, unlimbered, ran out picquet lines, tied up, ate our breakfast and then looked for a place to sleep: under a wagon or out in the open under a hedge. I did not know where it was that we stopped the first night, but it was a pretty little place nestled in among some hills. We kept under cover all day and again at dusk we moved south, keeping off the main road and winding around until I was again all mixed up in my directions.

Throughout the Canadian Corps there was a groundswell of emotion. "In the early years of the war the boys used to sing when they were going up to the line, but then they got in that sort of bleak, blank period and nobody sang," remarked Elmore Philpott, an artilleryman. "By some kind of spiritual osmosis or something, when our boys went up to that Amiens thing they all went up singing. There was an entirely different feeling in the air from the minute that we began to move south."[36]

Alan MacNab of the Divisional Cyclists recalled, "In the middle of the night we woke up and we heard this battalion coming up, a Canadian battalion, and they were singing at the top of their voices, just lifting, and they went by within ten feet of our heads — we were in this barn. I don't think there was a dry eye in the barn. You could hear some of the boys sobbing, just something was gripping us."[37]

SATURDAY, AUGUST 3

The day began with rain, but a sunny afternoon caused concern lest German reconnaissance planes penetrate the Allied fighter screen. However, there was far too much going on to worry for long about the weather. Conferences abounded. Haig met with Foch at Mouchy le Chatel. The Supreme Commander was anxious to begin the offensive because the Germans had commenced withdrawals in several sectors. Foch went so far as to state that the enemy was "breaking up." He appeared satisfied that August 8 had been decided upon, but urged Haig to insure that there would be no delays preparing defensive lines, but to press on to the limit. He also advised Haig that the French Third Army on the right of Debeney's First would extend the offensive even further south than had first been planned. Haig was disappointed to discover that General Pershing had refused to allow the U.S. 33rd Illinois Division, currently gaining experience with the Australians, to serve as a reserve because it was not yet fully trained.

Farther south, various reports had convinced General Debeney that the Germans opposite his French First Army were about to withdraw. Thus at noon he telephoned each of his corps commanders and advised them to be on the alert. "It is manifest that in several sections of the front, the Germans are straightening their lines. It is therefore very possible that they are withdrawing their advance posts on the right bank of the Avre.... Consequently in all Corps set patrols in motion to maintain contact."[38] As a result, when elements of the German Eighteenth Army drew back from their positions between Moreuil and Montdidier that afternoon, they were hotly pressed. But it also meant that plans for August 8 would have to be revamped.

During the day the Germans, having noted the Australians in the former French sector, had mounted a daylight raid looking for prisoners. The intended victims were the Queenslanders and Tasmanians of the 15th Battalion, but they drove off the raiders without suffering any casualties themselves. "Fritz" would have to try again if he wanted prisoners to question. It was certain he would — but where and when?

Meanwhile, numerous conferences were being held. Lieutenant H.R. Williams of the 56th New South Wales, along with the other battalion officers, arrived at the village school at Poulainville:

> We went expecting to arrange final details of a sports
> meeting, plans for which had tentatively been drawn up at
> a meeting on the previous day. The colonel duly appeared,
> and after the usual procedure we were told to make
> ourselves comfortable at the children's desks. He said that
> he had called us together to give us details of an attack that
> was to be launched within the course of a few days, and in
> which the Australian Army Corps was to play a major role.

The entire plan was revealed and the officers were warned of the necessity for secrecy. The conference touched on the fact that the corps was suffering from "line-weariness" and had every right to expect a rest. "But our colonel said that the opinion had been general at the Fourth Army conference that the Australians would forget their line-weariness if detailed to take part in a grand scheme of attack in which all five divisions were employed, especially if the Canadian Corps were to co-operate with them. Whoever so summed up our feelings must have known us well."[39]

Unlike the 3rd Australian Division, whose junior officers were being fully briefed, the Canadians were still completely in the dark. Many miles to the north, men of the 5th (Western Cavalry) Battalion were enjoying themselves with a pay parade and a bath when orders were received for them to entrain for an unknown destination. That afternoon these veterans marched off to meet fate. "A really impressive and touching incident occurred during the march," noted the War Diary,

> when the Battalion, approaching the village of Penin, found the streets lined by American troops, who cheered themselves hoarse as the Canadians went through. If the Americans could realize how delighted and moved the Canadians were by the spontaneous and whole hearted reception, they would feel well satisfied. We returned the cheers to the best of our ability, somewhat handicapped by full marching order, and in many cases a full heart. America and Canada have assuredly acquired a great affection and admiration for each other, which is one of the blessings which, strangely enough, are evolved from this war.

At the same moment other Canadian battalions, nearer Amiens, were training for the first time with tanks. "Turkey" Ross's 28th Battalion was one such. The "Nor'westers" had arrived at Ferriéres shortly before noon and found it full of men of the 2nd Canadian Machine Gun Battalion. Billets were few and it poured rain. However, negotiations eventually provided accommodation for both over-strength battalions. Then it was off to work. "A very busy and profitable day was spent practicing with the tanks, over tracks, trenches and in the open, riding on and in them and generally fraternizing with the crews of these strange weapons," Ross wrote.

Days earlier, the Australian, Williams, had viewed one of these demonstrations:

> Detachments of infantry were deployed into attack formation, the tanks were manoeuvred into position, and then the demonstration was opened.... The attacking waves came on, and at prearranged signals the tanks would diverge from their course to deal with a supposed strong point holding up the advance. These monsters

moved with surprising speed. Reaching the strong point, the tank would straddle the trench, swing around on its tractors, and obliterate the post by simply crushing it into the ground. These manoeuvres were a revelation to us, and we could fully appreciate what a wonderful asset they must have been to the infantry in the attack on Hamel.

The show was repeated several times with fresh detachments of infantry. Then the tanks halted, and we were told that they were for our inspection. Soon men were clambering over and into them. Lieutenant Musgrave and I entered one, and were shown the armament of the monster. A gun firing a small shell protruded from the front; the sides bristled with machine guns, housed in turrets, and capable of being swung over a wide field of fire.... Then we were taken for a ride in this land battleship. It was a queer sensation. Coming to a bank the machine reared upwards and clawed its way forward, even knocking down small trees in its path. Standing in the field was an old captured German tank. Its height dwarfed the new British models that we had just seen in manoeuvres, but it was cumbersome in appearance and had been as slow as a lame duck.[40]

The Canadian Corps was running into a critical supply problem. Ammunition was delayed by the late arrival of the Corps heavy artillery and its transport. Advanced refilling dumps were now discovered to be too far back, and the nearest army dump was a full day's journey from the forward area, resulting in only one trip per day per lorry. It was also on Saturday that the fuel supply almost ran out. The situation was so critical that Rawlinson placed a number of British transport units at Currie's disposal. But this expediency was short-lived, for these Category "B" men proved unable to stand up to the heavy work and stress expected of them. As a result, Currie returned these units after only a short time. One Canadian Transport driver, obeying orders to move up the supplies as fast as possible, was arrested for speeding by an overzealous military policeman. Only Currie's fiery intervention released the man and his lorry from custody. Doubtless, at least one MP's ears burned for days thereafter.

That afternoon the front lines in the southern sector were alive with Canadian staff officers and generals, preparing for the great offensive. Brigadiers F.O.W. Loomis and George Tuxford of the 2nd and 3rd brigades had gone forward to see their sectors. They ventured well into the 13th Australian Brigade's position opposite Hangard Wood and had worked forward without encountering trenches or cover of any sort. "We had not seen a soul since we had left the village, and the country appeared to be deserted, although we were in fairly close proximity to the Hun line," wrote Tuxford.

> I had just remarked that we must be very openly under enemy observation when we heard a voice hail us from our left rear, and telling us, in no uncertain terms to "get down." As there was no trench or other cover available, we made our way back in the direction of the voice, and dropped into a trench, to find an Australian officer who had established an O.P. there. He gave us a good deal of information regarding the features of the country, at the same time saying that it looked as though we were looking for trouble from the Hun, in the position that we had been in.
>
> Finally Loomis, looking towards our rear, which for a matter of some 1500 yards back, was on level plain, said, "I suppose it is all right to strike back overland?"
>
> "Well, I wouldn't advise it," the Australian replied, "for they sweep this level backwards with machine gun fire at any movement visible. They killed one of my men yesterday where you are standing."

SUNDAY, AUGUST 4

Early in the morning the generals were staggered by a report from the 51st Western Australian Battalion. At 3:05 that morning Germans had raided the Australian outposts astride the Amiens-Roye Road at Hourges. Amid the ruins a vicious fight had erupted that lasted only a few minutes. Ten dead and one mortally wounded German had been found, but five Australians were missing — presumably captured! Everyone who heard about the missing men waited in anguish. Canadian artillery had already taken up positions behind the Australian front and two Canadian brigades were scheduled to move into support the following night. How much did the captured Diggers know? Had they seen any Canadians? Would they remember the notice pasted in their pay books?

brigades had gone forward to see their sectors. They ventured well into the 13th Australian Brigade's position opposite Hangard Wood and had worked forward without encountering trenches or cover of any sort. "We had not seen a soul since we had left the village, and the country appeared to be deserted, although we were in fairly close proximity to the Hun line," wrote Tuxford.

> I had just remarked that we must be very openly under enemy observation when we heard a voice hail us from our left rear, and telling us, in no uncertain terms to "get down." As there was no trench or other cover available, we made our way back in the direction of the voice, and dropped into a trench, to find an Australian officer who had established an O.P. there. He gave us a good deal of information regarding the features of the country, at the same time saying that it looked as though we were looking for trouble from the Hun, in the position that we had been in.
>
> Finally Loomis, looking towards our rear, which for a matter of some 1500 yards back, was on level plain, said, "I suppose it is all right to strike back overland?"
>
> "Well, I wouldn't advise it," the Australian replied, "for they sweep this level backwards with machine gun fire at any movement visible. They killed one of my men yesterday where you are standing."

SUNDAY, AUGUST 4

Early in the morning the generals were staggered by a report from the 51st Western Australian Battalion. At 3:05 that morning Germans had raided the Australian outposts astride the Amiens-Roye Road at Hourges. Amid the ruins a vicious fight had erupted that lasted only a few minutes. Ten dead and one mortally wounded German had been found, but five Australians were missing — presumably captured! Everyone who heard about the missing men waited in anguish. Canadian artillery had already taken up positions behind the Australian front and two Canadian brigades were scheduled to move into support the following night. How much did the captured Diggers know? Had they seen any Canadians? Would they remember the notice pasted in their pay books?

moved with surprising speed. Reaching the strong point, the tank would straddle the trench, swing around on its tractors, and obliterate the post by simply crushing it into the ground. These manoeuvres were a revelation to us, and we could fully appreciate what a wonderful asset they must have been to the infantry in the attack on Hamel.

The show was repeated several times with fresh detachments of infantry. Then the tanks halted, and we were told that they were for our inspection. Soon men were clambering over and into them. Lieutenant Musgrave and I entered one, and were shown the armament of the monster. A gun firing a small shell protruded from the front; the sides bristled with machine guns, housed in turrets, and capable of being swung over a wide field of fire.... Then we were taken for a ride in this land battleship. It was a queer sensation. Coming to a bank the machine reared upwards and clawed its way forward, even knocking down small trees in its path. Standing in the field was an old captured German tank. Its height dwarfed the new British models that we had just seen in manoeuvres, but it was cumbersome in appearance and had been as slow as a lame duck.[40]

The Canadian Corps was running into a critical supply problem. Ammunition was delayed by the late arrival of the Corps heavy artillery and its transport. Advanced refilling dumps were now discovered to be too far back, and the nearest army dump was a full day's journey from the forward area, resulting in only one trip per day per lorry. It was also on Saturday that the fuel supply almost ran out. The situation was so critical that Rawlinson placed a number of British transport units at Currie's disposal. But this expediency was short-lived, for these Category "B" men proved unable to stand up to the heavy work and stress expected of them. As a result, Currie returned these units after only a short time. One Canadian Transport driver, obeying orders to move up the supplies as fast as possible, was arrested for speeding by an overzealous military policeman. Only Currie's fiery intervention released the man and his lorry from custody. Doubtless, at least one MP's ears burned for days thereafter.

That afternoon the front lines in the southern sector were alive with Canadian staff officers and generals, preparing for the great offensive. Brigadiers F.O.W. Loomis and George Tuxford of the 2nd and 3rd made a name for themselves with the 122nd Brigade when a patrol "went out to investigate a legend that there were a number of abandoned [British] Field Guns in one area. Back of Nameless Farm they found four 18 pounders. Two brand new ones passed by ordinance only as late as April 29th of this year."[43] Unfortunately, finding these lost guns had cost one company its commander killed and its second-in-command wounded. Captain T.W.E. Dixon, had risen through the ranks and had been very popular. His men had volunteered to carry his body out for a full military funeral early that morning. Now they were on their way south to join the Fourth Army. "This will make four armies we have been in in thirty-eight days," the War Diary marveled.

MONDAY, AUGUST 5

On Monday, His Majesty, King George V sailed for France on a tour of inspection that was scheduled to last till August 13. He landed that afternoon, but like the War Cabinet at home, he knew nothing of the undertaking afoot. At the same time at Flixecourt, thirteen miles northwest of Amiens, Haig met with his two Army commanders, Debeney and Rawlinson, and with Lieutenant-General Kavanagh, commanding the Cavalry Corps. Sir Douglas discussed Foch's plan to extend the operation by including the French Third Army and then issued operations orders to push well beyond the 1916 Amiens Defence Line. He feared that Rawlinson's orders on July 31 had laid too much stress on reaching this line as the final objective. Today Haig emphasized that although this position was to be put into a state for defence, the prime objective was to push reserves forward to capture the Roye-Chaulnes line. To make these orders workable Haig put a brigade of cavalry, a battery of Royal Horse Artillery, and several Whippet tanks under Australian Corps orders. This broadened the proposed penetration, for the Canadians had earlier been assigned the 3rd Cavalry Division and an entire battalion of Whippet tanks. The Canadian Corps would also be reinforced by the British 32nd Imperial Division. Kavanagh was also directed to pass the Cavalry Corps through anywhere between the Somme and the Amiens-Roye Road. By these measures, it was hoped that the imminent offensive would turn into a major breakthrough.

That night just before midnight the 3rd Canadian Brigade embussed at Hornoy and headed for Boves just behind their jumping-off positions. Brigadier Tuxford was appalled by the congestion on the roads, and the

Later a report arrived from their battalion stating that shortly before the raid the men had been "discussing the prospect of a long stay in the trenches."[41] This was mildly comforting, but did not remove the anxiety felt by the decision-makers. Orders for the two Canadian brigades to take up their positions were canceled. It would be inconvenient, but the Canucks could not now be allowed into the line till the last possible moment.

The 4th dawned rainy and overcast. It was the fourth anniversary of the British declaration of war and saw various open air services of "Remembrance and Intercession" behind the lines. For the troops in the front line or hidden in every copse, village, and hedgerow there were no church parades, no football, and no baseball. It was on this date that Canadian battalion commanders were informed of the operation, but were strictly ordered not to reveal them to subordinates, although every Australian subaltern had been informed the day before.

The Australians, gregarious, to say the least, had already started the "secret" on its rounds. One Australian war correspondent wrote in his diary that "officers of our 3rd Division have written to friends in hospital there in London and told them of what was coming off and all sorts of hints to details." He went on to tell how Hubert Wilkins, the Australian Official Photographer, had returned from a visit round the line of the 3rd Division bursting with news.

> He asked me if I had heard of the attack. Everyone up there at the front was full of it. On Wednesday night they were to attack and go as far as they could — Bapaume, they spoke of; and the Canadians were in it, and the British north of the Somme as far as Albert, and the French 50 miles south.... One officer told him that they were going through this time. The same officer was talking more freely to his men than to Wilkins. They asked him, "Where are we going to, Mr. _____? Berlin?" "Well, you always complain about being stopped," the officer said. "You are being given the chance this time of showing what you really can do. It's the right way to tackle the job."[42]

While these unnerving events were taking place around Amiens, miles to the north in Flanders the 27th (City of Winnipeg) Battalion and the 4th Canadian Mounted Rifles were marching towards Poperinghe. Two days of deception had not been cheap. The 27th had lost two men killed and nine wounded in the line near Locre. The 4th CMRs had number of troops packed into the village. "I stood by the side of the bridge and watched the never-ending tide roll by. Artillery, limbers, tanks, motor transport, wheeled transport of all description, lurched their way forward in the dark in one endless stream. I retired to the stone steps of the church, and slept until the rain wakened me."

Swelling the river of troops inundating Boves were the men of the 4th CMRs, weary after days of marching to and fro and their long train ride from Flanders. Now they sat three miles from the village stalled in what seemed like the grandaddy of all traffic jams.

Further south in the area to be taken over by the 3rd Canadian Division, the 9th Battalion, Canadian Engineers was working through the hours of darkness. The marshes surrounding the Luce had to be crossed in force by the attackers, and this posed a serious problem. For several nights now these sappers had been hard at it, constructing "bathmats" and foot bridges across the swamp and the river itself. In places the bridging had to stretch over three-hundred yards across marshes ten feet deep. "The difficulty, apart from the construction," records the War Diary, "is the necessity for silence, and the fact that the infantry do not hold the far bank of the river in strength, but merely have patrols passing every hour or so, where they join up with the French troops. There is also considerable enemy machine gun and shell fire" — a fact that could be attested to by Corporal Harry Brice at the Domart Bridge. However, his squad was still too isolated to know of their comrades' arrival or of the herculean tasks being performed.

Infantry tracks had also to be laid to guide the battalions from Gentelles Woods to the foot bridges being constructed. These tracks consisted of a line of stakes, fifty yards apart, joined along the tops by a single strand of wire. All of these tracks were several miles long and had been sign-posted, even to the extent of providing directions for the walking wounded who would inevitably return along these same tracks.

With these unfortunates in mind, the sappers were also constructing advanced dressing stations. One of the most impressive was built just west of Domart in a tunnel under the main road. At the same time a dry weather track was being constructed behind the front to enable ambulances to pass in a circular route across the front and back past the advanced dressing stations and on to Amiens. Meanwhile another company laboured on these roads to prepare them for the rush of traffic they would carry in a few days' time.

AMIENS:
DAWN OF VICTORY
TUESDAY, AUGUST 6

Early Tuesday morning while the sappers laboured in the marshes, and while Brigadier Tuxford cat-napped on the stone steps of the church, disaster was inexorably falling upon III Corps. At 4 a.m., as the 58th (London) Division was relieving the 18th (Eastern) Division near Sailly-le-Sec, a tremendous barrage opened up on them. Screeching shells by the hundreds tore into the trenches and burst with shattering roars amid the agonized screams of wounded men. After ten minutes of this the Germans appeared out of the darkness in swarms, overrunning the badly outnumbered 8th Battalion of the East Surrey Regiment. This 18th Division unit was about to be relieved by the 8th City of London Battalion (the Post Office Rifles) which had become mired in the muddy trenches six hundred yards behind the front line. The Surreys were shattered by the weight of the attack, and in moments the Germans had recaptured the ground lost to the Australians eight nights before. Brick Beacon Ridge was once again in German hands.

But this was only the first German objective. Men of the 27th Wurttemberg Division, a formation newly re-equipped and well rested, pressed on against steadily increasing British resistance, penetrating up to 1,500 yards beyond the front line to the old quarry on the Bray-Corbie Road. At this point they were in among the huge dumps of ammunition just accumulated for the offensive. The 6th Battalion of the Northamptonshire Regiment (18th Division) immediately counterattacked and by eight o'clock had driven the enemy back to the old Australian line. There the Wurttembergers held on, and the weary Tommies could push them no further.

At the various British headquarters news had been slow to arrive once the bombardment had commenced. At first everyone optimistically assumed that no serious damage had been done. But when a report finally confirmed that the Germans had penetrated right to the gun line, consternation burst like a delayed-action shell. What had the raiders seen? Had they taken any prisoners? Hours later another report confirmed the worst; British prisoners had been taken, two of whom were 50th Division artillerymen specially attached for the offensive and in charge of the ammunition dumps!

If this disaster was not bad enough, Headquarters now learned of a raid upon the French to the south. There the Germans had captured a corporal. What did he know? Would he talk?

Nothing could be done about these intelligence bonanzas now in German hands, but something had to be done about the strong-point they had captured. Brick Beacon must be retaken. Its loss would imperil III Corps' advance in less than forty-eight hours. The Australian Corps' left flank would be wide open. John Monash wrote, "I have made such an outcry on this point that Butler [commanding III Corps] has been told that he must keep on the battle and go on attacking all day if necessary till he takes it."[44] Rawlinson, with the Commander-in-Chief's approval, informed General Butler that for his corps the offensive had already commenced.

For the vast majority who knew nothing of these impending disasters, Tuesday was spent in humdrum activities — sleeping, gawking, hearing their orders for the first time. The *poilus* of the French First Army received General Debeney's orders today. Would they be encouraged by his closing exhortation? "I approve in advance all acts of initiative whatever may be the results."[45]

Throughout the Canadian Corps battalion conferences were being held in villages that by day, though they were packed with men and equipment, looked as innocent as they had before the war. Junior officers were for the first time being informed of what lay ahead, although even now objectives were not named. Officers were warned not to tell their men until all civilians had been left far behind.

At least one battalion was rehearsing its role in the offensive. The 41st Queenslanders were practicing their rather unique task under the critical eye of their CO, Lieutenant-Colonel Heron. Detailed to enter the valley in front of Cerisy, they would have to advance diagonally with their "right shoulder forward." Today they were rehearsing, using notice boards to represent the various features in the actual valley.

At some headquarters the clash of personalities was reverberating through the corridors of power. Major-General C.E.D. Budworth, Fourth Army's Commander of Artillery, visited the Canadian Corps' Counter Battery specialist, Andy McNaughton at Boves. The Canadians were new to Budworth, and he was growing more and more impatient as McNaughton described their incredibly detailed fire support plans. Finally Budworth broke into the discourse to dismiss it all as "over-complicated." The Canadian "light colonel" was not cowed by a British major-general. He had heard the same scorn from others. The young McNaughton icily asked for Budworth's alternative plan, but "was not enlightened." As McNaughton later recalled, "he turned on his heel and left."[46]

At Supreme Headquarters there was a more congenial mood in the air. Ferdinand Foch had been promoted Marshal of France.

The night of Tuesday, August 6, saw activity more intensive than any previous night. Those units that would make up the first wave of the attack moved forward into positions just short of the actual firing line. Brigadier Tuxford's 3rd Brigade left Boves and passed through Gentelles to occupy some poorly built, water-filled French trenches. His 16th Canadian Scottish sent an advance party to contact the 49th Queensland Battalion, who they were to relieve next night. These Aussies, they discovered, "knew nothing of the intended offensive, or of the fact that tens of thousands of Canadians lay under cover a few hundred yards behind it. No direct questions affecting the operation could be asked of its officers, a rather unsatisfactory state of affairs, as the jumping-off area bordered the outpost line, which was eight hundred yards ahead of the main trench and inaccessible by day."[47]

That night also saw movement back from the Australian lines. Americans from the 33rd Illinois Division had been attached to the 2nd, 3rd, and 4th Australian divisions, one battalion and one machine-gun company to each brigade. Both the Diggers and the "Doughboys" had expected this mutually popular program to continue for the allotted six weeks. Now the fresh-faced Yanks were being withdrawn after less than two weeks. As they encountered the columns of Canadians moving up they asked many questions, but few answers were forthcoming.

At the same time a unique armoured unit was just arriving after an all-day dash from Senlis, one hundred miles to the south. At nine that morning the 17th Armoured Car Battalion had been serving with the 6th French Cavalry Division north of Chateau-Thierry. As the cars had entered Senlis they had received orders to hasten to Amiens and there join the 5th Tank Brigade. The 17th was used to these fast movements, and held the record for shortest time into action. On April 23 of that year the 17th had been raised and equipped in England. Six days later they were in France dashing towards the front. Since then their armoured cars had seen action in many far-flung battles. Now they had to be hidden away for the night. Other armoured vehicles were also moving into secondary positions during the hours of darkness. Whippets of the 3rd and 6th tank battalions were now lining up on the Boulevard Pont-Noyelles in Amiens. Each had been snugged back under the thick trees that lined the street. Others were manoeuvred into the ruins of deserted villages or parked under the leafy canopies of small woods.

Some battalions moved in the traditional way. "The buglers have sounded assembly and we take station on the side of the road," wrote Jim Pedley of the "Mad Fourth" from central Ontario.

> In the field the band is dimly seen forming up. We are heavily laden, carrying rations for two days, extra

ammunition, bombs and the usual battle paraphernalia. The colonel and the company commanders take post. The battalion is brought to attention. A moment of silence and then the bugle sounds the shortest call, the Advance. *Come-along! Come-along!...* At the same moment the drums beat march time and *A Bachelor Gay* from *Maid of the Mountains* swells forth. We pick up the step, swerve on to the road. It is a great moment. "Good old band!" says someone derisively. "Listen hard, kid," a sour voice retorts. "It's the last band you'll listen to."[48]

WEDNESDAY, AUGUST 7

Wednesday, "zero minus one," dawned with a welcome feeble light. Low drifting clouds scudded overhead, insuring protection from prying airborne eyes. At a quarter past noon King George arrived at Haig's headquarters for an official visit. He looked "well and very cheery" and he brought a message from the Prime Minister. Lloyd George, certainly no admirer of Haig's, had apparently softened, according to the King, and assured Sir Douglas that the government was determined to support him "against the French Government." Lloyd George even sent suggestions for manning the entire Western Front, which Haig declared, "very excellent" — certainly a rare meeting of minds. However, Haig noted in his diary, "both the French and the Americans will be against us. Pershing wants to form one large American Army, while, of course, the French desire to keep the Americans as far away from the British as they can!" After this revealing aside, the Commander-in-Chief commented on the morrow's offensive almost as an afterthought. "However, I expressed the belief that the British front would be much further forward before winter arrived. And I explained in detail on the map in my study the forthcoming operation."[49]

At the same time Haig's counterpart, General Philippe Pétain, was issuing a message to the French Army. His attempt to stir the weary *poilus* revealed what hopes were uppermost in his mind: "Broken in his fifth attempt of 1918, the invader is recoiling. His effectives are diminishing, his morale is faltering, meanwhile at your sides American brothers, scarcely landed, have made the disconcerted enemy feel the vigour of their blows ... I said to you yesterday: Stubbornness, Patience, Comrades Are Coming ... I say to you today: Tenacity, Audacity, and You Will Take Victory by Storm."[50]

AMIENS:
Dawn of Victory

All day long III Corps struggled to regain the ground lost on Tuesday. At 4:30 in the morning an assault had been launched, but it had met a simultaneous German one and both had petered out after hard and inconclusive fighting. The 18th Division's 54th Brigade fought on in a series of savage little clashes, being repeatedly counterattacked by the Wurttembergers, so that the bloody ebb and flow through battered trenches, saps, and isolated outposts continued throughout the day. By 2:00 in the afternoon "D" Company, the 11th Royal Fusiliers, consisted of a wounded captain and three men. The other two battalions, the 2nd Bedfordshire Regiment and the 6th Northamptonshires, were only marginally better off.

Meanwhile, south of the meandering Somme, the Australians were trying to carry on as usual while the Canadians, the tanks, and the cavalry lay low. The Canucks had crammed Gentelles Wood to the bursting point. Lieutenant Jim Pedley of the "Mad Fourth" enjoyed an idyllic day:

> Between us and Fritz are the buildings on the east side of the street; we have a little garden in front of our cellar.... It is all very like a picnic.... Jolly and I grow bold, seize our moment to dash across the street into the *estaminet* opposite.... Inside the *estaminet* is a great deal of glass-ware, some broken, some intact. Little else. We climb to the second story, peep out through holes in the roof where tiles have fallen off. We have our maps with us and try to make out the ground we will be crossing tomorrow. There is Hangard Wood, that must be the Luce River. Over there, Villers-Bretonneux, where the Australians won fame. You can see the Boche trenches, silent, deserted-looking. Everything is desolate. Hard to imagine you are in the middle of a host crouching to spring. Hard to imagine this plain is more thickly occupied just now than the slums of a great city. The men must be hiding under blades of grass.[51]

Not everything was this idyllic. An entire platoon of the 2nd (Eastern Ontario) Battalion became casualties. The official water points had been crowded and one exhausted water-party had grown tired of waiting. They had filled up at a small creek that meandered through the shell holes, and soon the entire platoon was violently ill. Fortunately, the battalion reserve sent up men to replace Number 3 platoon and the 2nd did not suffer any lasting damage.

THE MAIN OFFENSIVE CAMPAIGN:
A RIVER OF MEN

This was the day for all last-minute jobs. Tank crews were busy topping up with petrol and stowing ammunition. Many an edgy driver puttered around with a spanner or an oil can while gunners fussed over their guns giving them yet another "last-minute check" while their tank commanders were absent, peering from observation posts into no man's land. This would be their one and only view of the ground they had to cover in the dark. Even battalion reconnaissance officers had not been allowed into the forward positions till "Z minus 4," and most others not at all. Fortunately, landmarks were abundant, the maps just received were accurate, and the oblique air photos provided by the French Air Service were of great value.

Today was the day to assign the men their individual tasks. For those who would have to go "over the top" tomorrow, there was the realization that this cloudy Wednesday in August might be their last ever. The young "Jack of all trades," Jerred Mansfield, had just been detailed to take his machine gun over with the second wave of infantry. He watched his mates.

> Some took it very seriously; it was a life or death matter to them. Others appeared not to care, or so hid their true feelings behind a mask, so you never knew what they thought. Some others again would laugh and say, "Oh, hell. What's the difference? You have only got to die once anyway, so why not now, eh? We'll be pushing up the daisies someday perhaps. Beats all, don't it? Give me a fag."

Not everybody was so philosophical; many had become bundles of nerves, and a few cracked under the strain. Captain D.E. Hickey of the 8th Tanks witnessed one such incident.

> I heard MacFarlane letting fly at one of the men of his section. Evidently the fellow was "windy" and was trying to evade going into action by saying he was ill. MacFarlane was openly incredulous, knowing the man was "swinging the lead." His reply to the would-be malingerer was forcible. Lifting a large tool, he said, holding it above the man, "I'll knock you on the head with this spanner if you do not go into action with your tank."[52]

For Lieutenant-General Currie and Canadian Headquarters, Wednesday meant another vanishing act. This time they reappeared in

Dury, a small cluster of houses and a chateau just south of Amiens. Currie, with obvious disdain for superstition, had chosen the site of Gough's Fifth Army Headquarters the day the German avalanche had thundered down upon that ill-fated command less than six months ago. Within hours Currie received a visitor. It was the Commander-in-Chief who was informed that the Canadian Corps was in position with the exception of two heavy long-range guns. Their platforms had been readied and they would be brought in that night.

Later in the afternoon Currie called a press conference to brief the two Canadian correspondents. J.F.B. Livesay wrote,

> One was struck with the speaker's simplicity and his quiet confidence and certainty. He, of course, knew the Canadian Corps and what it could do. It was a finely tempered weapon.... He knew his men — oh, abundantly he knew them and trusted them; he knew, too, their leaders, from Divisional Commanders down to the platoons, and had the assurance there would be no botching.... The biggest things in which the Canadian Corps had been engaged were but small affairs beside this; and then there was the memory of other shows that had promised great things but had turned out but half-successes or flat failures, had we but had the courage to admit as much. But confidence of that kind is infectious. After the talk was over we agreed on our luck in being in for the biggest thing yet."[53]

For the Australians also, this would be their greatest effort in the war. John Monash pointed this out to them, his message being read to his troops late that afternoon:

TO THE SOLDIERS OF THE
AUSTRALIAN ARMY CORPS

For the first time in the history of this corps all five Australian divisions will to-morrow engage in the largest and most important battle operation ever undertaken by the Corps. They will be supported by an exceptionally powerful artillery, and by tanks and aeroplanes on a scale never previously attempted. The full resources of our sister dominion, the Canadian Corps, will operate on our right, while two British divisions will guard our left flank.... I earnestly wish every soldier of the corps the best of good fortune, and a glorious and decisive victory, the story of which will re-echo throughout the world, and will live forever in the history of our homeland."[54]

The details of the great plan were now being studied by those entrusted with carrying them out. In its barest form, the operation was to move in three stages: At 4:20 the greatest barrage of the war would signal the commencement of the first stage, the advance to "The Green Line." There fresh troops would leapfrog the first wave and carry the assault to the second objective, "The Red Line." Against expected stiffening resistance, the final leapfrog would carry the last wave of fresh troops forward to "The Blue Line." Of course, it was anticipated that this "one-two-three combination" would lead to a knockout — a hole right through the German line — freeing the Cavalry, the Whippets, and the Armoured Cars to exploit the breakthrough. Possibly the infantry could press on even further, into the open country beyond the Blue Line!

Late that afternoon the sun broke through the clouds and basked the rolling plains in typical August warmth. The roads and fields soon lost their muddy guise, and the marshes and rivers glinted in the hours before sunset. For the waiting men the sunshine was a cheery omen and suggested fine weather for the morrow. Tranquillity wrapped the entire sector, outwardly without menace or any hint of the grand endeavour. Then an hour before sunset the illusion was shattered by a solitary German shell.

From the northern edge of Villers-Bretonneux, a short distance behind the 5th Australian Division's front line, a tremendous explosion was heard. A pillar of black smoke immediately towered above huge billows of wickedly crackling flame. There was a moment or two of shocked silence immediately followed by the whine and crash of a barrage from German guns of all sizes. The first vast explosion was repeated time and time again, and within moments an inferno raged in an orchard, silhouetting the shattered village. An enormous column of smoke ascended for thousands of feet and spread its vast inky shroud for miles over the waiting troops. Far behind the lines generals saw the pall and agonized — what disaster had struck? Had the Hun discovered the secret? The common soldiers in their hideouts watched the sun go down in a spectacular display of reds. The more philosophic among them must have pondered the symbolism of this blood-red sunset and the awesome black cloud that had suddenly shrouded them all, tomorrow's pawns.

CHAPTER FOUR
A Strange Delight

*"Were we on the eve of victory, or were the Germans waiting
in strength for us?... It was one of the magnificent moments
of the war and it filled one with a strange delight."*
Private Jerred Mansfield,
3rd Canadian Machine Gun Battalion

At Villers-Bretonneux the inferno raged beyond control. A few moments earlier Major Partington's No. 1 Gun Carrier Company had been nestled peacefully in the orchard on the northern outskirts. Each tank had been packed with supplies — mostly petrol and ammunition — and hidden in the orchard awaiting the moment to take forward their precious cargoes. Suddenly one of the sixteen carrier tanks had erupted in a sheet of flame as a chance German shell landed nearby.

The tank crews, braving hideous deaths, rushed into the doomed orchard to rescue their lumbering vehicles. But at the same moment a tremendous barrage descended upon the grove. Within minutes thirteen of the Gun Carrier Tanks were raging torches and many of their crews and the Australian infantrymen who had leapt to their assistance were casualties. Major Partington was wounded, but incredibly, three of the iron monsters lurched out of the hellish inferno unharmed. Above them an enormous beacon blazed to draw German eyes to Villers-Bretonneux and its not-so-innocent surroundings. Within an hour twilight's welcome shades had swallowed the shroud of smoke, and the flames had flickered out.

Just before darkness descended the battered 54th Brigade north of the Somme tried one last attack against the Wurttembergers near Brick Beacon. This gallant attempt to retrieve III Corps' lost position was organized and led by two young lieutenants, Leatherland and Wixcey. The dogged Tommies succeeded in recapturing a part of the line, but were finally driven back after both young officers were killed.

By now the 54th Brigade had suffered so severely that arrangements were being made to substitute the 36th Brigade (12th Division) in the morning's offensive. For the meantime, however, the decimated 54th was ordered to cling to its position to cover the 36th's assembly. Much shuffling among brigades and divisions would be necessary that very night, and an entirely new barrage plan would have to be devised on the spur of the moment. For III Corps the night of August 7-8 meant hours of hectic improvisation, to replace weeks of meticulous planning.

As night descended, the still countryside became a gigantic ant-hill of activity. An Australian who motored from the west into the seemingly deserted city of Amiens noted:

> We began to pass British cavalry — their horses lined at the right side of the road, heads towards us, evidently waiting to move off. As we got into Amiens itself (it now being practically dark) we found this cavalry moving quietly through the streets. It was wonderfully arranged. The paved streets were empty except for the cavalry column, and so they were able to move two columns abreast, and we were rushing past the side of them — making three streams of traffic all moving the same way.... The British cavalry columns were paired off exactly as in a review, always precisely abreast. If there was a cart beside us, there was a cart beside it, paired off almost wheel for wheel.[55]

This superb march discipline was necessary, for the column of three divisions was a very long one, making accurate timing essential because only one road through Amiens was available. Further forward the Cavalry Corps engineers and one battalion of American engineers were already building a special "cavalry track" that would take the squadrons through the waiting infantry reserves without confusion and without masking the artillery.

Now all along the seventeen-mile front the assault troops were moving into their jumping-off positions. It was the climax of weeks of staff planning.

THE MAIN OFFENSIVE CAMPAIGN:
A STRANGE DELIGHT

Tomorrow would be decided by the fighting soldiers — if tonight went well. Each formation moved on its own individual timetable. Consequently, some units were in position shortly after dusk while others did not arrive till a few minutes before zero — 4:20 in the morning. One of the first into its jumping-off line was the 33rd New South Wales Battalion. This unit of the 3rd Australian Division was in position by nightfall, and, as ordered, relieved the garrison battalion, the 38th Victorians. At 10:30 the new patrol ran into a strong party of Germans in the difficult sector looking down on Accroche Wood. The previous morning a German patrol had attempted to raid the Australians here and apparently they had planned to try again. Amid the flash and roar of bursting hand grenades, a vicious fight took place between the two almost invisible forces. The clash ceased as suddenly as it had begun and both withdrew, the Australians carrying five wounded. The 38th quickly sent its own patrol out to bring in any German casualties for questioning, but none could be found.

In the historic ruins of Boves Castle, high above the surrounding countryside and three and a half miles southeast of Amiens, Lieutenant-Colonel Andy McNaughton commenced an oft-interrupted letter to his wife:

> A constant rumble of traffic to the north where the tanks are moving into their battle positions and just now the music of a pipe and drum band leading a regiment which is moving up to its assembly area. I passed a battalion a few minutes ago as I came up from the village. Tall ghostly figures in the mist almost like creatures of another world.... The south wind blows fresh through the few trees in the courtyard or rather what was once the courtyard of the castle and the Very lights rise above the ground mist all along the front casting a sickly pale light around. There is no moon but the stars are bright.
>
> With any luck we should fairly swamp the enemy's batteries. I have very nearly gun for gun for Counter-Battery work alone and all this concentration of fire-power made undetected by the enemy. At least it appears to be undetected. Perhaps he knows of it and is waiting to catch us in a trap. Who knows? The next few hours will tell.[56]

The hours that lay ahead were critical, for if the enemy had discovered the truth he could inflict enormous casualties upon the Allies, packed as they were into every nook and cranny in the sector. Certainly now was the finest chance they would ever have to destroy the Allies' ace-in-the-hole, the Tank Corps. Along with it they could do irreparable damage to the two best fighting corps in the world — the Australian and the Canadian. Although Allied artillery had prepared for a German barrage with the most meticulously planned counter-battery operation in history, it would all be for nothing if the Germans had penetrated the secret. In this case they would have moved their batteries to other sites, and the Allies' counter-barrage would fall upon empty gun-pits, for it must be remembered that the preceding week of cloudy weather had also masked German activities from Allied eyes.

Had the German attack on III Corps been a deliberate attempt to disorganize the northern flank? Certainly it would provide them with superb positions to enfilade the Australians as they advanced on the lower southern side of the river. Had the ruse in Flanders worked? What about the secret spilled by the staff of the 3rd Australian Division four days ago? Had it reached the four men who were now German prisoners? And what about the British artillerymen captured on Tuesday morning? They had definitely known something was afoot. What had they told? Behind the front, generals agonized over these questions. Nearer the line the common soldier who knew none of these chilling facts merely went about his business. Lieutenant Williams of the 56th New South Wales Battalion recalled:

> In all the little dugouts, honeycombing the bank like birds' nests, candle-lights appeared, and men about them lifted up their voices in song. I shared a dugout with three other young officers. Laughter and merry talk was the atmosphere of this cramped shelter. For weeks I had had the premonition that I was to be wounded, and this was a topic which in army fashion was greeted as a great joke. To look back and remember how confident I felt that I was going to be knocked, and how I talked about it in the most light-hearted manner, makes me realize what fatalists the war had made of us all."[57]

From hundreds of similar hidden bivouacs men of several nations were moving forward in long files through a silent countryside. "D" Company of the 42nd Royal Highlanders of Canada made up one such file, and the men were conscious of a great rustle of movement all around them. "It was something we had not heard before. All at once no one was speaking or whispering," wrote Corporal Will Bird — in later years a well-known writer. On the night of August 7-8, 1918, Bird was the guide for "D" Company of the 42nd.

> Thousands of men were moving by us as quickly as possible, and the only thing audible was the soft sound of men jostling in the dark, the swish of feet in the grass. There was something in the night that seemed pregnant with sudden violence, as if at anytime some crashing chaos might envelop the entire landscape. No one complained as we threaded in and out in snaky fashion to avoid other companies and other units, and all were too amazed to say anything when we saw field guns being wheeled into positions. There were no pits or any camouflage for them, and it showed what expectations there were."[58]

Others were still far behind their assembly areas. The 10th Canadians from Calgary and the Alberta foothills were just entering a silent city. "Someone saw a sign which said 'Amiens' which to us meant just another name on the map," recalled Charlie Brown, one of the rare veterans of the Canadians' first action at Ypres during the first German gas attack back in April 1915.

> In the dim light it looked a deserted, dusty old place with gaping holes in some of its buildings. It all seemed so eerie — everything was so still and quiet as we marched through, not like other fronts where there was the intermittent rat-a-tat and the odd boom to tell you how close we were. Hardly a shot was fired, and about the only noise we heard was that of our footsteps as we trudged through the dusty streets.

Each incident that night stirred imaginations and speculation. "As we moved forward the enemy was shelling the area, in a desultory manner, with some high velocity shells, a rather extraordinary thing, as our forces were by now well within ordinary artillery range. Naturally this suggested in our minds the idea that the Boche might have withdrawn his lighter artillery," wrote Alex "Turkey" Ross of the 28th "Nor'westers." His battalion eventually reached its position and the opportunity to rest, "but," as Ross observed, "it was doubtful if many slept. The next two or three hours were bound to tell the tale."

The 2nd (Eastern Ontario) Battalion discovered just how well the secret had been kept in some Australian units. "Are you relieving us?" asked one Aussie officer, obviously suspicious of the new arrivals. "No, we're relieving nobody," was the bewildering reply. "Then what are you doing here," he retorted, thinly disguising his scorn for these lost sheep. But at that moment he was called to his own headquarters where presumably he was let in on the secret. Presently he returned and cheerfully announced to the Canucks that he was "buzzing off" and extended them a warm "good luck!"[59]

Once marshaled in their allotted assembly areas, the troops waited while a very tricky preliminary operation was carried out. This was "taping," which consisted of laying strips of white tape marking "the start line" for each wave of infantry as well as lines straight forward towards the enemy position to insure that the troops, on advancing, did not lose direction. It was a touchy business for the tape-laying parties because the tapes had to be absolutely straight, and had to end reasonably close to the German line. They could not allow these preparations to be discovered by the enemy. Consequently, strong patrols covered no man's land.

When these preliminaries had been completed, the infantry formed up once more — in absolute silence — and filed forward to take up their positions along the appropriate tape. In silent lines, completely without shelter, they lay in no man's land till zero hour, protected only by the veils of darkness.

It was around 3:00 when the mist thickened to an almost impenetrable fog. Within moments it became difficult to see more than twenty yards in any direction. By this time most of the troops were in position alongside their jumping-off tapes. Nevertheless, several of the last units to arrive found themselves in difficulty. The 57th Victorians solved their problem ingeniously. Just as the leading elements were becoming anxious as to their direction they suddenly saw an amazing sight — their numeral, "57", in lights high above the fog ahead of them. On arriving they found that some quick-thinker had punctured the numerals into empty petrol tins, placed candles inside and then mounted them on poles along the route.

North of the Somme III Corps began the relief of the 18th Division's shattered 54th Brigade. In the darkness amid confusion and returning streams of stretcher cases, the 36th Brigade on loan from the 12th Division moved up to take over. The 9th Royal Fusiliers, 7th Royal Sussex

Regiment, and 5th Royal Berkshires had earned reputations for dogged tenacity. That quality was now severely tested, for out of the darkness came the dull pops of hundreds of German gas shells! Their targets were the roads and river-crossings in the Mericourt area, and the troops were forced to struggle along the tracks wearing gas masks, a monstrous handicap even in daylight. Now darkness and mist rendered hand signals invisible while the uncomfortable respirators made verbal commands inaudible. Confusion and casualties multiplied. At the same time, in the rear areas, regular bursts of high explosive and gas shells caused mounting casualties particularly among the artillery. Nevertheless, despite the fact that over two thousand mustard-gas shells fell upon III Corps, the British guns remained silent. The code-word "Hell" would authorize the artillery to hit back only if the Germans commenced counter-preparations.

Throughout the night there was intermittent artillery fire. A short barrage in one spot would be followed by a long period of silence, then in the distance another burst of fire could be heard falling on some other location. The outburst that caused the most consternation took place shortly after the fog had settled in. At Boves Castle Andy McNaughton had just begun another installment of the letter to his wife:

> 3:27 a.m. Just been walking up and down outside. It is getting perceptibly lighter. The volume of traffic on the roads has dwindled to practically nothing. The troops and tanks must now be pretty well into their battle positions. One tank on the opposite hill has apparently got into trouble as his petrol is burning brightly. I hope the men are out of it.
>
> Very quiet — just an occasional thump on the line.
>
> The first aeroplane of the morning has just passed along the lines going, I think, to bomb the Hun signal centres.
>
> Feeling very tired but confident. Just 50 more minutes till several hundred of our guns will open up.[60]

Now McNaughton heard in the distance the sound of sustained German artillery fire. Obviously, the Germans were laying down a heavy bombardment somewhere. In his letter to Mrs. McNaughton he confides his anxiety.

> I will not open up unless it becomes very heavy

and general. I can start the guns in a moment by a
signal which all can see if it is necessary.

About 20–30 shells a minute now, but local, opposite
_____, largely trench mortars, I think. Just been outside.
It is off our sector to the north and dying down.

This barrage fell on the Villers-Bretonneux-Marcelcave rail line at the
junction of the Australian and Canadian positions. The Australian front
trenches at this spot had just been vacated by two companies of the 21st
Victorian Battalion and by elements of the 50th South Australians, which
had been covering the 2nd Canadian Division. The men in the attacking
waves dispersed themselves among various shell-holes and trenches to wait
out the unwelcome attention. Said the Aussies, "They're having their fun
now, but wait till our barrage starts." The Australians suffered between
twenty and thirty casualties, and the 19th (Central Ontario) Battalion on
the Canadian left flank also lost a handful. Even when this savage little
barrage tapered off continual German flares kept the men on edge.

Shortly after this bombardment had broken out a similar one hit III
Corps north of the Somme. An observer at Sailly-le-Sec, a mile behind
the front reported:

A number of very distant batteries began to rain small
shells on to the British front or support positions ahead of
us. From ever so high up these little shells came whining
down and then burst with a swish, as if they were shrapnel,
or a pat, as if they were gas. This lasted about five minutes
and seemed to be certainly a counter-preparation by the
Germans against a suspected attack from the British front
north of the Somme.[61]

Did this indicate that the Germans knew about the offensive, or did
they only expect another British attempt to regain Brick Beacon? Whatever
the answer, a steady shower of shells probed III Corps' sector, and machine
guns began to chatter brutally through the dense fog as 4:20 drew closer.

At this moment, a lone Handley-Page bomber cruised up and down the
front above the fog-shrouded landscape. Lieutenant G.A. Flavelle of 207
Squadron had the early morning sky to himself. Plans had called for a
number of the huge biplanes to cruise over the area to drown the sounds

of tanks assembling. But the fog had made it almost impossible to get the heavy planes off the ground. Flavelle had achieved the impossible in taking off through the "soup" and then patrolling his sector. But now it was almost time to head home.

With zero hour only minutes away, the infantrymen made their final preparations, both physical and spiritual. Most of these men were fatalists. Months, and, for some, years of carnage had convinced them that there was nothing they could do when the inexorable hand of fate singled them out. Will Bird of the 42nd Royal Highlanders shook the hand of an old chum, Sergeant Cuvilier, and said, "Good luck, Eddie."

> Eddie shook his head. "This is my last trip," he replied.
>
> Many words tumbled out vaguely, and he smiled again. "I know all you want to tell me," he said. "But this is my last morning, and I wanted to say goodbye to someone from home."
>
> He turned abruptly and left. What could I say? And he was no more than gone when Bob Christensen, the stretcher-bearer and one of the best came over.... He smiled and shook hands. He said he hoped he would get to my heaven, but was going that day anyway. We shook hands warmly and he went. What could one say to him?[62]

The tanks were also now in position. When darkness had fallen they had begun their approach from harbours four miles in the rear. Progress had been slow with the engines throttled down to prevent them from being heard. Now they were in assembly points only a thousand yards behind the infantry jumping-off tapes. There they lurked in the foggy silence. At 4:08, twelve minutes before zero, the monsters coughed into life and, almost purring, crawled forward through the crowded formations of infantry. "In the impenetrable mist we started off for Hamel to fall in with the Australians," Captain Hickey of the 8th Tanks remembered. "I was responsible for getting my section there. It was impossible to see where we were going, and it was more by good luck than good guidance that when the mist lifted a little we found ourselves in Hamel. Eventually we reached a field where tanks were lined up."

At all the various headquarters the approaching zero-hour was awaited with equal measures of excitement and apprehension. Cyril Falls, liaison officer with the 42nd Division of the French First Army, witnessed a strange ceremony in General Deville's spartan command post. The hero of the Marne was not the usual dapper French general, indeed he was nervous, unpretentious, and careless of his appearance. When Falls entered the dugout he found Deville, in his scruffy uniform, standing by the telephone waiting to speak to the Corps Commander, General Toulorge. "It appears that this is a sort of ceremony with him before battle," records Falls' diary. "We all stood around waiting patiently for some time, I expect old Toulorge was being hauled out of bed. Then Deville said solemnly: 'My General, I have to report that my troops are in position. The assembly has passed off without a hitch.'"[63]

It was almost at this same moment that Corporal Harry Brice of the Canadian Engineers first saw the line of tanks about to cross Domart Bridge, which his squad had cleared of explosives. For a moment Brice stood in awe, then stepped up to the first of the monsters idling softly in the foggy darkness. These were the tanks of "A" Company, 5th Tank Battalion. Climbing up on the tank, he was accosted by a young officer who opened a hatch and asked politely, "How far am I from bridge number 64?"

"About twenty yards," replied Brice.

"This is it, boys," the young lieutenant reported excitedly to his crew. "We'll be the first to go over!" Then remembering his manners, he invited the Canadian corporal inside his iron landship — and just in time, too!

"Darned if that machine gun didn't open up just then," Brice would recall later. "It sounded like a hailstorm outside."

Brice laughed and said to the lieutenant, "You hear that? You might run into a lot of that when you get over there."

"That's what we're for," replied the officer confidently. "That's where we're going."

Years later Harry Brice was still impressed by the crew's spirit. "They were raring to get at it. The first tank to go over!" Brice could not stay long, he was told, for zero hour was very close now. "I wish you luck, boys. I sure wish you luck," he said. "I hope nothing happens to you and I hope you get back."

He climbed out of the warm tank, smelling of oil, into the chill fog and walked along the road till he had counted ten tanks, but he could detect even more looming out of the white vapours. Returning to his men in their post he told them what he had learned. "Watch out there. They're waiting for the signal," he told his squad, trying not to sound excited. "The signal is the largest gun we have. When it's fired, the officer said, you'll see the flash, but you won't hear it, for it'll be drowned out. *Everything* will be drowned out by the barrage."

In an open field before Hangard lay the former Jack-of-all-trades, Jerred Mansfield of the 3rd Canadian Machine Guns.

> The hands of the watch crept nearer and nearer to the hour. Our officer came around and gave each man a small shot of rum. I, for one, was trembling with suppressed excitement. Were we on the eve of victory, or were the Germans waiting in strength for us? Had all our precautions been in vain? We would soon know. It was one of the magnificent moments of the war and it filled one with a strange delight.

PART II
THE POWER OF THE NATION

"The power of the nation and that of the armed forces were so intermingled that it was impossible to separate them."
First Quartermaster-General Erich Ludendorff
My War Memories, Vol. IV, p. 4.

CHAPTER FIVE
PARALYSIS OF COMMAND

"At the head of the German army during these critical days was violent rage, indiscriminate blame, fundamental panic, paralysis of command."
Correlli Barnett[64]

W eeks before Amiens, on July 15, the German offensive against the French had burst across the River Marne east of Chateau Thierry, less than forty miles from Paris. But the offensive was only a partial success, for east of Reims no ground was seized at all, and the major gains were achieved against two Italian divisions. When these were replaced by British troops the advance ceased. This was the fifth such German offensive. Each had achieved initial surprise and had made substantial gains in territory, materiel, and prisoners; but each had failed to achieve the desired strategic result — the "knockout." Nevertheless, General Erich Ludendorff, in effective control of the German military machine, confidently advised the Secretary of State von Hintze, "I hope to make the enemy ready for peace with my next stroke."[65] Three days later at Tournai in Belgium, Ludendorff held a conference to discuss his ultimate knockout blow, "Hagen."

Ludendorff was pure soldier. He understood war and nothing else, and his narrow outlook reduced even that knowledge to the absurd. Professing to be a follower of Clausewitz, "he evolved the theory according to which war was not an instrument of policy. On the contrary, politics were ... a part of warfare."[66] Ludendorff was aggressively self-confident and contemptuous of almost everyone — even Field Marshal von Hindenburg, his senior partner. "In Hindenburg he saw, on his own confession, nothing but a serviceable symbol, and he believed that the masses needed some symbol of this kind — which amounts to saying that Ludendorff considered Hindenburg a man of straw."[67]

Ludendorff rose to sudden prominence at the age of 49 when he captured Liège in the opening phase of the war. He soon became the Chief of Staff for General Paul von Hindenburg, and the team went on to achieve several stunning victories over the Russians on the Eastern Front. Eventually von Hindenburg was given supreme command of the German war effort with Ludendorff as his "First Quartermaster-General" — a designation chosen by Ludendorff despite his domination of strategy. Initially depressed by the disappointing results of his five recent offensives, Ludendorff soon rebounded and regained his old confidence.

"Hagen" was Ludendorff's "baby" and he pinned all his hopes on this "decisive" offensive against the British in Flanders. However, at noon the "Hagen" conference was interrupted by the shocking news that the French had that morning launched a surprise counter-offensive against the new German salient on the Marne. General Mangin's French Tenth Army, which included several British and American divisions, had counterattacked with no preliminary bombardment. In total surprise a creeping barrage and swarms of French light tanks had fallen upon the Germans. By noon the French had advanced four miles. German losses were staggering and could not be replaced, but the worst news of all was the number of *feldgrau* who had surrendered rather than fight to the death. Although Ludendorff did not then know the final figures, 26,413 men and 609 officers had been captured. Losses in materiel were almost as serious — 612 guns, 221 mortars, and 3,330 machine guns. As well, the French had retaken 181 guns and 393 machine guns lost by their forces in the previous three days. The First Quartermaster-General was badly shaken by the news.

Later that day Ludendorff met with von Hindenburg at Supreme Headquarters at Avesnes. The entire General Staff was shocked by what followed. Ludendorff lost control of his emotions and insulted his superior! Both men abruptly stalked from the room, leaving their colleagues dismayed. Another embarrassing performance took place next morning at a second conference. General Bernhard von Lossberg, the acknowledged expert on defense in depth, recorded the following scene: "When I reported I found Ludendorff in a really agitated and nervous state. To my regret, he made some very unjustified remonstrances against the Chief of Operations Section [Lieutenant-Colonel Wilhelm Wetzell] and others of his colleagues who, he implied, had 'failed' in their assessment of the fighting forces. This scene was a really painful one."[68] Paralysis of the supreme command had set in — camouflaged ever so thinly by rage and accusations.

It was the threat to Hagen that had caused Ludendorff's panic. Hagen was the life-line to which he clung. He had been collecting all his best resources for this offensive. This cherished hammer-blow, he was convinced, would destroy the British and close the Channel ports to "the Entente," as the Germans called the Allies. The U.S.A., despite its potential, could then have little effect upon the war. But time was short; already American divisions had appeared in the line. If Ludendorff employed his carefully husbanded resources to shore up the front he would have to postpone Hagen. To postpone Hagen could mean abandoning it forever. Abandoning Hagen meant that Germany could not win the war by purely military means.

Reluctantly, Ludendorff gave up his hard-won bridgehead beyond the Marne and withdrew his forces on the night of July 20–21. Thus his tactical crisis was solved; the French counter-offensive had been held. To try to solve his strategic crisis he sent Lossberg and others to investigate and report on the state of the troops. Lossberg returned to burden Ludendorff even further. Using relentless logic, he recommended that all troops in the front line be withdrawn to the Siegfried Line (known to the Allies as "the Hindenburg Line") thus abandoning all the areas captured in the brilliant spring offensives. Only this action would release enough troops to permit Hagen a chance of success. For Ludendorff, the worst shock was to discover that Lossberg, one of his most able officers, had already relegated Hagen to a merely tactical role, and considered Germany's best hope to be a retreat to a strong defensive line followed by negotiations.

Ludendorff held out against Lossberg's relentless logic. "I consider your suggestion relevant, but I cannot carry them out — for political reasons." When pressed by Lossberg, he explained that the "political reasons" were: "Consideration of the impression that would be made on the enemy, on our army, and on the people back home."[69]

Such was the paralysis at OHL that no decision was reached until July 22. That evening it was decided on a further retirement from the Marne to the Vesle. The withdrawal would take place on the night of July 26–27. Reluctantly, Ludendorff came to a second, more momentous decision. "The offensive in Flanders could not bring a rapid and decisive success. According to all indications, the enemy was ready for it. If he avoided the attack, as he had done east of Reims, we should be unable to force a decision.... O.H.L. therefore decided to abandon this offensive."[70] Ludendorff had given up on Hagen. That evening, one of his staff, Mertz von Quirnheim, summed up the eventful day in his diary — "His excellency quite broken."[71]

Kaiser Wilhelm II had imperiously and impulsively led Germany into the war expecting a rapid and overwhelming victory. But he had proven unequal to the demands of real leadership and soon gave up all but the trappings to his chancellor, Bethman-Holweg. The latter had favoured a negotiated peace and attempted to find a peaceful end to the war. However, the military, led by Hindenburg and Ludendorff, protested that "defeatists" were at the helm, and demanded Bethman-Holweg's dismissal. The Kaiser caved in when his two military titans threatened to resign. As a result, Bethman-Holweg was replaced by the first of a series of puppet-chancellors controlled by Hindenburg and Ludendorff, who henceforth made all decisions — military and political. The Kaiser felt relieved by this arrangement even though his two military "advisors" now treated him with disdain. For his part, the once-bombastic monarch escaped into a world of fantasy and adopted "his well known, impossible victory mood," as it was described by Admiral von Müller.[72]

On July 22, the second anniversary of Bethman-Holweg's dismissal, the Kaiser received a nasty shock. His year-long sojourn in "cloud cuckoo land" had been harshly terminated by a conference at OHL. Admiral von Müller recorded the event in his diary: "July 22, 1918. This afternoon the Kaiser drove over to Avesnes to hear a report. He was told the bitter truth which conflicts with the optimistic communiqués. The Field Marshals admitted total failure."[73]

Wilhelm's reaction was typically selfish. At Spa later in the day, Müller recorded: "After dinner His Majesty spoke of himself to a small circle ... as a defeated War Lord for whom we must show consideration." Next day the Kaiser's thoughts were still of himself: "After lunch in the train the Kaiser admitted that he had not closed an eye all night. He had seen visions of all the English and Russian relatives and all the ministers and generals of his own reign marching past and mocking him. Only the little Queen of Norway had been friendly to him."[74]

The common citizens of Germany were sheltered from such disturbing dreams by the realities of malnutrition and hunger. Their dreams were similar to one described in the *Vienna Witzblat*. "I had a wonderful dream last night," said a woman to her neighbour. "I dreamt that the war was over."

The other replied, "What did you have to eat?"

"I don't know," admitted the woman.

"What a stupid dream!"[75]

Four long years of the British naval blockade had achieved drastic results. It had been hoped by all Germans that the long-delayed Treaty of Brest-Litovsk imposed upon the defeated Russians would start a flow of foodstuffs into Germany. Unfortunately, the results proved to be so meagre as to be unnoticeable to the average citizen. Two examples of the effects of the British blockade will suffice: (1) The *minimum* amount of fats scientists considered necessary for the individual for one day now had to be stretched to last for two weeks; (2) The milk shortage: The lack of fodder formerly imported for dairy cattle had cut the number of milch cows drastically. The meat shortage had resulted in a further reduction as milch cows were slaughtered for beef. The severe tin shortage meant that tin containers could no longer be provided to ship milk to the populated areas. Finally, this shortage of suitable containers plus the low quality of the milk produced by poorly fed cows meant that much milk spoiled before it ever reached the cities. The net result was that every city of thirty-thousand or more now suffered a *daily* shortage of half a million litres of milk.[76]

Bread now made up almost 70 percent of the average German's diet. And what bread it was! "Flour" was ground from such wheat substitutes as rye, beans, bran, beets, and potatoes. The government commission that studied the problem later reported, "When the main article of diet is available only in half-rations and then eaten only reluctantly and badly digested owing to its poor quality, this must inevitably have ill effects on the health and strength of the population."[77]

Even the upper classes were relatively hard-pressed. In June Princess Blücher wrote,

> We ourselves have little to eat but smoked meat and dried peas and beans, but in the towns they are considerably worse off. The potatoes have come to a premature end, and in Berlin the population have now a portion of 1 lb. per head a week, and even these are bad. The cold winds of this wintry June have retarded the growth of the

vegetables, and there is almost nothing to be had. We are
all waiting hungrily for the harvest and the prospect of at
least more bread and flour.[78]

One proposal, much talked about, was "The Common Pot." This was the suggestion that everyone, regardless of rank or occupation, should eat the same food as the German frontline soldier. Nothing came of the proposal: though each faction agreed to take part, they agreed to do so only if another rival group agreed to do the same. This tone of self-denial was well illustrated by the German General Staff. After avoiding the issue for some months, General Ludendorff reported in October, "Even the Supreme Command would eat what the field kitchens provided, if all the Secretaries of State and the whole of Berlin would eat nothing else." He recorded with satisfaction, "The Chancellor, Prince Max, declined to do so."[79]

Other disturbing signs of a breakdown in the nation's spirit of self-sacrifice were abundant. Spectacles not seen since before the war were reappearing in Berlin.

> Men dressed in tuxedos, accompanied by wives in flowing
> evening gowns bedecked with jewelry, alighted from
> chauffeured limousines to spend a night on the town, their
> apparel and demeanor symbolizing a disdain for the spirit
> of sacrifice that had flourished in 1914.... War veterans,
> upon boarding street trolleys, found themselves jostled by
> civilians who also refused to give their seats to those who
> had lost a limb for the Fatherland.[80]

Germany was changing. On Wednesday, August 7, *Berliner Tageblatt* reported on "a gala Fashion Show" — the first of the war years — that had just opened to dense crowds in Berlin. "This show attracted not only the elite of Berlin society but hundreds of foreign buyers as if it were a normal peacetime commercial exhibit of fall fashions. With models dressed in ornate silk dresses and rich furs, viewers could easily forget that most Germans were contending with primitive paper-made clothing."[81]

In stark contrast to the frivolity of the upper classes was the newly awakened class-consciousness of the German workers. Disgust with the war and the Reichstag's total inability to cope with its military rulers drove the workers to strike. They had before them the example of Russia's workers rising *en masse* to remove an oppressive government, and the sight was heady stuff. Nevertheless, the "Great Strike of January '18" had been totally crushed by the government. The official reprisal had been swift but incredibly inept — strikers were conscripted into the army. "The government was kind enough to send excellent agitators to revolutionize the front," exulted one revolutionary. "Every man who was then sent to the trenches or to prison or punished in any way for refusing to work was an agitator for revolutionary Independent Social-Democracy and a man who explained to the soldiers their duties as men, as sons of their country, and as soldiers."[82]

Crushing the strike had not settled the grievances, nor had it poured oil upon the troubled waters of class-consciousness. Germans had endured worse — for instance, the dreadful winter of 1916–17 — but then there had been a feeling of unity and purpose. That old feeling had vanished by the first days of 1918 to be replaced by the cancer of distrust and even animosity among the classes of German society.

Germany possessed a Reichstag, an elected assembly, which in most countries would have clamoured for the necessary changes. However, by its very constitution the Reichstag held no decision-making role in the conduct of the war. Edicts of the Supreme Command in no way depended upon the Reichstag's confidence or approval. According to the theories of the General Staff, "it was the business of the leading statesman to make prompt use of the success of the military commander."[83] After the war the General Staff accused Germany's "political leaders" of not utilizing German successes in 1918. "Even the period between the offensives of March, 1918, and up to July which brought us a series of great successes and inflicted severe blows upon our opponents and during which the success of our submarine campaign caused the British the greatest anxiety was not sufficiently utilized from the point of view of the statesmanship."[84]

This accusation is misleading, for it leaves the crucial point unsaid. Germany's "political leaders" were in fact her two military titans, Hindenburg and Ludendorff. *They* made and unmade chancellors, and it was their own political ineptitude that had lost Germany the chance for a favourable negotiated peace. After their first offensives they had been convinced that Germany was about to win a crushing victory over the Allies; therefore talk of negotiation was almost traitorous. Even as late as June when the Secretary of State, Richard Kuhlmann, had stated in the Reichstag that "a conclusion by military decision without diplomatic negotiations is improbable," the generals had been horrified. Most Germans however, echoed the thoughts of Princess Blücher when she wrote, "It has fallen like a bomb. Everyone seems to agree that what he has said was the truth, and nothing but the truth, but that it was a heinous offense to say it."[85] The enraged Ludendorff had demanded that Kuhlmann be fired and replaced by

Paul von Hintze, and the obedient Kaiser had done so. Now, less than a month later, OHL itself was not certain of a total military victory.

There were serious shortages of just about every military item. Airplanes were one production problem. Although the Fokker DVII was generally considered to be the finest craft in the air, Germany's production figures were being surpassed by the Allies. It has been estimated that German factories were now able to manufacture only one-third to one-half the number of planes produced by the Allies.

Transport had also become a crucial factor. Every transport item was in short supply — especially horses. On July 10 secret orders stressed this severe shortage. "We must take care of our horses as they cannot be replaced. The men must thoroughly understand that this is absolutely necessary in order to continue the war until victory is reached."[86] Mounts were now being collected from officers of all arms to provide the artillery with sufficient horses to keep operating.

Of all the shortages the most critical was the shortage of men. As early as July 9, OHL had ordered rear units to comb their ranks for men capable of serving at the front. Previous orders exempting soldiers from families suffering severe losses and soldiers over forty-three years of age having served more than six months were to be ignored. For some time the main concern of the High Command had been to maintain the number of infantry units even though it was necessary to weaken each battalion numerically to do so. Thus German infantry battalions had been reduced from 980 to 880, although machine gun companies continued to employ 130 men each. The actual trench strength of most battalions when those on sick parade and leave were discounted came to 600. Now in late July OHL was forced to break up ten divisions because of recent losses.

The only other means of bringing infantry units up to strength was to conscript the undesirable or to rob future armies. Both were done; convicts and "strike comrades" from the factories were dispatched to the front. At the same time the youths not due for enlistment until 1919 were drafted, and even the 1920 class was being called to the depots.

Desertion had become a major problem. Large numbers of German soldiers were giving up without a fight to escape from the front. But the most astonishing fact was that the majority of desertions were organized from *within* Germany by revolutionaries determined to force Germany out of the war. As one deserter later stated:

> The organization of desertion was quite systematic and
> was worked out down to the smallest details. The main

bases of this organization were in Berlin, Hamburg, Cologne, Stuttgart, and Munich. Here the deserters were provided with food cards, forged papers, lodging, money, and directions how to reach the frontier, and also found an excellent postal service. At the same time these bases were always kept fully informed by comrades regarding the reliability of the officials at frontier posts which had to be passed, so that the frontier was passed without difficulties.[87]

In Holland, "deserters' associations" were formed to assist others in making their way over the border.

This rampant desertion was indicative of the morale both at home and at the front. OHL had been able to ignore this problem by isolating itself from the troops, but lower down the chain of command a more realistic picture emerged. Censors reading the men's letters home found sentiments such as "It is time that our Government got peace. More and more Americans are coming out and we are having a foul time: too many hounds are the death of the hare," or "The war will end when the great capitalists have killed us all," or, "You at home must strike. But make no mistake about it, and raise revolution. Then peace will come."[88]

Officers supervising rail transport were well aware of the problem of morale. A year earlier reports had begun to come in complaining of the undisciplined conduct of men in troop trains moving towards the front. By February shots were being fired from the train windows and men disappeared at every stop. For example, in May one party of seventy-six NCOs and 555 men lost three NCOs and eighty men en route to their division. By June violence had become common, and revolutionary graffiti such as "We're not fighting for Germany's honour but for the millionaires," and "Slaughter Cattle, Wilhelm and Sons" had become commonplace on trains heading to the front. The Eighteenth Army south of Amiens had been forced to arm railway guards with rifles and even machine guns after several trains had been attacked by armed bands that had looted them before vanishing into the countryside.

Not all generals chose to ignore this malaise. Prince Rupprecht, the fifty-year-old Prince of Bavaria, had written on May 26 concerning the drafts his Army Group was receiving: "Unfortunately it is not unusual that in these journeys up to twenty percent of the troops absent themselves without leave, for which, when again apprehended, they are mostly punished with from two to four months imprisonment. This, however, is exactly what many of them wish, as they thus avoid one battle or another."[89]

When units of the German Navy had mutinied twelve months earlier OHL scoffed at the suggestion that it could happen to the German Army, and they continued on as though nothing had changed. Now in July 1918, many generals still refused to see the demoralization of their men. Possibly they were like the Kaiser when he visited the front in May after Ludendorff's spectacular advances. He had started the day in high spirits, but by lunch, "spoke very harshly of the brutality of our men, who made no effort to help badly wounded English soldiers, although right in their path. He had seen to it personally that they were bandaged and carried down the line."[90] It seems not to have occurred to the Kaiser that his men's lack of concern stemmed from their complete exhaustion and lack of reasonable food.

A major reason for the demoralization of the German soldier was the Allies' complete mastery in tanks. German generals had scoffed at the tank as a useless weapon, but that did not fool the common soldiers who soon were calling the tanks "*Deutsch's Tod*" — "Germany's Downfall." The *Neue Freie Presse* of Vienna expressed the fears of the frontline soldier when it speculated: "Hitherto tank squadrons containing hundreds of tanks have been employed.... It is conceivable that the enemy and the world's almost unlimited war industry may produce this arm in unprecedented masses. As human shock-troops advance in waves, solid tank waves might also advance."[91] When at last the construction of *fifteen* tanks had been authorized by OHL, Hindenburg commented (while visiting the tank factory at Charleroi), "I do not think that tanks are any use, but as these have been made they may as well be tried."[92]

Anti-tank tactics and weapons had been ignored. The General Staff dealt with the problem by issuing the following instructions: "The infantry must not let itself be frightened by tanks. The fighting capacity of the tank is small.... It has been proved that tank crews are nervous and are inclined to turn back or leave the tank.... The hostile infantry follows tanks only half-heartedly."[93] The French Army's brilliant success in using masses of Renault tanks during their counterattack on the Marne now reversed OHL's thinking. Ludendorff's order of July 22 stated: "The utmost attention must be paid to combat tanks.... Our earlier successes against tanks led to a certain contempt for this weapon of warfare. We must, however, now reckon with more dangerous tanks."[94] It was a difficult admission to make, but OHL's past neglect had to be explained away to the army and to the public whose faith in their leadership had already begun to waver.

Desperate attempts were now undertaken to remedy the omission. Special officers were appointed to staffs from brigade level up whose sole duty was to deal with anti-tank measures. An anti-tank rifle had just been developed. Unwieldy and conspicuous, it was five and a half feet long and weighed thirty-six pounds. Although it fired a 530-calibre armour-piercing bullet that could easily penetrate the Mark IV at several hundred yards, it was unpopular with the infantry who had to use it because it was a slow single-shot weapon and had an unbelievable kick. The field gun firing over open sights was at last recognized as the most effective weapon available. OHL now instructed that three measures be carried out to provide defence against tanks. First, outpost guns were to be hidden well forward and reserved solely for anti-tank work. Second, reserve batteries were to be given sectors that they were responsible for occupying and defending in case of tank assaults. Third, all batteries, even howitzers, were ordered to take up positions from which advancing tanks could be engaged by direct fire.

The infantry's anti-tank role was not so well defined. Some were instructed to take cover and allow the tanks through: "Tanks must be dealt with behind the front. The chief object is the repulse of the enemy infantry." Other orders advised, "infantry should move to a flank." How this was to be done on a wide front was not explained. The only consistent instruction given to the unfortunate infantry was "to keep their heads."[95]

General Ludendorff began to recover his spirit and his composure after the conference of July 22. He had been badly shaken by the Allies' response to his latest offensive, and even worse, by being forced to give up Hagen; but Ludendorff had not been crushed. As the situation along the front returned to normal so did his composure. The French advance had bogged down and there was no indication of its renewal. The planned German withdrawals had gone off without a hitch: the first, the major retirement from the Marne to the Vesle; the second, before Amiens and Montdidier (which caused Foch and Haig such concern); and the third, several minor pull-backs in Flanders. All were carried out to secure more defensible positions requiring fewer men.

With each of these small successes Ludendorff's paralysis of the will waned, and his confidence increased. After the war he wrote his memoirs in which he ignored his own panic and stressed that of his troops. With monumental lack of understanding Ludendorff identified August 1 as the turning point: "The shadow cast by the events of July 18 had passed. After that day, in spite of the heavy demands made upon him, the German soldier had fought well, and felt himself a better man than his enemy."[96]

OHL expected only minor local attacks, believing that the Allies had lost too heavily to be capable of a major offensive. Nevertheless, a sharp lookout was kept for the Canadian Corps as the following secret document indicated: "The Canadian Corps, magnificently equipped and highly trained in storm tactics, may be expected to appear shortly in offensive operations."[97]

On Friday, August 2, Ludendorff issued orders to prepare to resume attacks both in Flanders and east of Montdidier. This was a concrete step, but confusion still clouded his mind, as evidenced by this incoherent strategic directive:

> The situation demands that on one hand we should place ourselves on the defensive, on the other that we should as soon as possible go into the attack again.... In our attacks ... it will not so much be a question of conquering further territory as of defeating the enemy and gaining more favourable positions.[98]

Contrary to popular belief, the German intelligence service had been decidedly ineffective throughout the war. August 2 was no exception. Based on reports by intelligence, OHL issued an appraisal of the situation listing five possible targets for Allied attacks — Amiens was not mentioned.

On Sunday, August 4, Ludendorff issued an order of the day that he hoped would both inspire his troops to a spirited defence and spread any blame for the defeat of July 18.

> I am under the impression that, in many quarters, the possibility of an enemy offensive is viewed with a certain degree of apprehension. There is nothing to justify this apprehension, provided our troops are vigilant and do their duty ... the French were only able to obtain one initial tactical success, due to surprise ... and this success ought to have been denied them.... It was not the enemy's tactical successes which caused our withdrawal, but the precarious state of our rearward communications. The French and British infantry generally fought with caution; the Americans attacked more boldly but with less skill. It is to the tanks that the enemy owes his success of the first

day. These, however, would not have been formidable if the infantry had not allowed itself to be surprised, and if the artillery had been sufficiently distributed in depth.

Ludendorff then reassured his men that their new defensive positions were stronger and in greater depth than ever before. He concluded with a flourish. "We should wish for nothing better than to see the enemy launch an offensive, which can but hasten the disintegration of his forces."[99]

The same day General von der Marwitz commanding the Second Army opposite Amiens received an alarming message at his headquarters: "Apparently two Canadian divisions have been relieved from their hitherto front position after a short tour; particular attention should be given to ascertain their whereabouts.... The front of the British Third and Fourth Armies require particular attention."[100]

On Wednesday, 7 August, Ludendorff attempted to remove the effects of his own paralysis and panic by issuing a secret order to his staff:

> To my regret the existence of despondent outlooks and rumours has been established and their source traced to Supreme Headquarters.... The O.H.L. is free from despondency. Sustained by what has previously been achieved on the front and at home, it prepares stout-heartedly to meet the challenges that are to come. No member of O.H.L. may think and act in a manner other than this.[101]

Ludendorff had regained his aloof serenity, and looked to the future with confidence. Intelligence finally reported that the Canadians had been located in Flanders, but added that there was no sign of an immediate Allied offensive. Consequently Ludendorff issued orders advising his commanders to expect attacks of a purely local nature. Not everyone was convinced. Lieutenant-Colonel Wetzell, Chief of the Operations Section, and the butt of Ludendorff's bad humour just days ago, submitted a memorandum that pointed out that "if the Commander-in-Chief of the Entente had even a reasonable knowledge of his business he must attack us ... on the Somme front."[102] The First Quartermaster-General was not convinced.

CHAPTER SIX
ISOLATION IN A "QUIET SECTOR"

"The feeling of numerical inferiority and isolation has a very depressing moral effect on the men."
Crown Prince Rupprecht, July 30, 1918[103]

"This sector was called a quiet one and the troops were reproached with not having carried on enough work at building trenches."
History of the 247th Reserve Infantry Regiment[104]

The weary men in "coal-scuttle" helmets crouched in their shell holes and stretches of trench peering into the inky blackness and listening for suspicious sounds. It was the night of Wednesday, August 7, and the sentries in their field-grey uniforms, huge stove-pipe boots, and fearsome helmets were men of the 109th Division of the German Army. They held the sector opposite Amiens, from the Amiens-Chaulnes railway three miles in front of Villers-Bretonneux to the Amiens-Roye Road, 8,500 yards to the south.

Shortly before sunset a most singular event had taken place opposite them. While their artillery was firing off its normal quota of searching shots a chance shell started an enormous fire on the outskirts of Villers-Bretonneux in what appeared to be an orchard. Immediately several batteries brought down a rain of shells on the innocent-looking orchard and it erupted into a huge conflagration that sent up a pillar of smoke that could be seen for miles until dusk swallowed it. The consensus among the men was that the Allies had stored their petrol and ammunition too close to the front and that some British staff officer would pay for the mistake with his job.

But as interesting as this sight had been, there was only one topic that occupied the minds of these *feldgrau*: in a few hours the weary 109th Division would be relieved by the crack 117th.

Like most of the so-called "trench divisions," the 109th was badly understrength — only three thousand riflemen, most of whom were apathetic and listless. The few veterans had been over-extended too many times and now regarded themselves simply as survivors. Physical hardship had also sapped them — poor rations caused by the British blockade, topped off for most by a savage bout of "Flanders Fever." This was the same "Spanish Influenza" that had been sweeping over the world with such deadly effect, but its results were even more devastating here on the German side of the Western Front because of the soldiers' poor diet, their exhaustion, and poor sanitary conditions.

The German Army of August 1918 was vastly different from that of August 1914 — much more cynical and crafty, but without the dedication and élan that existed at the beginning of the war. The last vestiges of dash and ferocity had been used up in the German offensives early in 1918. For these mobile operations on a massive scale all the best troops had been stripped from the divisions and united as "Storm Troopers." These highly motivated and splendidly equipped units had at first succeeded magnificently. But now they too had been worn away, and the depleted "trench divisions" had been left with the dreary task of holding quiet parts of the line.

Certainly there was a shortage of the old aggressive spirit. German troops were now very reluctant to carry out night raids on their foe. This was the time-honoured method of obtaining information by capturing prisoners. Now it was necessary to offer three weeks leave or large monetary rewards to persuade the *feldgrau* to cross no man's land. The news had spread regarding the daring and good fortune of three men of the 203rd Reserve Infantry Regiment of the 43rd Reserve Division. These had received two hundred marks for capturing two "Tommies" from the 18th British Division recently arrived opposite Morlancourt.

Among the numerous new replacements were many who talked incessantly of injustice, revolution, and peace. Especially vociferous were men from the Eastern Front, sent to France now that the Russians had finally been knocked out of the war. Many of these men had been infected by the virus of revolution now sweeping Russia. "That socialism has already gained the upper hand in everything is characterized in our battery, by the fact that a so-called soldiers' council has its hand in everything," wrote a gunner from the Eastern Front.[105] A soldier in a labour battalion wrote, "The longer the war lasts the more obvious it becomes that the officers of all arms of the service consider it as a most favourable opportunity to enrich themselves.... An institution on the model of the Russian soldiers' councils would be a great blessing for us and a good education for them."[106]

Other new arrivals included "strike comrades." These were leaders of "the Great Strike of January '18." Formerly factory workers exempted from military service, they had been conscripted and sent to the front as punishment. Here they talked constantly of desertion, and even passed out pamphlets. "Our enemies are not the French, the Russians, or even the English people," declared one, "but the German Junkers and the capitalists."[107] These men were nearly all activists of the Independent Social-Democratic Party, and their aims were simple — revolutionize the front, organize mass desertion, and bring down the old regime in Germany.

Recently, despite this widespread disinterest in glory, there had been renewed speculation of another offensive. Only two days earlier the *Berliner Tageblatt* had carried a statement by General Baron von Ardenne: "The German offensive has suffered an unpleasant interruption, but it will certainly be resumed.... Apart from other factors, the happy confidence of our army leaders, which has recently been described by our war correspondents, guarantees that this freedom of initiative will, at the right time, be utilized."[108] Such reports were read glumly by men of the trench divisions.

Many of the *feldgrau* on duty that night of August 7 undoubtedly let their thoughts wander back to loved ones at home. Visions of those wan, pinched faces brought waves of despair. The children were slowly starving, and the government was either unwilling or unable to do anything about it. The number of children who died each day in the Fatherland had soared already, and there was no prospect of improvement. In contrast, *Courier de l'Air* daily reminded the weary soldier of a better life. Millions of these shrewdly worded British leaflets had been dropped upon the front lines and in the bivouac areas over the last year. At first designed to provide inhabitants of the occupied areas of France and Belgium with accurate news of the war through extracts from Allied and neutral newspapers, the *Courier* had become popular contraband for the *feldgrau*. In it, German prisoners of war wrote glowingly of the food and of their treatment in prisoner of war camps far from the fighting.

Certainly it was a fine summer night for such dreaming — a shade chilly, but the air was clear and the stars sparkled, remote from man's ghastly war. It had also been deliciously peaceful so far, with only a few shells going the other way. The enemy had been unusually quiet, although in the distance the sounds of lorries were often detected. Many of the newer men — suffering from "tank fright" — averred that it was tanks that they heard.

It was true that even in daylight there had been an extraordinary number of lorries moving about beyond no man's land over the last few days. From Hangard, Lieutenant Hammer, Adjutant of the 217th Reserve Infantry Regiment, had counted eighty of them in and around Boves yesterday. Today he had counted 120! Without doubt, Boves had seen more traffic in the last few days than it had in all previous years. Hammer had, like many other officers, sent his baggage home. It was only in the way during an attack, and besides, all the officers' servants had been withdrawn to beef up the forward companies.[109]

Among the front-line troops the daily talk concerned the probability of an Allied offensive. The heavy traffic and the shouting of orders during the night could lead to no other conclusion said some, while many reasoned that it was simply the Australians taking over this part of the French line. Things had seemed less ominous when the French had held the sector opposite. Now that the Australians had extended south into the area almost anything could be expected. The men from down under had earned a reputation as fierce and wily adversaries, prone to raiding and raising havoc. The *feldgrau* of the 109th hoped and prayed that these unreasonable warriors would leave them in peace for just a few more hours. That was all it would take because the 109th should be well out of the way by dawn.

PRIOR TO AUGUST 7

The Amiens sector was the responsibility of the German Second Army. General von der Marwitz, its irascible chief, was not impressed by the troops in his command. Known to his officers as "The Automatic Boiler," von der Marwitz did not mince words. He reported that three of his divisions, the 107th, 109th, and 43rd Reserve were "in urgent need of relief." Of the remainder, the 192nd and 243rd were only "fit to hold a quiet front," although the 14th Bavarian, 41st, 54th Reserve, 108th, and 225th were "fit for trench warfare." Fortunately for von der Marwitz, two fresh divisions had also been allotted to him, the 27th Wurttemberg, and the 117th. These he glowingly rated as "of outstanding quality."[110]

At OHL it was believed that the Second Army's defences were in excellent shape. Had not Ludendorff himself issued orders on July 6 detailing the pattern for all defences on the front? First there had to be an Advanced Zone covered by outposts and patrols extending to a depth of between five hundred and one thousand yards. Next came the Principle Line of Resistance, which had to dominate the Advanced Zone and contain a garrison comprising the main fire-power. In expectation of localized attacks in the Amiens sector, Ludendorff had reinforced the artillery. The new batteries were to arrive that week.

To insure that these orders were being faithfully carried out, staff officers had been sent out to the headquarters to inspect the results. Sent to confer with "the Automatic boiler" at Second Army was General von Kuhl, Chief of Staff to Crown Prince Rupprecht. Von Kuhl claimed to be satisfied, and Ludendorff accepted his report at face value. All the reports turned in by Ludendorff's staff officers were in a similar vein. At the various headquarters they had found detailed maps with the required positions marked in blue as stipulated. These chair-borne staff officers seldom ventured closer to the front, so after pleasant visits they returned to assure OHL that all was well. If these staff officers had gone forward into the front line they would have received rude awakenings.

South of the River Somme were three lines of shallow trenches, poorly wired, and lacking shelters. Behind these lay nothing more than the long-abandoned trenches of the Inner Amiens Defence system dug by the French three years earlier. Four miles beyond this lay the once formidable Outer Amiens Defences dating from the Battle of the Somme in 1916. This system included strong belts of wire, but of course, faced the wrong way! The one real strength of the entire Second Army position was its vast number of machine-gun posts. These ranged from carefully constructed platforms that could be raised or lowered below ground, to unprotected sites concealed only by the ripening grain. This same grain often completely masked the Advanced Zone from its support in the Principle Line of Resistance. Why were these German defences in such poor state? Although regiments in the 41st Division complained that their trenches were only disconnected lengths giving cover only to breast height, their divisional commander stated that his men would not do the work ordered to strengthen their own positions. Some divisions were in such poor physical shape that there was no one available or capable of doing the manual labour required.

The 13th Division was in just such a situation south of the Somme. These veterans had spent the last five weeks in the line and had been the Aussies' victims during the Battle of Hamel on July 4. The defences shown on OHL maps did not exist in the 13th's sector. The division had only twenty-seven field guns and twelve howitzers instead of the standard thirty-six of each. Only six infantry battalions were in the two lines — a total of twenty-four companies. Contrary to OHL orders, thirteen of these were in the Advanced Zone instead of the Principle Line of Resistance. This had been forced upon the weakened 13th by Australian raids.

The troops' lack of confidence and their feeling of isolation manifested itself in rumours of disaster and enemy raids. Numerous reports had been sent back telling of tanks heard each night. Reconnaissance revealed no tanks, but still the rumours persisted. Supreme Command, safe behind the lines, scoffed at the constant nervousness of the trench troops and labeled their claims "tank fright."

However, von der Marwitz took these reports seriously, and because they had increased alarmingly since August 1, had ordered a "stand-to" on the morning of the 4th. The expected attack did not materialize, however, and the troops were too tired to continue this practice every morning. Besides, it seemed only common sense that the enemy would not bring tanks up to advertise themselves days before their attack. If tanks were there, they would have been employed by now.

"The Automatic Boiler" had organized a large raid on the Australians at Hourges for that night (4–5 August). He had already surmised that the Australians had extended their front southwards, but he desired proof. Consequently, four parties of twenty-five each slipped out into no man's land. They were supplied by the 373rd Infantry Regiment of the 225th Division. One of the parties discovered an Australian post in the ruins of Hourges and fought it out with rifles and bombs. Four of the 373rd crept behind the Australians and shot one of the defenders before rushing the survivors, capturing four and a sergeant. These prisoners were very unco-operative and threw themselves on the ground. The NCO in charge had to shoot one, lightly wounding him, before they could be dragged back across no man's land. A second raiding party also had an encounter, but took no prisoners. The captives made "a good, soldierly impression," according to a German War Diary, and their sergeant, "refused to make any military statement, and could not be shaken in his resolve by any means employed." The others were recent arrivals to the 51st West Australian Battalion. "Whether their statements are pretence or truth there is no means of proving: all were reticent and only after a lot of talking did their tongues become loose."[111]

Not much was learned from these Australians, but it now seemed obvious to Second Army Headquarters why there had been so much transport activity of late. The Australian takeover of the French position between Villers-Bretonneux and the Amiens-Roye Road must account for it. This stretching of the Australian line could only mean one thing: French troops were being withdrawn to use in an attack at some other point on the front. So reasoned many staff officers.

The *feldgrau* at the front remained unconvinced. Even from positions as far back as battalion headquarters it was possible to see impressive amounts of traffic around the eastern exit from Amiens. The historian of the 26th Reserve Infantry Regiment summed up the belief of the front-line soldier: "After August 4th there could no longer exist any doubt of the enemy's intentions. From 9:30 p.m. onwards throughout the whole night not only heavy train and road traffic, sounds of voices and neighing of horses, but actually the strong noise of motor-engines at Cachy and Villers-Bretonneux were heard by all sections of troops in the forward lines. All measures for defence against tanks were therefore again carefully tested."[112]

Von der Marwitz had planned an attack of his own in the meantime. It took place early Tuesday morning, August 6, south of Morlancourt, astride the Bray-Corbie Road. On the night of July 28–29, the Australians had taken a large area around Brick Beacon. Von der Marwitz judged that he must put a stop to any further advances in the area by striking back hard. With the arrival of one of his two "outstanding" divisions, the 27th Wurttemberg, "the Automatic Boiler" now had the means at his disposal. Just as planned, the Wurttembergers sliced through the British trenches and into their gun positions. Despite British counterattacks, the operation was a great success and showed what well-disciplined troops could accomplish. Eight British officers and 274 other ranks — all but two from the 18th and 58th Divisions — had been captured. The two exceptions were men of the 50th Division taken at "the Quarrie," quite deep in the British position. Both described themselves as "machine-gunners," although they gave no further information.

That same day at noon Crown Prince Rupprecht had issued a situation report for his group of armies. One curious note read, "Results of reconnaissance: about a hundred tanks were observed on the Ailly-Moreuil road." Nothing more was said about the report — not even a warning. As one LI Corps staff officer commented, "Not even a request to keep a sharp look-out. We were anxious because anyone who brings up a hundred tanks is not planning a joy-ride. The Army Staff was astonishingly indifferent."[113] So were the subordinate staffs — corps and divisional both. However, the most remarkable thing about this report is that it was completely false! The area in question was in the French XXXI Corps area, but their ninety Renaults were all in Fouencamps, miles from the Ailly-Moreuil road.

Equally groundless were *all* of the other reports of tanks in the Amiens sector! *No* Allied tanks were anywhere near the front line. The *feldgrau* were indeed "crying wolf"!

WEDNESDAY, AUGUST 7

While Berliners were reading about the "slick and elegant" finery displayed at last night's "Gala Fashion Show," von der Marwitz and his staff were wondering what was going on across no man's land. The bad flying weather coupled with the exceptionally effective blanket put up by Allied air forces had prevented any glimpse behind their lines. To remedy this situation, the famous Flying Circus once commanded by the late "Red Baron," Manfred von Richthofen, was to be transferred from the Seventh Army into Second Army's sector. Younger brother Lothar, accompanied by his "wingman," the great ace, Loewenhardt, would, in fact, be flying over that evening to inspect the arrangements.

Heavy road traffic was obvious, yet no tanks were in the neighbourhood. That must be assumed despite the constant unfounded reports. The Allies could not have risked keeping tanks in the area for several days. No, they would already have attacked if the "tanks" had been anything other than imaginary. Besides, any major British offensive would have to include the Canadians, and their wireless transmissions had been detected near Ypres in Flanders. Despite these reassurances, von der Marwitz was still puzzled. He decided to send out patrols that night to penetrate the veil of secrecy. Accordingly, the 13th Division opposite Accroche Wood and the 41st Division astride the Villers-Bretonneux-Chaulnes rail line was ordered to probe the Australian line that night.

Evening, of course, was made memorable by the spectacular conflagration that erupted on the outskirts of Villers-Bretonneux shortly before sunset. But it was merely a spectacle to be relished. Serious work commenced at 10:00 p.m. when the first German patrol went out. Near Accroche Wood it encountered an Australian patrol and a short, vicious battle ensued. However, the Australians made off and no prisoners were taken.

Shortly after 3:00 a.m. von der Marwitz received an alarming report from north of the Somme. Captain Rechtern of the 265th Reserve Infantry Regiment near Brick Beacon had reported that "Tommy," in fighting kit, was lying out in no man's land in front of his battalion's positions. On the right another battalion reported hearing troops and even engine noises. Therefore it seemed inevitable that the British were preparing a major attack against Brick Beacon. Rechtern requested a barrage and began machine-gun fire into no man's land while awaiting daylight. It was not until 3:40 that the requested barrage came down. This was the one noted by Andy McNaughton in his letter to his wife.

At about the same time an operation by the 41st Division was producing surprising intelligence. Code-named "*Ernte*" ("Harvest"), the operation was carried out by the 148th Infantry Regiment towards Villers-Bretonneux. The program began with an intense artillery barrage at 3:30 in the area of the rail line between Villers-Bretonneux and Marcelcave. The point raided was in the Allied front trench just south of the tracks. "The raiders made their rush, and find — nothing," reported General Kabisch. "Not once does the enemy artillery answer.... The 148th could only report that they had found the foremost trenches of the enemy empty."[114]

It was now 4:00. From somewhere far above the fog-shrouded battlefield came the annoying drone of a lone British bomber. For three hours it had cruised back and forth dropping the occasional bomb which had burst somewhere in the invisible distance. The bombs had produced little or no effect, but the plane itself was a hindrance, preventing all attempts to listen for sounds from across no man's land. The fog, too, was unfortunate, for it obscured the unfamiliar landscape from the men of the 117th Division who were now all in position.

As dawn approached, "the Automatic Boiler" and his staff felt that everything was under control. In fact, the situation was undoubtedly better than it had been for several weeks. Von der Marwitz's remaining "outstanding" division had entered the line. The superb 117th had just completed its takeover from the weary and demoralized 109th. The 117th's colourful and vigorous commander, the one-armed General Hoefer, had already settled into his new headquarters near Harbonnières. This was shared with the 14th Bavarian and the 225th, but it was not crowded. Formerly a row of sunken huts built by the British along the grassy slope southeast of Harbonnières, it included extensive underground galleries. Hoefer's 117th was one of the freshest and most battleworthy divisions in the German army. All its regiments were at full strength — each company being two-hundred strong. What was more, these splendidly equipped troops had recently come off four months rest, an unheard-of luxury for trench divisions. Everyone expected great things from the 117th.

Overhead, the noise of the bomber began to recede into the distance. The newcomers who looked at their watches noted that it was almost 4:20. Dawn was not far away and within an hour the 117th would be able to stand-down and settle into the quiet routine of trench life. But today was August 8, 1918, "the Black Day of the German Army." Within an hour the elite 117th Division would cease to exist, and these fresh *feldgrau* would nearly all be prisoners of war or dead.

PART III

The Black Day

"August 8th was the black day of the German Army in the history of the war."
First Quartermaster-General Erich Ludendorff[15]

CHAPTER SEVEN
THE GREEN LINE — WHAT A DAY!

"Zero hour, 8th of August. Four hundred tanks along the Amiens front. Is there a man alive of us who forgets? What a day!"
L.G. Morrison,
The Tank Corps[116]

THE CANADIAN CORPS

Along no man's land thousands upon thousands of khaki-clad figures huddled in the mist and fog waiting for zero hour — 4:20. The loud engine of the single bomber was receding into the distance when a new sound — the one it was intended to cover — became audible. "We could hear the tanks coming up," recalled Ed Hunter, a blond, boyish-looking twenty-year-old veteran of Vimy Ridge, Hill 70, and Passchendaele. In the 1st Canadian Mounted Rifles' position in front of Hangard, the young Lewis gunner began to worry. "Surely the Krauts will know what's coming off with all that noise back there! You could tell the noise of a tank when it was miles off, 'specially when there was a whole slew of them. They sounded like the diesel passenger engines you hear in the railyard nowadays."

"On the tick of 4:20 a.m. the barrage burst with all its fury, a hissing, screeching rain of shells," recalled Jerred Mansfield. "The savage roar of thousands of guns along the line was like wild and wonderful music, played upon a gigantic key board twenty miles long, and the piece they played was the 'Prelude to VICTORY'!"

AMIENS:
Dawn of Victory

From his vantage point in the rear, the war correspondent, J.F.B. Livesay, wrote of that incredible outburst: "There goes up a mighty flare, and simultaneously[117] all along the line, ten miles to north and south of us, other flares light up the countryside. At the same instant there breaks out the boom of our heavy guns, the sharp staccato of sixty-pounders, the dull roar of howitzers, and the ear-splitting clamor of whizz-bangs — a bedlam of noise. Shells whistle and whine overhead; they cannot be distinguished from one another, but merge into a rushing cataract of sound."[118]

From the German lines — now a fiery furnace of bursting shells — came frantic signals for help. Spluttering high into the inferno scores of Very shells burst silently into twin red balls of light — the distress signal. "The prettiest sight you ever saw," remarked Harry Sheppard, an eighteen-year-old artilleryman from Lachine, Quebec. "Some of them were just like incandescent lights on parachutes. And they would just hang there — like they were installed in the sky — with the smoke billowing up from the explosions. I could see hundreds of them along the front." But the German reply to these pleas for assistance was feeble; the Allied counter-battery work had already been overwhelmingly successful.

At the vital Domart Bridge Corporal Harry Brice watched the activity. "Away went these tanks, full speed over the bridge. We were watching them going by — getting lots of fun out of it, you know — when a shell came down, just short of the bridge about twenty feet, on the north side of the road. Three or four seconds and another came over and landed under the rear tank and turned the tank part-way over and killed all the crew. And a third shell came over — it was short, right on the road, but it didn't hit anybody. Then Fritz was silent. He only got away three shells on the bridge. He didn't last long."

Brice's new-found friends of "A" Company, 5th Tank Battalion, were destined to be sadly disappointed by their role in the attack. The last tank across had been knocked out 150 yards from the bridge. Due to heavy shelling farther back, the remaining thirteen tanks were deployed off the road and three immediately bogged down in the swamp. By the time the first objective, Hamon Wood, was reached, six more had received direct hits. One of these had come upon a German 5.9 howitzer. The German gun crew had not panicked, but had depressed their enormous barrel to engage the tank with direct fire. At only fifteen yards range they had fired! The tremendous explosion had utterly destroyed the tank *and* the gun-crew together.

THE GREEN LINE — WHAT A DAY!

9th Brigade, the 3rd Canadian Division

The Canadian infantry had much more satisfying success. The 43rd Cameron Highlanders from Winnipeg were on the right, the only Canadians south of the Amiens-Roye Road, and their first objective, Dodo Wood,[119] lay at the top of a steep hill.

On the extreme flank along the Andrea Ravine an "International Force" insured liaison with the French. Lieutenant Rouaud and his platoon of the 94th Infantry Regiment had been teamed up with Number 5 Platoon under Lieutenant H.B. Holland. They had met less than four hours earlier at the five crossroads south of Hourges. "The whole of their attack was a splendid exhibition of Gaelic [*sic* — "Gallic"?] dash and highland fury in assault," enthused the Cameron's War Diary. "The kilts and the horizon blue swept all before them. The 43rd part of the platoon alone captured 11 machine guns, and 5 trench mortars, dashed into hand-to-hand fighting with the astonished enemy and carried the little wood in front of Dodo Wood, the southern end of Dodo Wood, and Hollan Wood."

Meanwhile the remainder of the battalion was heavily hit by the German counter-barrage which, although it only lasted a few moments, caught the Camerons in their jumping-off areas. In overwhelming confusion and heavy fog (thickened by smoke from their own mortar bombs, damaged in the German barrage) the four companies surged up the steep hill towards Dodo Wood. Somehow they made it to the top where the fog thinned noticeably. "From the time the top of the hill was gained the operation became almost a field [day] for the men who were laughing and joking and in a state of high spirits and enthusiasm," records the War Diary. "By this time the tanks were up, though not without an unfortunate incident on the way. In the mist one tank had mistaken our men for the enemy and had opened a hot fire on them until Lieutenant Hanson dashed up to the tank, and by beating on the door, persuaded its occupants that their fight was not with us but with the Hun." This Mark V was from "B" Company, 5th Tank Battalion, which had crossed the Luce in the French sector at Thennes. By now three were ditched in the swamps, one stopped by gas fumes, and four detailed to assist the French. The remaining five helped to clear the woods scattered across the front.

Although German machine-gun fire was extremely heavy, it was poorly aimed and caused few casualties. Invariably the machine gunners surrendered before the highlanders were within one hundred yards of them although a battery of 5.9's put up a more determined defence until outflanked. Dodo Wood was reached by 5:30 and the Camerons pressed on despite resistance that lingered there for two more hours. Two other small woods lay ahead — Hollan Wood on the right, and somewhat farther ahead, Vignette Wood on the Green Line. These were reached around 7:10 a.m. The Camerons' booty included over four hundred prisoners, a battery of 5.9's plus a 4.1, sixteen trench mortars, and thirty-three machine guns. Twenty-one Highlanders had been killed and another 173 wounded, mostly in the opening minutes of the German counter-barrage.

Beside the 43rd Camerons the 116th (Ontario County) Battalion advanced under heavy fire. The leading company lost all of its officers and sixty men before outflanking Hamon Wood. This cleared the way for the other three to seize the Wood with relative ease. By 7:30 the 116th occupied its first objective. This was heartening for the men from Oshawa and district. The battalion had replaced the veteran 60th (Montreal) Battalion eighteen months earlier, and had suffered by comparison with the brigade's more experienced battalions. Now under Lieutenant-Colonel Pearkes, a former Mountie, homesteader, and bronc-buster, the 116th displayed great confidence and considerable swagger. "Every one of the 116th Battalion carried a piece of chalk with him," related Harry Brice,

> and everything that was captured he wrote on it "Captured by 116th Battalion". *Everything* was marked, and it was really a joke, and the boys were having a whale of a time. Here was one of our 43rd Highlanders in a kilt come marching down the road and he had about twenty prisoners and half of these prisoners were marked on the back, "Captured by 116th Battalion". We started to kid him, "What's the idea? Stealing prisoners, eh?" He just laughed. But there was wagons and guns, and even toilets, "Captured by 116th Battalion".

The men from Oshawa reached the Green Line after capturing sixteen artillery pieces, forty machine guns, and 450 prisoners.

The left battalion of the 9th Brigade, the 58th from central Ontario, fought its way into the town of Demuin in close co-operation with the tanks. The advance ran like clockwork here and was entirely successful. Corporal Harry Miner from Cedar Springs, already severely wounded in the head and shoulder, rushed a machine-gun post single-handedly, killed its entire crew and turned the gun on the retreating enemy. Next, with two comrades, Miner disposed of another gun. Finally the twenty-seven-year-old corporal rushed a German post, bayonetting two of the enemy before the rest fled. At this moment a "potato-masher" grenade wounded Miner again. He died of these wounds later in the day, and was posthumously awarded the Victoria Cross.

8th Brigade, the 3rd Canadian Division

On a narrow front next to the 9th Canadian Brigade was the 8th Brigade, made up of four battalions of Mounted Rifles, converted to infantry two years previously. Two of these, the 4th (just back from its brief visit to Flanders) and the 5th were in divisional reserve. That left the 1st supported by the 2nd to advance on a one-battalion front through the village of Hangard to Cemetery Copse. The boyish veteran, Ed Hunter of the 1st, was a native of Moose Jaw, Saskatchewan. He never forgot the last time he went "over the top." "Our sergeant jumped up and shouted. He had his gat in his hand, firing in the air and swearing."

Through the fog the plainsmen charged, capturing swarms of Germans. Having earlier learned the route by "going over the tapes," the men did not feel lost despite the fog and darkness. Through the shattered village shrouded in swirls of thick fog they scrambled. Dashing towards Cemetery Copse, they could distinguish the huge gateway to the grave yard. From the top of this gate a flurry of machine-gun fire tore into the Canadians who took cover and returned the fire. Hunter stood firing his Lewis gun from the hip, but when that proved ineffective, he dove for cover. Resting the Lewis gun on a stump, he opened fire. "I was so sure I was gonna' knock them guys out. I could tell by them tracer bullets that I was going right into his nest, bullets from the Lewis machine gun were ricocheting all over up there. But soon as I'd quit he'd start right in again. So I told the guys, 'Look, you'd better get a tank over here and let them fix that guy.'" Several of the Mounted Rifles held up their rifles with their helmets balanced on top — the accepted signal to call for a tank. It seemed a feeble hope in the fog and semi-darkness.

Of the Mark Vs six were now out of action — only two by enemy fire. Two had ditched themselves, one had stalled with its gears seized, and another had gassed its entire crew with its fumes. Nevertheless, a tank arrived at that moment, and after being directed towards the gate, churned into action.

He went on over, butted that thing a couple of times, and walked on over it. From where I was I could see a pile of rubble, sandbags, and corrugated iron where he'd knocked the thing down. I was getting up to go on when I got a piece of shrapnel in my leg. So I told Sergeant Brooks that I was hit. "Hang on to your gat, your water-bottle, and your gas-helmet," he says and he shook my hand. "Hope to see you again," but it was the last time I ever saw him.

As Hunter hobbled to the rear he appeared to be one Canadian in a sea of Germans — prisoners streaming to the rear. "There were a lot of trenches there we'd crossed over, and I got back and sat down in one. The Krauts were coming in there, by golly. Kids! Just kids, many of them! They were scared of me too. I think they lost a lot of their battle there too — these young kids," marveled the twenty-year-old veteran.

Ed Hunter was one of only forty-seven wounded CMRs. Another ten of the men from the prairies died in the attack, but everyone agreed it was a small price to pay for such a leap forward. Nevertheless, even this orderly advance produced some ghastly memories. The second wave certainly saw some terrible sights. Into Hangard, Jerred Mansfield and the machine gunners of the 3rd Canadian Machine Gun Battalion trudged, strung out in single file past a destroyed tank and two more mired in the Luce marshes. The buildings had been pulverized into rubble, but there was much worse.

Dead and dying were scattered about, some stretched out full length on their faces as if they were trying shut out the awful sight. I saw a group of five German soldiers outside a doorway. They were all in a heap and I thought likely they had been struck by a bomb. They were horribly wounded; some of them were dead and lay in great pools of blood. One looked as if his entrails were protruding from a great gash in his abdomen. His face was as white as chalk. Another chap had a terrible gash in the thick of his leg which he was trying to bandage. They seemed completely dazed and unaware of our passing.

Also passing through were the men of the 2nd Canadian Mounted Rifles from British Columbia. They leapfrogged the 1st and made for Demuin to secure a bridge over the Luce. But although it had been kept under a protective fire of shrapnel, the bridge was found to be blown up. This was soon remedied by means of a "crib" carried by one of the tanks that arrived shortly after the 2nd CMRs. As a result, by 6:30 even the second echelon had crossed, and the British Colombians were clearing the village of Demuin.

Sergeant Tom Peck would never forget a conversation with one of his prisoners in a captured dugout. "This fellow was sitting there and says, 'What are you guys fightin for?' I said, 'Christ, to beat you guys!' Then he says, 'You know, I was fourteen years in London, and six months before the war broke out I got orders to come home. We've got nothing against each other. This is a rich man's war and a poor man's fight.'"

3rd Brigade, the 1st Canadian Division

Alongside the 3rd Division was the 1st Division, with Brigadier Tuxford's 3rd Brigade in the lead. Its right battalion was the 16th Canadian Scottish which advanced north of Hangard, beside the 1st Canadian Mounted Rifles. The 16th had a particularly difficult task because the ground was very broken and unsuitable for tanks. Due to the fog and the nature of the ground, fighting took place simultaneously all over in isolated pockets. The 1st Canadian Division was up against one-armed General Hoefer's crack 117th Division.

Into the fog the kilted figures wafted silently through the din of the barrage. "I could see something that looked like an emplacement," reported an officer.

> Piper Maclean of Number 2 Company was with my party at the time. I told him to play "The Drunken Piper", and to the strains of this tune, played in quick time, we charged. It was an emplacement sure enough, of heavy trench mortars. Jumping into the trench we saw in front of us the entrances to two dug-outs each guarded with a machine gun mounted and well camouflaged. We shouted down to the enemy and up they came — one officer and about sixty men. They were taken completely by surprise; some of them were in their stocking feet and partly clad. Arrived above ground they seemed determined to "dish up" their daily rations and make themselves comfortable before starting the journey to the rear, but after some

gentle persuasion we settled that matter and sent them quickly on their way at the double."[120]

The main body of the 16th advanced across no man's land, quite wide here and untouched by shelling. All at once a dark mass loomed directly ahead in the fog. What was it? The maps gave no indication, so Lieutenant-Colonel Cy Peck, who was in the first wave gave the order to charge. The battalion historian noted,

> The men at once rushed forward, some thirty yards or so, only to find themselves up against an almost perpendicular bank. For a moment all ranks were nonplussed. A doubt arose as to whether the Battalion was on its right course. Groping its way over this slope, where it was most easily negotiable, the main body of the Battalion advanced to the attack. Piper Paul mounted one of the tanks named "Dominion"; the pipes skirled out the "march past" of the Battalion, "The Blue Bonnets Over the Border"; and with this dramatic lead the troops on the right flank moved towards the enemy.
>
> Daylight had now come. The fog was growing thinner. It became possible to see some little distance in front. Anti-tank guns and trench mortars were standing around in the open with their covers still on, but no enemy was in sight.
>
> For some hundred yards the advance proceeded without interruption. The fog gradually lightened, until just as the leading wave of the Battalion's attack was moving up the long grassy slope above the Aubercourt road north of Demuin, the mist cleared without a moment's warning.
>
> The Commanding Officer, who for observation purposes had again come forward into the first wave, hastened ahead to the crest of the ridge, and as he reached it an enemy machine gun opened fire in his direction at point blank range, killing Piper Paul, who was marching alongside of him. Simultaneously revolver shots rang out from the right front, the enemy gun ceased firing and Captain Alec MacLennan, the Battalion Intelligence Officer, appeared in the enemy's post.[121]

THE BLACK DAY
The Green Line — What a Day!

MacLennan with his sergeant, Frank Durham, was on "a roving commission," and had just come upon a very old and decrepit line of sandbags. As he recalled years later:

> Around the corner was a most beautiful V in the fog, right to the ground. It was wide enough at the top so that I could see the whole hill-side. On the hillside was a panorama of the battalion. Where they were there was no fog. Right then a machine gun opened up nearby and nearly deafened me. The bugger sounded as if he were right under my elbow.
>
> Out in front was the body of Jack Paul, the colonel's piper. Right away I thought, where's the colonel? At the same time I noticed that I was on the top of kind of a ramp. At the bottom of the ramp I could make out the German machine gunner bent over adjusting the sights. Next to him was number one, then number two, and so on. So in a line were five of them spread out.
>
> I just knew I had to get to the gunner before he had his sights adjusted 'cause I figured if the colonel's piper is laying there, the colonel can't be far away. My idea was to jump down that ramp as far as I could and get that gunner on the run. I'll swear to the day I die that when I jumped I heard a shout. Anyway, when I took off I pulled the trigger, and he hit the ground about the same time that I did. Then I kept going. I was quite used to high jumping and long jumping, and as soon as my toes touched the ground I was away — number one, bang — number two, bang.
>
> When I shot number three he was sprawling towards me so I grabbed his collar and heaved him back onto the last two. Number four, the bugger, he had me in his sights, but I got him first. When I got number five there was a hell of a yell behind me. It was Frank Durham, "You got 'em all, sir!"

Another isolated fight reminded those who saw it of the wild west. Lieutenant Mackie and an unknown Lewis gunner had sniped a German machine-gun post of four guns into submission until a German officer waved to Mackie to advance. Each regarded the other suspiciously, hesitated, and then advanced slowly towards one another. At thirty yards the German reached for his pistol, but Mackie was faster, dropping him in his tracks. Mackie broke into a run and accompanied by the Lewis gunner captured the entire post and its survivors.

The 16th also took a quarry — not shown on the maps — that sheltered a regimental commander and his entire staff. Mainly responsible for this capture was the indomitable Alec MacLennan, two Lewis gunners, and a Mark V of the 4th Tank Battalion. The Canadian Scottish pushed on and reached the Green Line before nine. But where was Number 1 Company? It had set off at zero on the left flank next to the 13th Royal Highlanders of Canada, but the entire company had apparently vanished. It was not till after 10:00 that Captain Lyons and some of his men appeared. They had had quite a morning. Having advanced too far to the left they had captured a German who led them to a strong point, which they took from the rear. Here Lyon found his company to be well ahead of the advance and far to the north. Thereupon he led his men southeast to where he calculated lay the deep valley they were to take.

Suddenly the fog lifted, revealing a stunning panorama. "To the right lay the valley of the Luce, filled to the brim with a white bank of fog," records the Battalion History.

> Beyond this lake of mist was visible the high ground east of Dodo Wood; over it lines of khaki-clad soldiers were pursuing a panic-stricken enemy. To the left rear still more troops were coming forward.
>
> In front there was not a sign of the enemy. Without any warning the party found itself right on the edge of a deep ravine, which was crowded with German batteries. The crews were coming out of their dug-outs, and, standing on the running boards at the sides of the guns, were hastily pulling off the covers, and preparing for action without the slightest idea that the foe was standing right above them.
>
> Raising one rousing cheer, the 16th lads made a wild rush down the bank on to the frightened enemy, who fled precipitately into the dug-outs and gun emplacements, and northwards up the valley. Lyons and one section of the platoon rushed after the fugitives who were escaping up the valley; another section got hold of a

cluster of bombs which were lying beside the guns, ready for use against tanks, and flung them down into the dug-outs where a perfect babel of talk was going on; and the remainder of the party ran around emplacements, chasing, hide-and-seek fashion, the Germans who were in hiding there.

The enemy who had taken refuge in the dug-outs and the emplacements were soon rounded up and placed under a guard on the top of the bank, but the party of Germans who had fled up the ravine gave a great deal of trouble.

Making good use of the short start, they got in touch with a German machine-gun crew, who placed their gun on top of one of the steep sides of the draw and directed fire against the 16th section, who were working their way up along the foot of the opposite side. Lyons rushed his men across to dead ground under the bank from which the hostile machine gun was firing, but there they came under fire from the northerly end of the ravine, where a group of the enemy had rallied, and were forced to retreat towards the guns.

Meanwhile, the prisoners, at the top of the slope, becoming aware of the turn which events had taken in their favour, endeavoured to take advantage of it. One by one, unknown to their escort, who were absorbed in the progress of the battle, those nearest the bank slipped over, and were making for the gun emplacements to get rifles, when the movement was noticed by the 16th section who were retreating down the draw. They fired on the escaping Germans and raised the alarm. The prisoners' guard woke up to their responsibility and rounded up their charges, with the exception of a few who hid in the undergrowth on the side of the ravine.[122]

Farther north in the middle of the 3rd Brigade sector the 13th Royal Highlanders of Canada from Montreal were hit by their own barrage and within moments had lost thirty men. On the 3rd Brigade's front the tank support proved more effective than it had further south. Twenty-one tanks reached the plateau ahead of the 13th and the 14th Royal Montreals on their left. Only one Mark V was ditched, although it later extricated itself and joined its mates. The tanks looming up through the mist instilled panic among the Germans who fled, many of them only half-dressed. However, it was a different story in the intervals between the tanks.

In one of these gaps Charlie "Bubbles" Hughes, a teenaged "old salt," advanced. Charlie had run away from his native Liverpool to go to sea when he was only fourteen. In 1916 he had jumped ship in Saint John, New Brunswick to enlist. Now he was a nineteen-year-old "kiltie." With him was a Newfoundlander by the name of John Croak.[123]

> Now this Johnny Croak was a remarkable man. There was not a phoney bone in his body. He was a roly-poly guy, feared nothing, and didn't give a shit for anybody. He always carried a revolver on his hip and I don't think he would have been afraid to use it on *anyone* who crossed him. It was a saying in our company that if you went on a patrol or out on a working party with Johnny Croak you'd come back.

At this point "A" Company had been held up by the fire of a machine gun. Croak had already bombed and captured a machine-gun crew single-handedly. Once again Captain Christie's men swung into action like a machine. The "old salt," Charlie Hughes, was the flank guard on the left. "Well they went at those machine guns and demolished everything — port and starboard — wiped out the crews. Just then another machine gun opened up from a patch of fog and Johnny went after that." By now Croak was severely wounded, but he did not hesitate. After him went the entire kilted platoon pell-mell for the trench — really only a gully with dugouts scattered along it. The Newfoundlander was the first to jump into the enemy position.

"I began throwing my bombs along the trench," recalled Hughes, "but the machine gun got Johnny." Private John Croak was awarded a posthumous Victoria Cross for his gallantry. His comrades followed him into the trench in reckless ardour. "I jumped into the trench — of course we had our bayonets fixed — and when I came down I skewered a German in the neck. He had been lying there wounded already, so I gave him a drink and a cigarette and tried to patch him up."

Not all prisoners received such gentle treatment. "Just ahead, Kent and I came across a little fellow named Dickinson. He had captured two big — and I do mean *big* — Germans, but they were sitting down." It transpired that the two refused to move although the wee kiltie had ordered them to head to the rear. Hughes's partner suggested shooting them, but Dickinson was shocked. "No, I can't," he said.

"So," recalled "Bubbles" Hughes, "Kent just put up his rifle and shot one guy right between the eyes. Well, the other fellow took off to the rear in a hurry then."

One of the most remarkable captures of the day involved Corporal Herman Good, a 13th Royal Highlander from South Bathurst, New Brunswick. Good had already taken three machine guns single-handedly, but now the 13th had run up against a battery of 5.9's firing as fast as they could reload. The New Brunswicker was unimpressed. He and three privates charged with fixed bayonets. Good later explained that the gun crews were probably "not trained in hand-to-hand fighting and that, once at grips, he and his stout-hearted companions would have the advantage."[124] Incredibly, the entire battery surrendered to the four highlanders, and Good survived to wear the Victoria Cross he was awarded.

The 14th Royal Montreal Regiment to the north of the 13th advanced with little difficulty at first. Although Morgemont Wood and Tittle Copse offered some resistance, it was not until they came upon "Czech" and "Croat" Trenches that they were halted. At this point the tanks came up, wheeled upon the German trenches and made a trip along them firing into the massed Germans and crushing the parapets in several places. The tanks then moved on, having over-estimated their effect upon the *feldgrau* of the 117th Division. The fire from the Czech and Croat Trenches resumed almost undiminished and the 14th men were forced to begin flanking moves. These were successful and white flags appeared from the German trenches. Several Royal Montrealers then advanced to receive the Germans' surrender, but when they were almost over were cut down by rifle fire. The Montrealers, enraged by this treachery, reopened their fire. Ignoring two further white flags the Canadians attacked with the bayonet and took no prisoners. When the 14th reached the Green Line a few minutes later they had suffered 18 men killed, 107 wounded, and 34 missing.

4th Brigade, the 2nd Canadian Division

The Canadians' left wing was led by the 4th Brigade, made up of four Ontario battalions. The 18th Western Ontario Battalion suffered thirty killed and 120 wounded but reached its objective three hundred yards southeast of Marcelcave by 7:45. To their left, the 19th Central Ontario Battalion advanced beside the Australians along the railway from Villers-Bretonneux.

However, there was one complication in this plan; to thicken the line prior to tackling Marcelcave, the 21st Eastern Ontario Battalion would move up between the 18th and the 19th. Everything went according to plan right from zero hour. "The shells came over our heads with an appalling shriek into the fog ahead," W.S. Macklin of the 19th later recalled. "We simply lit cigarettes, shouldered our rifles, and walked after the shells."[125]

The left flank received excellent support from the Aussies of the 7th Brigade with the result that only one really serious problem was encountered. A German machine gun held up the Central Ontario men, but was immediately rushed by Lieutenant Burton and Acting Sergeant Hollidge. The officer was shot down, but Hollidge killed the entire six-man crew and turned the gun on the grey figures who were now retreating.

Large numbers of outposts had been by-passed in the dark and fog so the 20th Central Ontario Battalion in close support also had its share of fighting and took its share of prisoners. One sergeant, while checking a cellar, discovered a German major so badly wounded and in such agony that it was evident he would not live. The officer swore forcefully that he would never be taken by any "swine of an Englishman" and told the sergeant to shoot him — with a German rifle. The sergeant, realizing that only an agonizing and lingering death lay ahead for his enemy, carried out the man's last request.

The tanks were isolated by the mist, each crawling forward blindly. "Somewhere about 5:15 our great chance came," wrote Lieutenant J. Robertson in his diary. His tank, "*Oblivis Caris*" ("Oblivious to Care"), was one of the 14th Tank Battalion Mark V's attached to the 2nd Canadian Division.

> We had at last found touch with the main advance and came across a company of Canadians taking cover from strong machine gun fire from a harvested field. Almost as we got there one of them gave the S.O.S. We didn't wait to ask questions but passed through the infantry and in two minutes found ourselves right among the Boche. One lot tried to beat it for a wood but Gunner McKellars, to his huge delight, got them all. We reached a trench crowded with Jerries and all our guns got right busy. The effect of case shot in a crowded trench isn't pretty. All this time some machine gun had been beating a devil's tattoo on the old bus. We located the trouble and dealt with it.[126]

THE BLACK DAY
THE GREEN LINE — WHAT A DAY!

Oblivis Caris was supposed to reach its first objective, the town of Marcelcave, by 6:23 and it was already 5:45. So Robertson gave the "all clear" signal to the infantry and headed in a northeasterly direction where he hoped Marcelcave was.

A special barrage had been concentrated on Marcelcave. At zero plus 123 minutes (6:23 a.m.) it lifted and men of the 19th and 21st rushed the shattered village. Acting Sergeant Hollidge again led the way, a machine gun cradled on his arm, firing into dugouts and cellars and clearing the streets. The men knew that a German headquarters was located in the town, so there was the added incentive of souvenirs. "We found this German headquarters alright," F. Stitt of the 19th recalled with satisfaction. "After we got the betabbed Generals up the stairs from this deep dugout we investigated the place and found the porridge warm on the table — that's how badly we surprised them."[127]

In the meantime the Australians' two extreme right companies had been stopped by fire coming from Marcelcave. At that moment up came a tank commanded by Captain C.R. Percy-Eade, in better times a lawyer in Taunton, Somerset. The Diggers explained the problem and Percy-Eade swung south churning along the outskirts of the village, blasting away with his six-pounder. Then he wheeled and plowed into the village from the north, followed by the two companies of the 26th Queenslanders. After evidently subduing all resistance, Percy-Eade, in true legalistic style, obtained an official receipt for the village before turning it over to the Australians. The gesture was slightly premature for the southern portion of the village had not yet been cleared. "Behind the right rear, an uproar of shots and bombs resounded for five minutes," records the Australian Official History. "Then out came the Canadians, to the admiration of all, advancing as if on parade to their objective."[128] It was the 19th and 21st Ontario battalions moving onto the Green Line.

Casualties were moderately heavy. The 18th lost 150, the 19th 158, the 20th 109, and the 21st 88 including their RSM and their Commanding Officer, Lieutenant-Colonel E.W. Jones. The 21st deeply mourned their CO, an original, and a native of Brockville in the heart of Eastern Ontario. Despite failing health, Jones had stayed to fight his last battle and was hit by a German machine gun half way to Marcelcave. But Jones lived long enough to see the streams of German prisoners who passed him on the road — a great day for his beloved 21st.

If Colonel Jones had but known it, August 8 was proving to be a great day for the entire Canadian Corps. As the summer sun began to disperse the banks of mist, "Foch's Pets" found themselves firmly established all along the Green Line preparing to make the next lunge forward. On their left, the Australians too had been enjoying success.

THE AUSTRALIAN CORPS

"Bang! Clang! Blatter! No words can describe it," marveled L.G. Morrison within his Mark V when the barrage burst at 4:20.

> Just the whole world heaves, rocks, tumbles, turns upside-down, ricochets, and runs off at a tangent. We can see, hear and feel nothing.... Millions of lights flash and stab and crisscross.... The driver is on his seat, his hand on the clutch. The handle [crank] is rotated by four burly gunners; she snorts, coughs, stutters, and catches.... Soon she is humming low and sweet. I depress the pedal, and she roars ... magnificently, like the great man-eater that she is. Each man at his appointed post, six-pounder gunner to his shoulder piece, Hotchkiss gunner along his sights ... naked to the waist, pistol at belt, steel-lace visor over the straining, bloodshot eyes.
>
> Off! She gives a lurch and a roll, the gunners spread their feet apart for balance, and we are off. Lurch, dip, slide down, nose up, heave forward, amble along ... blindly in the darkness, pitching and rolling.[129]

At the opening crash of the barrage excited Australians cheered. Then nearly every Digger lit a "fag" as the leading companies rose and strode into the fog, unhurried and confident. Visibility varied from fifty yards down to ten as the dust thrown up by the shell-fire mixed with the fog and the smoke shells used to mask enemy positions. Consequently, direction was lost in some instances despite the white tapes and officers with compasses. No one faltered, however. Many groups simply advanced on their own guided by the sound of the barrage, even though shell bursts were not visible. "I had a feeling," wrote a man from Koo-wee-rup, Victoria, "of being behind a curtain of rushing noise."[130]

Some platoons managed to keep together, but most became separated and advanced in small groups. Often an individual pressed on blindly, trusting his own sense of direction. Ahead, German machine guns chattered uncertainly — firing blind. Now and then a group of Diggers would walk straight up to a German machine gun crew. Only at the last moment would the two parties see one another — the rangy Australians striding along with rifles and fixed bayonets pointed straight ahead, the Germans huddled low in their shell holes with scared, bewildered faces, clammy hands gripping their weapons. In most cases the latter would throw up their hands with cries of "*Kamerad!*", but here and there a brave *feldgrau* would open up and keep firing until outflanked and shot.

The tanks, led by the Mark V*s, were supposed to advance through the infantry and take positions just behind the leading screen of scouts. Unfortunately, the fog slowed some of the iron monsters to such an extent that they would not catch up with the leading elements till the Green Line had been reached.

7th Brigade, the 3rd Australian Division

On the Australians' right, next to the Canadians, the 7th Brigade advanced along the rail line towards Marcelcave. At first there were only scattered posts, then came a belt of well-constructed barbed-wire entanglements where resistance stiffened suddenly. No tanks had arrived as yet, and the wire was impenetrable under such heavy fire. The 26th Queensland Battalion was stopped in front of Card Copse.

Suddenly, well behind the German wire a lone figure could be seen striding along the enemy's parapet, firing his pistol into the defenders. An entire company of fifty men and four machine guns immediately surrendered to Lieutenant Alfred Gaby of Tasmania. For this action Gaby was awarded the Victoria Cross. Not far away, Lieutenant Shorrock, a former policeman from Perth, performed a similar feat, capturing twenty men and two machine guns.

The German 41st Division's Main Line of Resistance had been breached. An officer of the 18th Infantry Regiment later told how it had happened. The forward troops had at first assumed that the barrage was in retaliation for that which had accompanied the raid by the 148th Infantry Regiment earlier that night. Soon bursts of machine-gun fire from their outposts brought the realization to them. The growl of engines drew nearer through the dark fog. Then all at once on their flank the terrifying shape of a tank passed. Shadowy figures in British helmets materialized only yards in front, and the Captain's men opened fire. Out of the fog on his left rear came more figures hurling bombs. After a brief and confused fight the officer and his men surrendered. Of the 715 men of the 18th Infantry Regiment only eight officers and fifty men escaped.

A short distance behind the 26th came two companies of the 21st Victorians and a liaison platoon of the 19th Central Ontario Battalion. This combined force worked along the railway tracks. Heavy opposition came from the Canadian side of the rail line and several fierce machine-gun duels ensued. Near Marcelcave one German post in an orchard near Jean Rouxin Mill resisted strongly. Lieutenant Mason, a one-time tram-conductor from Prahran, crossed the tracks to reconnoitre and met some of the 19th Canadians. Together the dominion troops drove out the defenders after a savage scrap in the fog. One Australian company, known affectionately as "The Brewery Company," remained to mop up and discovered that the post was the headquarters of a battalion of the 18th Infantry Regiment whose CO had escaped but had left behind a mass of interesting documents. At that moment, an Australian mounted orderly appeared out of the fog. He was sent racing back to the 7th Brigade Headquarters with the haul.

Tanks were now able to steer by sight and took a more effective part in the advance, joining in a successful assault on Labastille Mill and a factory, part of the Old Amiens Inner Defences. L.G. Morrison recorded what it was like:

> "We should be almost there," the crew commander bawls in my ear. The machine gun in the turret begins to bark. "Rat, Rat-tat! Rat-tat-tat!" The aeroplane-spotter has seen something. Hope it isn't our own. No, our sides are being hail-swept with bullets. They are flying very low, sweeping down alongside us, climbing, looping, and swooping back again. If they find our pin-holes, look out for a shower of molten lead.
>
> The machine-gun stops. The gunner is peering through the slit in his turret, fascinated. A duel in the air, he signals. They are riddling each other with machine guns, seeking each other's petrol. Ah! Both burst into flame simultaneously, and crash to the ground together.
>
> The front line now. A low parapet of earth looms ahead.... Now, a few wavering bayonets protrude. Swing her around. The epicyclics behave beautifully. Round she slews, broadside on, to the enemy trench. The right six-pounder roars. A flash illuminated the dusky cabin as a canister of shrapnel is poured on the huddling field-greys.

We trip merrily on, the six-pounder volleying shell after shell into the trench, and the two Hotchkiss machine gunners raking fore and aft as the Germans run for it. I spot a sister tank approaching from the opposite direction. Our little trip here is over. I swing the old bus round again and put her to the jumps. Over she goes, belly slithering forward, nose coming up in the air, hot on the scent, sniffing after the enemy.[131]

Tanks of the 2nd Battalion, the Tank Corps, now made straight for resistance wherever they saw it. Forty or so of the giants were still with the infantry heading into a long deep valley on either side of the village of Warfusee. A short distance ahead, they knew, stretched "the valley of the guns" where several German batteries were positioned. In the meantime four tanks had been disabled rather mysteriously, with tracks torn off. The surprised infantry noted that a small explosion took place beneath one of the Mark Vs just north of the Roman Road. One track had been broken and now the monster sat, otherwise undamaged, but out of action. It was discovered that it had run over a nest of contact mines. "They were in containers like kerosene tins, and were buried in groups of half a dozen, with the tops a few inches above the ground."[132]

Farther north near Warfusee the 28th and 27th battalions overran several German artillery batteries. Some were surprised still firing on their "S.O.S. targets" from zero hour. Others recovered and fired point-blank into the advancing infantry. Of the four batteries and their brigade headquarters captured, only one officer and two NCOs escaped. Although it had run into the most serious resistance encountered by the Australian Corps, the 7th Brigade arrived on the Green Line first, the 26th Queenslanders reporting in at 6:25. Almost every move had been made according to the timetable. Only the two companies beside the Canadians had been held up by the stubborn resistance of General Hoefer's fresh 117th Division.

5th Brigade, the 2nd Australian Division

Next in line to the north, the 5th Brigade had a narrower stretch of no man's land to cross. Consequently, the fog still lay thick when its leading battalions approached the Old Amiens Inner Defence Line. Diagonally across their route lay a Roman Road. The 5th Brigade, made up entirely of New South Wales battalions, was to start off with this road on its left and finish with it on the right. The 19th and 20th battalions had been instructed to seize the Old Amiens Defence Line, whereupon the 17th and 18th were to pass through beyond Warfusee. "The road was the one sure guide to the objective, and here the jumble of units was bewildering. Tanks had been carefully allotted for tackling each sector of the old trench-line, but the force now consisted of intermingled groups of several brigades with a sprinkling of tanks wandering forward through fog, and the old inner Amiens line was taken by those who stumbled upon it."[133]

"It took a little while to get these trenches cleared," wrote Captain Lane of the 18th. "There were a good many bits of communication trench and so on in which there were Germans. Occasionally bombs had to be used." The process was informal: "someone telling any one he met that there were some Germans down in some corner he had passed or where he had seen them; collecting a few men and going round and grabbing the Germans, generally from the rear."[134]

The confusion along the Roman Road was incredible. Besides the four battalions of the 5th Brigade, hundreds of prisoners and parties from four Australian divisions were pushing along the ancient thoroughfare. Groups of the 34th Battalion of the 3rd Division blundered by — a mile south of their proper sector. Also on the road was the 46th Victoria Battalion of the 4th Division, which was supposed to leapfrog the 34th.

> The leader of the 46th and several other stray officers were standing with their compasses placed on the cobblestones and their steel helmets carefully laid aside, arguing out their position. At that moment there loomed from the mist ahead an Australian escorting back a dozen Germans. "Where did you get them?" they asked. "In Warfusee." "Where's that?" "About a kilometre and a half up the road." This settled the location — the leader of the 46th took his unit in single file northwards along the old trench-line. At one of the redoubts it ran into a force of Germans facing a broken-down tank but missed by attacking divisions.[135]

The Victorians took out their built-up frustrations on the surprised Germans and within moments had their own sizeable bag of prisoners to send to the rear.

THE GREEN LINE — WHAT A DAY!

The Germans in front of the 5th Brigade were to the south the 41st Division, and to the north the 13th Division. The 41st's right flank was held by its strongest regiment, the 152nd, each of whose battalions had an average "fighting strength" of 482. One captured company commander told how he had ordered his men to fire into the mist until only ten rounds per man remained. After a further half-hour wait tanks were heard approaching from the rear. Then hard after them at the double came a swarm of Australians, cheering wildly. The 152nd's two forward battalions were swept away.

In most of the captured sectors the Germans showed little fight. For instance, Captain Portman's company of the 20th outflanked and captured a party of sixty-five Germans and six machine guns with no resistance at all. In moments, another ninety had been winkled out to swell the stream of prisoners. Twelve men of the 17th Battalion captured one hundred prisoners and many machine guns in a matter of minutes. All these prisoners were taken without the assistance of tanks.

Daylight had begun to dissipate the mist, reducing the confusion among the Australians but increasing it among their foe. On the southern edge of Warfusee, Captain Harnett, formerly a shipping clerk from Newcastle, led his company through a gully and the back gardens of Warfusee to capture numerous infantrymen and several batteries including one of 5.9s from which not one man escaped. From the village a battery of 4.2s could be seen abandoned on the plateau ahead. A young tank officer took his Mark V across the open, hitched up one of the guns, and brought it back to Warfusee although hit twice by guns still manned near Bayonvillers. Meanwhile in "the valley of the guns" the 18th had found two more batteries abandoned. By seven o'clock the 5th Brigade occupied all of its objectives on the Green Line.

9th Brigade, the 3rd Australian Division

The 3rd Australian Division was responsible for the northern half of the Australian sector. Its 9th Brigade had to take the difficult ground around Accroche Wood, and stiff fighting had been expected. But the fog and the unprecedented barrage had kept the forward elements of the German 13th Division in their dugouts. As the Diggers swarmed over no man's land they encountered almost no resistance. Most of these dugouts were surrendered without a shot being fired, and by 5:00 a large number of "field-greys" from the 13th, 15th, and 55th Infantry regiments were being herded meekly to the rear. OHL's instructions to hold the forward zone lightly and the Main Line of Resistance strongly had been ignored. It was well for the 9th that they had been, for this brigade consisted of only three battalions from New South Wales. Due to the fog and the thick wood, all three became hopelessly mixed, and fell well behind the barrage. Luckily, at only one point was there serious resistance. In a maze of trenches just north of Accroche Wood, the 35th ran into savage fire. Captain A.E. Yates, a rare member of the Australian Permanent Forces, was shot in the leg leading the assault. In the fog he was lost to sight, and the mixed company moved on. It was not until next day that his body was found, wounded and gassed.

Groups of Diggers pressed on to Gailly Ridge, a long wheat-covered spur east of Accroche Wood. Here lay the German's Main Line of Resistance, but by now the tanks of the 13th Battalion had caught up with the infantry, and the German machine guns — seven in one wheat field — were easily overcome. Only a handful fought to the bitter end.

By 5:45, as the fog began to thin, the 9th Brigade started its descent into "the valley of the guns" where the men hoped to find trophies. Few were disappointed; a battery of the 58th FAR stood silently, with the gunners sitting on the tails of their guns awaiting capture. By 7:15 the Green Line was occupied without serious casualties. Only the 35th had suffered losses when at two minutes after zero a solitary shell had put out of action the entire staff of one company.

11th Brigade, the 3rd Australian Division

The Australian left flank was provided by the 11th Brigade. Its advance through the Somme flats was complicated by the low ground and the meandering river on the left. The right-hand battalion, the 44th West Australians, attacked on a very wide front with Gailly Ridge as their objective. There they would be leapfrogged by the 41st Queensland Battalion.

When zero hour arrived Captain Longmore of the 44th reported that "it was impossible to see one's outstretched hand, and any form of control except self-control was out of the question."[136] Undoubtedly the fog in the Somme flats was thicker than anywhere else, but the troops had been well briefed so they set off — individuals determined to do the job alone if necessary. The unfortunate *feldgrau* of the 108th Division, equally isolated by the fog, did not know what was happening. The West Australians picked their way through the dense cloud, bagging scores of bewildered prisoners. All this time tanks could be heard but were seldom seen. A steep incline told the Diggers they were climbing Gailly Ridge. Soon they were crossing a wide, wheat-covered plateau until the 44th, scattered and in small groups, reached its objective, the Warfusee-Gailly Road.

During the confusing advance, several parties of Germans had been by-passed and these were encountered by the 41st on its way up to leapfrog the 44th. One particularly valiant defence was put up by the headquarters of the 3rd Battalion, 97th Infantry Regiment at Spur Fork. The commander, Captain Schoning, directed a courageous resistance against the dimly seen figures in front and on both flanks. Soon, however, Schoning was mortally wounded by a shot from the rear and Spur Fork fell to the Aussies. Another Captain, having been frisked, escaped his captors in the fog but was immediately retaken and, as he put it, "gone through by a horde of drunken Australians." Again abandoned, he heard a call in German and discovered a machine-gun post forty yards away. With a wounded companion the Captain made for the post, only to be set upon and frisked for a third time by Aussies. This irritating procedure was interrupted belatedly when German machine gunners opened fire. Their outburst lasted only seconds and resulted in more Germans being "gone through" for souvenirs.[137] To German officers, the effrontery of the enlisted men of Australia and Canada, who invariably searched their "betters" for "swag" or "loot," was past all belief. This predilection for souvenirs reflected the dominion troops' remarkable "tourist" attitude to the war.

As the fog began to disperse under the warm August sun, the 41st Queenslanders swarmed down the eastern edge of Gailly Ridge and captured two batteries. On this day no one begrudged the hours of practice ordered by Lieutenant-Colonel Heron, for the companies "keeping their right shoulders forward" advanced diagonally across the valley through the diminishing fog to end up exactly on the Green Line. True, they had been slowed so effectively by the fog that they were nearly an hour behind time, but it had been a well-executed, almost bloodless advance. As a finale, Lt. J.B. Lawson led a party with one tank into Hamilton Wood, which lay immediately ahead of the objective. In a few moments they returned escorting two hundred more prisoners.

The 11th Brigade's other attacking battalion was the 42nd from Queensland. This unit advanced next to the Somme itself where it had been straightened and dredged to form a canal. Because of the bend in the canal, only a few yards from the jumping-off trench, the 42nd was forced to advance through a bottleneck with only one company in front.

AMIENS:
Dawn of Victory

Even before zero the 42nd had endured the edge of the barrage put down by the Germans and aimed at III Corps. Then as false rumours will, the story spread among the men that the British had been driven back. Consequently, all ranks expected heavy casualties from being fired upon from across the Somme.

Splashing and struggling through the mud and marsh grass the 42nd advanced in near silence. One by one, isolated German posts were surprised and seized without resistance. Captain Jack, a former dental student from New Farm, led his men on to their objective at 6:10 — only half an hour late. They had seized numerous bridges and the canal lock at Gailly. Their lone adventure had been the last minute rescue of a tank that had almost driven into the Somme. Incredibly, Captain Jack's company had suffered not one casualty while the company beside his had only one. The 42nd was ecstatic.

Meanwhile on the north side of the canal, two platoons of the 39th Victorian Battalion (10th Brigade) had been detached to reconnoitre. Without losing a man, they captured forty Germans and five machine guns.

By 7:00 the Australian Corps had completed one of its longest advances of the war — and at a lower cost in lives than ever before or ever again. German artillery fire had been almost negligible, and most of the infantry had resisted only briefly, if at all. The average casualty figure for the Australians was less than fifty per battalion. In this sector the Germans too had suffered few fatal casualties, but their loss in prisoners was severe. The Diggers had been surprised and elated to encounter practically no German trenches or barbed wire. Certainly few "field-greys" had been prepared to fight it out, and many had been discovered standing disarmed, hands raised, awaiting capture. Knowing the habits of their adversaries, quite a number already had their watches and other souvenirs ready in hand when the Aussies arrived.

Due to the fog, the tanks had played a lesser role than had been envisioned. However, as daylight dissipated its white veils, the tanks' importance increased. It is doubtful if the German infantry would have surrendered so easily if it were not for the ominous growl of the Mark Vs and the terror spread when their huge forms were glimpsed through the fog. The tanks themselves had suffered only minor losses. Four had been knocked out by contact mines, but, of course, were repairable. In all, fourteen nests of mines had been discovered before the Green Line, most of these near the Roman Road.

Meanwhile, at 7:40, sixteen armoured cars entered Warfusee. These were the much-travelled vehicles of the 17th Armoured Car Battalion.

Tanks towed them through the rubble that blocked the streets of the village. Just beyond, several large trees had been felled across the road. The procession, joined by lorries and touring cars, came to a halt while the tanks dragged away the obstacles. Now the road into enemy country was clear, and the 17th dashed off into the blue, vanishing from knowledge of headquarters for almost sixteen hours.

On the Green Line at this time, the Australians' own protective barrage was falling short. This forced the 5th Brigade to withdraw three hundred yards in places while the 7th drew back fifty yards. All the while, German batteries, beyond the protective barrage, continued firing upon the Green Line. Then suddenly, at 8:00, like a curtain on a vast stage, the mist lifted revealing a scene that would never be forgotten by those who were there.

> Scattered parties of Australian infantry, some still digging, others looking out from their new-dug trenches, others strolling or standing between the groups in the easy attitude by which Australians were recognizable on all their battlefields.... Behind them was every arm of the Fourth Army's offensive in motion. First ... were the infantry of the 5th and 4th Divisions.... Beside them, or sometimes still filing across country ... were processions of the tanks, sixty machines in all, that were allotted for those divisions, many having the colours of their infantry painted on their sides or on plaques hung by chains from their fronts. Farther back in the gully about forty other tanks, which had already taken part in the first phase, were assembling to follow and assist in the second. Behind these ... came battery after battery of field and horse artillery, chains jingling, horses' heads and manes tossing.... In streams across the open, rolled the ammunition waggons, water-waggons and the waggons with engineer stores hurriedly packed to replace those lost in the carrier tanks twelve hours before. Parties of pioneers and engineers who had pushed out along the roads as soon as the advance started were still at work upon them.[138]

Shambling in the opposite direction were droves of prisoners in field-grey. Through the cheery throngs they trudged wide-eyed, gaping about in astonishment. Relief was written large upon their faces, many smiling for the first time in weeks.

AMIENS:
Dawn of Victory
III CORPS

At 4:20 the Tommies of the 58th London and 18th Eastern divisions climbed to their feet after what seemed like hours of lying by their jumping-off tapes. Close behind the barrage they walked, oblivious to the machine-gun fire. It was almost a relief after hours spent trudging forward in gas masks, losing their bearings in the fog, and enduring shelling and gas. Five hundred and fifty British guns of the 58th and 25th divisions fired a creeping barrage — two minutes for the first one hundred yards, slowing to four minutes thereafter. This barrage was most effective and many of the enemy guns were knocked out, making German retaliatory fire weak and ineffective. However, III Corps faced an entirely different situation than did the Canadian and Australian Corps. Here the enemy was ready and expecting an attack. Only minutes before, the Germans had been shelling the British rear areas, so when the thunderous barrage broke at 4:20, they took it to be simply retaliation although they were surprised by its strength.

174th Brigade, the 58th London Division

On the right, next to the Somme and the Australians, the 2nd Battalion, 10th County of London Regiment (Hackney) advanced towards Sailly Lorette. The 10th London was actually part of another brigade (175th), but had been assigned this task to allow the 174th a straight run to Malard Wood, which was somewhat to the left. The Hackney's were to seize Sailly Lorette and the small wedge of land formed by the northward bend in the Somme. Without the aid of the two tanks that were to have supported them, the Londoners surprised the garrison of the village, which they cleared by 6:30 — except for the church, which was held by two courageous machine-gun crews until the arrival of the tanks. Against stiffening resistance, the Hackney men pushed on, securing a commanding position along the spur northeast of Sailly Lorette and establishing contact with the Australians on the other side of the Somme. By 9:30 the 10th Hackney had captured 285 prisoners, twenty-three trench mortars and ninety-eight machine guns.

Farther north the 6th City of London Rifles fought their way to Malard Wood with the help of a solitary tank. Here they encountered the heaviest resistance in the woods *behind* the German front line. Beside the 6th, the 7th City of London advanced against even less resistance. Both battalions were in position east of the wood on the Green Line by 8:00, although scattered pockets of Germans still held out behind them.

The 58th London Division had thus achieved the Green Line without suffering unduly. It's opponent, the 43rd Reserve Division, on the other hand, reported being "nearly entirely liquidated." Having lost four and a half batteries and having buried one gun to save it from capture, the divisional commander retired and assembled his remnants on Chipilly Spur.

36th Brigade (attached from the 12th Division), the 18th Eastern Division

In the centre of III Corps the 18th Eastern Division ran into difficulty. Due to a variety of circumstances, this division was forced to cobble together its operation using troops from several other formations. The Divisional Artillery had not yet arrived from its sojourn with the French, so artillery support was being provided instead by the guns of the 25th Division. Its own 54th Brigade, which had been scheduled to launch the offensive, had been used instead to counterattack the Wurttembergers two days earlier after Brick Beacon had been seized. This had made it necessary to replace the battered survivors with the only brigade available, the 36th from the neighbouring 12th Division. Consequently, these weary Tommies had spent the night trudging towards the front line through a steady rain of shrapnel and mustard gas, arriving barely in time to cross the startline without reconnaissance. Theirs was an unenviable task. Exhausted and battered, the "Brigade" consisted of only two understrength battalions, the 7th Royal Sussex and the 9th Royal Fusiliers. None of the assigned tanks appeared at zero hour so they set off alone into the fog. They re-crossed the ground lost two days previously, but on approaching the former British front line, ran into strenuous resistance from the waiting Wurttembergers, and a fierce struggle ensued in the darkness and fog.

At this critical juncture the 10th Battalion of the Essex Regiment arrived from the rear. This 53rd Brigade unit had been scheduled to leapfrog ahead *after* the Green Line had been taken. Instead, the Essexmen attacked immediately, sweeping the other two battalions along with them. It was touch and go, but they all reached the Green Line together just as the barrage lifted to move on to the second objective. Still no tanks had appeared. Nor could contact be made with troops on either flank. The Essex were scheduled to step off immediately, but evidently they were alone. What had happened?

55th Brigade, the 18th Eastern Division

On the left, the 7th Queen's Royal West Surrey Regiment ran into even stronger opposition. As the forward battalion of the 55th Brigade, the Queen's had been ordered to form a defensive flank. Without tank support the one understrength battalion pressed forward to hunt down the enemy. Suddenly, out of the mist two battalions of Wurttembergers hurling grenades burst upon them. The Queen's were stopped in their tracks and fought for their lives — the hunted rather than the hunter. A wild melee ensued in the dark and fog — individuals versus a dimly discerned foe in overwhelming numbers. The situation was critical, but at the last moment reinforcements rushed onto the mist-shrouded battlefield. It was the battalion commander, Lieutenant-Colonel Bushell, with every remaining available man. These "odds and sods" were enough to swing the tide of battle, and the Wurttembergers were driven back. "Infantry, machine guns, and trench mortars were fleeing to the rear in flocks," reported the German Monograph.[139] In the half-hour between 7:00 and 7:30, two-thirds of the 120th and 123rd Infantry Regiments had been swept away.

Despite this victory, III Corps' objective was far off. The British barrage was well ahead by now, and drastic steps would have to be taken to catch up. It was at this moment, however, while making arrangements for the final stage of the advance that Lieutenant-Colonel Bushell was killed. In the fog few knew of the tragedy, with the result that the battalion stayed where it was in the old front line, well short of the Green Line. Had III Corps' attack failed?

THE FRENCH FIRST ARMY

General Toulorge's XXXI Corps held the key to the French role in the offensive. Its task was to cover the right flank of the British Fourth Army by advancing between the Amiens-Roye Road and Avre. Toulorge's four divisions — the 42nd beside the Canadians, the 37th in the middle, the 66th on the right, and the 153rd in close support — were to initiate the French attack. Further advances were to take place in succession to the south as the gap opened up in front of Amiens. It was even planned to extend the advance as far as the French Third Army south of Montdidier. But for the moment, it was all the 42nd Division's show.

In the spartan underground headquarters of General Deville's 42nd Division his staff officers had gathered. Some looked at their watches. It was 4:20. Suddenly an incredible, ear-splitting crash shook the dugout. "Ah, there it is," Deville exclaimed, shouting into the phone through the tumult of the barrage. Then he turned to his staff and read a homily which they had heard a dozen times before. "Liaison, messieurs! Liaison first and last and always," he exhorted. Cyril Falls' diary noted, "the old boy's face was radiant. During the past few days his nerves had been a nuisance; he has screamed with impatience and nearly driven his Chief of Staff mad. Now the impatience has passed, and though the excitement remains, it is the right kind. He is simply keyed up to concert pitch."[140]

Of course, for the majority of the French First Army the real excitement would not commence for another forty-five minutes. Not till 5:05 would the French assault begin. However, for Deville's famous 42nd Division on the right flank of the Canadian Corps an unusual preliminary advance was launched sharp at zero hour.[141] Here the *poilus* climbed over their parapets and made a six-hundred yard advance in which they met no opposition and captured an officer and twelve startled men of the 4th Bavarian Division. This novel manoeuvre had been arranged to avoid the mustard gas, which it was assumed would inevitably deluge their front line in retaliation for the barrage. On the Canadian flank the 94th Infantry Regiment, assisted by a British tank, easily overcame negligible opposition. The advance could have continued were it not for the wall of French artillery fire falling a few yards ahead, so here the 94th would wait another forty-five minutes.

General Deville had by this time interviewed a number of captured German officers, all of whom addressed him respectfully as "*Eure Exzellenz.*" He began to fidget about the lack of news from the left," wrote Cyril Falls, who was sent to find out what the Canadians were doing. Falls could learn few details, although he was assured that "things were going well." However, what he saw on the Amiens-Roye Road clinched the matter. "A long column of prisoners was approaching, those at the head carrying wounded of both sides on stretchers. In front of all was a magnificent young Canadian, carried shoulder high by four Germans, lying on his stomach with his chin propped on his forearm, obviously enjoying his position and making me think of a victorious Roman general in triumph."[142]

CHAPTER EIGHT
THE RED LINE — SAILING THROUGH

"We just sailed through that morning. It was unlike anything we had known — no trenches, blazing sunlight and absolute gaiety among the troops."
Gus Sivertz
2nd Canadian Mounted Rifles[143]

O rders had stressed that there be no pause on the Green Line. Consequently, sharp at 8:20 the protective barrage laid down in front of the Green Line lifted. Near silence followed for a few minutes, broken only by random shots from German guns as troops of four nations rose to their feet and advanced towards the second objective — the Red Line.

Back in the wagon-lines at Boves Wood, P.J. Campbell of the Royal Field Artillery had been awakened at 4:20 by the barrage, but went back to sleep, troubled by the terrible memories of that morning in March.

When I woke again the noise had almost stopped and this was surprising; battles lasted for more than an hour or two — whether we won or lost. The silence was rather disconcerting; I could interpret noises, but silence, even this comparative silence, was a new feature in a battle.... I saw Hughes and Durham ... and I shouted to them, "What's happened? Who's winning?"

"We are," said Durham. "Forty-love."

"Jerry's on his way back to Berlin," Hughes said.[144]

The Allied barrage had weakened by this stage. The long advance had left the smaller guns out of range and now they were trotting forward over roads and across bridges already being repaired by the engineers. Other artillerymen had come up immediately behind the infantry to take over captured German batteries, which would supplement the dwindling fire-power. It was gratifying to discover that there were more captured guns than crews to fire them.

So far air power had played an insignificant role in the offensive, although the German Air Service had been out in small numbers and had successfully attacked an Australian artillery unit as early as five o'clock. The RAF had achieved marginal results, but now the dispersing mist revealed an incredible number of targets, and the entire force swarmed into the August sky shortly after nine. For the remainder of the morning the skies above the battlefield were alive with S.E.5a's and Sopwith Camels, swooping, diving, and strafing. Further south over the French sector, heavy cloud still prevailed and the ceiling remained low. This, plus the thick ground mist, kept the vast majority of French planes on the ground.

THE CANADIAN CORPS

The 3rd Canadian Division

At 7:33 Brigadier Brutinel's "Canadian Independent Force" had begun its approach to the front along the Amiens-Roye Road. The advance had been led by Number 8 Platoon, Canadian Corps Cyclist Battalion, screening six of the 1st Canadian Motor Machine Gun Brigade's armoured cars. The leading section of cyclists did point duty, the remaining four pedaling with hundred yard gaps between them. Soon they had passed the leading elements of the Royal Canadian Regiment on the left and the French 94th Infantry Regiment to the south.

"About 9 a.m. we encountered sniper fire from the wood at D-19. This was cleared by the points and one armoured car," reported Lieutenant McKague of the Cyclists. "At 9:30 a.m. we reached the cross-roads at Maison Blanche and here we took a few prisoners and accounted for several snipers. One machine gun came into action on us on this corner from the direction of Mézières." This village was to the south, in the French 42nd Division's sector, and McKague received orders to enter it with an armoured car. "On reaching the first house we found several Germans, and one machine gun could be observed getting into position about two hundred yards in front of us. The points here were able to reach the 5.9 guns located on this road, and after reporting back the information that the village was apparently strongly held, it was decided not to enter it with the armoured cars until the French should come up on the right." This setback, minor as it seemed at the time, was the first of a series that would snowball along the junction of the Canadian and French advances.

To the north of the Amiens-Roye Road, Brigadier "Daddy" Dyer's 7th Brigade made a rapid advance. The Canadian components of the "International Force" now consisted of a platoon of the Royal Canadian Regiment, which had leapfrogged the 43rd Camerons on the Green Line. "The Shino Boys," permanent force soldiers famed for their spit and polish, advanced with clock-like precision. In this they were assisted by tanks and airplanes, which literally swarmed over this sector. Shortly after 10:00 the RCR had occupied the Red Line without problem.

Beside the RCR, the 42nd Royal Highlanders had jumped off from Hamon Wood promptly at 8:20. They had barely made it on time, the hurriedly constructed "bathmat bridges" proving a tougher obstacle than the enemy. Now the kilties from Eastern Canada were met with machine-gun fire and artillery firing at point-blank range. The platoons advanced spiritedly in section rushes without regard for the fire. Ahead lay several batteries including one of 8-inch howitzers. Their crews kept firing despite the swarm of "ladies from hell" charging down the slope, shouting wildly.

"All at once a German popped up directly in my path," wrote Will Bird. "He rose so suddenly that I shot without taking aim.... As the German dropped he gave a fearful groan, and to my dismay I saw he was a wizened old chap with steel-rimmed spectacles and a scraggly beard. Probably he used to do mean chores around the battery position, maybe as a sanitary man, and in all probability he was trying to surrender."[145] The highlanders swarming into the position were met by frightened horses, rearing and neighing. Twenty gunners who tried to escape were shot down and the rest surrendered on the spot. The 42nd had cleared the valley; ahead lay the Red Line.

"From this point onwards," records the unit historian,

> progress to the final objective was more or less of a route march enlivened by the sight of the panic-stricken enemy running in every direction. Crossing the crest of Hill 102 the Battalion emerged on a plateau of rolling fields unscarred by signs of warfare, most of them covered with standing crops. By 10:20 all the companies

were in position along the Red Line while patrols had
been pushed forward.[146]

The 49th Edmonton Regiment made its advance in record time,
reaching the Red Line at 10:00. Its only opposition came from machine
guns in Cerfs Wood. However, despite the rapid success of the 7th
Brigade, the supporting tanks had become sadly depleted; only eight of
the nineteen reached the Red Line.

Individuals with no special assignment went in search of souvenirs.
Jerred Mansfield, his horses tethered, strolled into a nearby wood. He
found an abandoned German battery, but the pickings were poor.

> I picked up two small bombs of the kind that explode on
> contact, with the intention of pulling the fuses and saving
> them to take home with me. Stuffing them into my
> pocket, I started across the woods in a different direction.
> About a hundred yards farther on I heard voices and
> stopped to listen, but could not make out who it was or
> what they were saying. Thinking it was someone else
> looking for souvenirs, I went on about my business.
>
> I came out into another little clearing and looking
> around saw that there was another machine gun post, in
> a pit, with the gun all mounted and the belt in position
> for firing. It was surrounded by barbed wire
> entanglements, but a path led into it from the opposite
> side. It appeared to be a good place for loot and I started
> to walk around to the other side. Someone spoke — he
> was almost beside me — and I turned to see who it was.
> I looked into the face of a German — two of them! One
> was standing up in the gun pit looking at me, and the
> other was swinging the machine gun around in my
> direction. Letting a yell out of me, I dived behind a
> stump, just in time to miss a burst of bullets. I was
> trapped. If I made a move, they would riddle me, and I
> was too far away from my group to call for help. I wasn't
> over thirty feet away and there wouldn't be a ghost of a
> chance even if they threw a bomb at me. Bomb?? It burst
> on me all of a sudden that I had the two German stick-
> bombs in my pocket. I rolled over on my back, carefully
> took out the bombs and worked my way out of my coat.

I pulled the safety pin out and threw my coat off six feet to one side to draw their fire. I took careful aim and threw the bomb where I thought it would do the most good. A burst of bullets riddled my coat and suddenly stopped. The bomb burst with a sharp crack and then silence. I jumped to my feet and to one side before throwing the other bomb. It landed beside the wrecked gun. One German came tearing out of there and across the clearing at a great speed. The other lay across his gun.

The 1st Canadian Division

In the Canadian centre the 1st Division's advance had been taken over by the 1st Brigade, made up of four Ontario battalions. On a three-battalion front — 2nd (right), 4th (centre), and 3rd (left) — the brigade advanced behind schedule, having arrived late on the Green Line.

The 2nd Eastern Ontario, as it turned out, had already experienced most of their adventures prior to reaching their jumping-off position, and had captured several large parties of Germans by-passed in the fog by the 16th Canadian Scottish. Although their tank support had been left far behind in the mist, the 2nd had occupied their objective by 11:00.

Finding a German dugout with its commanding officer lying mortally wounded and unconscious outside, the adjutant and the orderly room sergeant decided to appropriate it for Battalion Headquarters. Exploring down a long, dark stairway, Sergeant Sample became convinced that they were not alone. "What should we do?" he asked the adjutant.

"Shoot your pistol downstairs." The roar of Sample's pistol, amplified by the echoing walls, had barely died away when a cry of "*Kamerad!*" was heard, and "two amazingly grubby fists" appeared around the corner. As their owner was being directed outside a veritable babble of "*Kamerads*" introduced twelve more equally grubby "field-greys," who were also shepherded up the stairs. The Adjutant and the Sergeant felt quite pleased with themselves until Sergeant Sample discovered that he had forgotten to insert the magazine in his pistol that morning.

"Sample, how many cartridges have you left?"

"None, sir. I just had one in my pistol, and that was the one I shot down the dug-out stairs."[147]

The "Mad Fourth" also went over the top five minutes late and without tank support. They encountered much heavier opposition. "I am running neck and neck with Private Moreau, Number 2 on the Lewis-gun," recalled Lieutenant Jim Pedley.

> He carries a wallet filled with spare parts for their gun; also two panniers of ammunition besides his revolver and web equipment. It is too much for him to run far with.
>
> "Here, give me this," I shout, reaching for the panniers of S.A.A. slung on his shoulder. He misunderstands me, thinks I am hit, reaches to hold me up as we run forward together. "No, I'm all right," I yell, and shift the panniers to my shoulder. He is grateful and smiles a moment; then we are down together in the ditch.
>
> God! how the bullets crack, just above our heads! They break the twigs all around, they thud into the little bank of earth.... Moreau is on my left, and beyond him is Proctor, with the Lewis-gun. The gun is jammed; he is working feverishly with it.... Cautiously Moreau and I raise our heads a foot apart until our eyes can see through the long grass. But we do not have time to see anything.
>
> Crack! Moreau is hit. He falls back, and I with my arm around him. My hand is wet with blood that spurts from his breast. What a flow of blood, a fountain of blood! Moreau gasps and chokes three or four times, his whole body heaving, then stiffens in a final convulsion and collapses. It is all a matter of a few seconds. The corpse is heavy and I push it from me.
>
> Over on the left is a whirring noise as a great tank lunges ahead. Its six-pounders are firing and the din of the bullets on its iron walls mingles with the roar of the guns and the smashing of trees.
>
> "Get ready to rush!"
>
> Our Lewis-gun is at last in shape.
>
> I wave my hand, shout to Armstrong to come with us. "Away you go!"
>
> Somehow we scramble up, run up the hill. I take a few steps wondering why I am not hit, then realize that the firing from the hill has stopped. Fritz's nerve has failed him in the pinch.
>
> "Come on, boys!"
>
> The others take up the shout and we sweep up.[148]

Scattered between the Green Line and the Red Line are "The Mad Fourth's" 135 casualties.

On the left of the 1st Brigade the 3rd Toronto Battalion had become hopelessly scattered before even arriving on the Green Line. Battalion Headquarters had arrived first at 7:35 after suffering heavier casualties than any of the companies. Now as their own heavies dropped around them causing several more casualties, they waited for their missing companies. 8:20 came and passed, but still there were too few men to advance on the Red Line. Eventually at 8:40 five platoons had been assembled and these now went forward to take the battalion's objective. Five minutes later another three materialized out of the dissipating mist and they too pushed on.

The Torontonians were soon pinned down by machine-gun fire and suffered numerous casualties. At last a lone tank rumbled onto the scene, and although the *feldgrau* of the 117th Division fought bitterly, the advance resumed and the Red Line was occupied shortly before 11:00. The 3rd had captured eleven artillery pieces, fourteen machine guns, and 450 prisoners, but the cost had been high — 41 killed and 164 wounded.

After only two and a half hours in action the 1st Brigade men looked out over a peaceful landscape reminiscent of their own Ontario — no trenches, no barbed-wire. There was only open rolling countryside in which peaceful villages nestled. Under the warm August sun fields of ripening grain rippled in a light breeze, while at the foot of a gentle slope the Luce sparkled and murmured beneath drooping willows.

The 2nd Canadian Division

The 2nd Canadian Division continued its advance alongside the 5th Australian Division. The two leading formations were the 26th New Brunswick Battalion on the right and from Montreal, the 24th Victoria Rifles of Canada. Here the assault went like clockwork, with efficient tank support being provided by the 14th Tank Battalion. The New Brunswickers carried off their advance in great style, and despite point-blank artillery fire and a blizzard of machine-gun bullets, reached the Red Line at 10:15.

On the left flank the 24th Victoria Rifles had also moved along rapidly, although the Montrealers did encounter several difficulties on their left at the junction with the Australian line. It had been agreed that a platoon of Canadians would operate on the Australian side of the railway line and vice-versa. This, it was hoped would securely interlock the two "Victorias," the Victoria Rifles and the 57th Victoria Battalion from "down under." The Australian liaison officer had been uneasy however, and appeared to doubt the Canadians' ability to keep up with his own battalion. Lieutenant Clark-Kennedy of the 24th assured him that the Canucks would keep up, and even suggested a race to the Red Line. The Australians, gamblers by nature, could not resist, and the contest was scheduled to begin at 8:20.

Exactly on time the Victoria Rifles bounded out of the Green Line led by their CO. Despite the usual storm of machine-gun fire, the Montrealers swept forward with surprising speed. Their tank support never faltered, and within half an hour they were through Pieuret Wood. Here the Diggers spotted several German guns and lined two platoons along the railway cutting to rake the enemy in enfilade. The 24th took only time enough to secure their trophies — four 4.2 howitzers, two 5.9s and several anti-tank guns — before moving on. The wager had not diminished the co-operation between the two dominion battalions.

Wiencourt village lay on the railway a short distance ahead. It was taken easily by 9:20, only an hour after the assault had begun. South of the village an enemy concentration was broken up by a single tank. The Germans held their ground until the monster was only fifteen yards distant, then they broke completely, fleeing in all directions.

The next village along the rail line was Guillaucourt. Fortunately for the Montrealers, the 60th Australians provided covering fire, and nine Whippet Tanks appeared in the nick of time. These medium tanks from the 6th Tank Battalion were somewhat in advance of the 9th Cavalry Brigade, which was coming up from the rear. The medium tanks crawled around the village with six coming in from the south and three from the north. The 24th rushed the battered buildings at the same time, and there ensued some vicious house-to-house fighting, but Guillaucourt was cleared by 9:50.

Now there remained only a 1,500-yard advance to the Red Line. For the 24th it was the most trying portion of the day. Here enemy resistance stiffened as the resting battalions of the fresh 117th Division were encountered. These last few yards cost the 24th dearly, and most of their 189 casualties fell here. Nevertheless the 24th Victoria Rifles were in place on the Red Line before 10:15.

The 5th Australian Division

Meanwhile, the Australians were advancing over much flatter ground, the plain of Santerre, which stretched three-quarters of the way along the front. On their right, adjacent to the Canadians, the 57th Victorians ran into trouble from their own artillery. Lieutenant-Colonel Deneky sent three urgent messages by pigeon requesting a correction in range. At last, when he was about to ask his artillery to cease fire completely the gunners traced their problem to its source and made the necessary correction. Despite this hitch, the advance was rapid — and for the 57th, made more exciting by their wager with the Canucks. The 15th Brigade's two leading battalions were opposed only by German artillery, but facing these guns firing over open sights could be enervating. "As the shells tore past, each one of us imagined that they were passing within a foot of him," wrote Captain McKenna from Coburg, Victoria.[149]

The 5.9s of the 8th Battery, 15th Foot Artillery opened up on the three tanks leading the Victorians. The centre tank raced straight for the guns, firing until it was hit eighty yards from the battery. By this time, however, the two surviving tanks and parties of infantry had outflanked the German gunners and captured them all.

The 57th and 59th had now reached the German military railway, which ran across their front. A halt was called because Australian artillery was still firing onto the slope immediately ahead. While waiting, the Diggers pulled out their rations and dined almost leisurely. The 59th Victoria Battalion had spent a very easy morning so far, passing just south of Bayonvillers. Their only opposition had been a battery of the 27th Foot Artillery Regiment, which had fired upon the 59th while deployed in the controversial "artillery formation." The sections strung out in short columns had proven vulnerable under direct artillery fire for they offered the enemy the chance to rake an entire file with one shell. Two of the 59th's little section columns were hit and almost destroyed. Yet upon the arrival of the tanks, which forced the gunners to take cover, the battery were easily taken by one platoon.

Now as the 15th Brigade waited for its artillery fire to lift, the men munched their breakfast and watched the cavalry come up. "What a glorious sight they presented! The sun shone on their well-groomed horses, the burnished harness and the oiled tin-hats of the riders," marveled Lieutenant Williams, enthusiasm having overcome his premonition. "The troopers' smart-fitting uniforms looked brand-new beside the stained clothing of the infantry, and their long sabres, bucketed rifles and bandoliers made a most warlike equipment. In long lines they came on through the brown stubble of crops, and then deployed into wave after wave to harry the German rear-guards."[150]

It was about 9:40 when the cavalry, led by two twelve-man patrols, passed Bayonvillers. Presently they crested the rise where the Australian barrage still played. Shells burst among the horsemen and several were seen to fall. From a factory and some huts north of Guillaucourt, machine-gun fire broke out. At this the patrols broke into a gallop, and wheeling and darting, soon outflanked and silenced the guns. In this they were assisted by Australian infantry and by a tank that charged straight at the buildings. By 10:15 the 15th Australian Brigade took up positions on the Red Line. But for the 57th Victorians it proved to be several minutes too late. They found grinning Canucks of the 24th Victoria Rifles quietly waiting there for them.

The 8th Brigade advanced on the left of the 15th. Its route was devoid of natural obstacles, being completely level. The 31st Battalion made up of Victorians and Queenslanders simply marched five miles to its objective. For the tanks spearheading this advance, however, the open country proved deadly. What happened in those few minutes in the fields between Lamotte and Bayonvillers is related by a survivor of the German 13th Division. He was a gunner in the 6th Battery, 58th Foot Artillery Regiment, half of whose guns had been knocked out in the opening bombardment.

> A light tank was roaring toward us with great speed, plunging into craters and climbing over trenches, while his machine guns kept firing at our battery. Bullets were whizzing all around us. Our men feverishly set the sights and fired one, two shells in rapid succession. Before us, there was a shattering roar followed by a dark cloud the size of a house: the tank had been destroyed. But this was only the beginning. Two large tanks emerged from the ruins of Lamotte, flames flashing from their steel turrets. Their projectiles were exploding around our battery. Our pointers aimed at them hurriedly, fired a few shells, and disposed of the two tanks as rapidly as they had wiped out the first. But three new tanks were approaching in single file through the high grass on our right, and had arrived within several hundred yards.

Their guns opened fire on us, and again four men of our battery were badly wounded.

As we had only two guns, we first fired at the tank on the left, then on that on the right. The order, "Fire at will!" was followed by a desperate cannonade. Our left gun ... destroyed its tank almost at once. Its fuel tank exploded with a blinding flash and a big black cloud, tossing pieces of iron and human remains high into the air. The tank in the middle, which had approached to within three hundred yards, was destroyed in a few seconds. The tank on the right had a broken tread, and kept turning round and round.... In Bayonvillers, a village behind the front, we heard the tumult of battle. Our situation was becoming critical, as we risked being cut off. Suddenly, one more warning cry rang out: "Tank on the right!" A large male tank, the seventh in a matter of minutes, came speeding straight toward us and opened a murderous fire when only two hundred yards distant ... Sergeant Wessel's gun was disabled while being trained on the new enemy. Its commander was badly wounded, its crew either wounded too, or killed. Our last gun's shield and sights were seriously damaged in the attack, but its crew did not give up the fight. Crouched behind the steel shield, under a hail of bullets, they turned the gun-carriage. The cool-headed pointer took aim and, at the very instant the tank plunged into the sunken path ahead of us, the fatal shell crashed through its side. Nothing other than dense smoke and flying pieces of iron could be seen. The tank's destruction was our last-minute salvation. Now it was time to fall back.[151]

The "tumult of battle" heard coming from Bayonvillers by this gunner was very real. There at the entrance to the village a battery of 4.2s belonging to the 27th Foot Artillery still fired unceasingly. In several minutes the battery had knocked out three of the Mark Vs as they advanced at the head of the infantry. At that moment the first cavalry patrols were arriving, and behind them rumbled "Musical Box," a Whippet of the 6th Tank Battalion. It was commanded by an audacious twenty-four-year-old from Llandudno, Wales, Lieutenant C.B. Arnold.

We came under direct shell fire from a four-gun field battery of which I could see the flashes, between Abancourt and Bayonvillers. Two Mark V tanks, 150 yards on my right front, were knocked out. I saw clouds of smoke coming out of these machines, and the crews evacuated them. The infantry following the heavy machines were suffering casualties from this battery I turned half left and ran diagonally across the front of this battery at a distance of about 600 yards. Both my guns were able to fire on the battery, in spite of which they got off about eight rounds at me without damage, but sufficiently close to be audible inside the cab, and I could see the flashes of each gun as it fired. By this time I had passed behind a belt of trees running along a roadside. I ran along this belt until level with the battery, when I turned full right and engaged the battery in the rear.... The gunners, some thirty in number, abandoned their guns and tried to get away. Gunner Ribbans and I accounted for the whole lot.[152]

The last few minutes of savage action had barely touched the 31st Battalion, but had reduced its tank support to a lone Mark V. A thousand yards ahead another German battery retired slowly along the road to Harbonnières, unlimbering at intervals to fire over open sights. Aussie Lewis gunners picked off the horses for one gun, which then had to be abandoned, and the remainder of the guns (1st Battery, 79th Regiment) withdrew to Rosières for ammunition. To the south of Harbonnières a German observation balloon could be seen being hurriedly towed away by its motor-wagon. The 31st advanced at a brisk walking pace led by its one remaining British tank. Finally on its left, from the scrub brush marking the beginnings of Morcourt Valley — which ran northwards down to the Somme — machine-gun fire crackled — the first serious opposition for the infantry. Upon the appearance of the battalion's one tank nosing about through the scrub, the enemy was seen "running about like ants from a disturbed nest."[153] By 10:25 the 31st Battalion was in position in Buchanan Wood, its portion of the Red Line.

Enemy fire in front of the 30th New South Wales Battalion was sufficient to cause the support battalion, the 32nd, to move into the gap between the 31st and the 30th. Well-supported by the five surviving tanks, men of the 8th Brigade swept through feeble opposition to take their place on the Red Line at 10:40. German morale in this sector was indicated by the fact that one hundred prisoners were escorted to the rear by a solitary Digger. Another, about to take back a further eighty, was asked in polite English by one of the *feldgrau* whether they might "visit" their quartermaster's store. "As long as you don't run away, you can do what you ___ well like," he replied. The prisoners happily treated themselves to new underwear, uniforms, and boots to begin their lives as POWs in style.

The 4th Australian Division

Next to the 30th New South Wales Battalion was the 12th Brigade led by the 46th Victorians and the 45th New South Wales. The progress of these units had been rapid and without problem to this point. They had crossed several gullies, each of which became deeper as it dropped northwards to the Somme — and found tiers of German artillery dug into the slopes. These they took without incident. The 45th alone had captured twenty-nine guns.

The 12th Brigade reached Morcourt Valley, the sides of which had been terraced with bivouacs, huts, and horse standings. German reserves, despite the barrage, now lined the topmost tier of shelters firing into the Australians. Tanks rolled forward, but the first to attempt the steep slope rolled over. Helpless to advance, the remaining tanks resorted to firing from the crest into the valley. The Australians now assaulted by section rushes. It was at this moment that further assistance arrived in the shape in the 16th Brigade, Royal Horse Artillery, which raked the valley with shrapnel. Even more dramatic was the appearance along the old Roman Road of the 17th Armoured Car Battalion. The cars roared into Morcourt Valley pouring machine-gun fire into the rows of Germans lining the tiers of bivouacs on both sides of the road. Combined with the Diggers' determined advance this encouraged many of the Germans to break for the rear. But at this juncture the *feldgrau* also received support. An anti-aircraft gun mounted on a truck quietly drove up the Roman Road and pulled into position beside the red-brick "Hussar Farm." It opened fire at the tanks, quickly hitting three. Several RAF planes then dove low along the valley crest dropping smoke bombs which screened the tanks. The anti-aircraft gun was reduced to firing blindly along the road. Despite machine-gun fire from a large tented hospital, and from across the valley at Hussar Farm, the 46th's men were already into the gully, ferreting out the enemy, who began to scatter. The anti-aircraft gun truck started up and drove off eastward as a tank and an armoured car emerged from the smoke on the road. Another tank fired across the valley into Hussar Farm, and the red-brick buildings broke into flames even as the 46th reached the eastern crest and surged into their objective, Richmond Wood. The time — 10:00 — the 46th Victoria Battalion was the first to reach the Red Line — ten minutes ahead of schedule.

To the north, the 45th had continued its advance without even deploying, simply sending Lieutenant Vincent and Sergeant Brown with five scouts armed with stripped-down Lewis guns to reconnoitre. They advanced into the valley occupied by the 201st Reserve Infantry Regiment. Here the seven Diggers found total confusion — German soldiers, having thrown away their arms, were running about intent on plundering the canteen and clothing stores. When the seven opened fire a large numbers of looters ran towards them begging to surrender. Two hundred prisoners were sent back as the 45th entered the valley — still undeployed. A German machine gun opened up on the neighbouring 46th, but after one grenade exploded thirty yards from it, the crew and fifteen more *feldgrau* surrendered to Vincent, including one who ran forward shouting, "Don't shoot me! I'm an Alsatian. *Vive la France!*"[154] The 1st Battalion, 201st Reserve Infantry Regiment had been captured in its entirety! Only their commander survived to report that the 201st had "fired away its ammunition and then defended itself with bayonets and spades."[155] Still without bothering to deploy, the 45th New South Wales reached the Red Line by 10:19. There they watched as to their left a "rabble" of a thousand or more Germans streamed in full retreat towards Mericourt. Meanwhile, a private carrying a paint pot and a brush was following the battalion. It was his job to mark each gun or trophy taken, "Captured by 45th Bn. A.I.F." While busily at work in some gun-pits near "Hamilton Wood," he was interrupted by several Germans begging to surrender to him.

In this second phase of the offensive, by far the most difficult task on the Australian front was that assigned to the 4th Brigade, the 4th Australian Division. Although its planned advance was not long, it covered a wide front and included several steep riverside gullies. Thus the brigade went with three battalions in line and only one in support. On the right the 13th New South Wales Battalion started off with great success although only one tank made the advance with them. When a German machine gun opened up, Sergeant Sexton[156] of Malvern, Victoria, stood up in the wheat field and watched for the tell-tale muzzle flashes, then hosed each German position, firing his Lewis gun from the hip. In this style the 13th crossed three valleys almost without casualties, although the left company held itself back somewhat to keep abreast of its neighbour.

On the far side of Morcourt Valley, straddled by bursting shells of the bombardment, stretched three tiers of huts, a jumble of German transport wagons, and a line of picketed horses, a continuation of those encountered by the 12th Brigade on their right. As soon as the bombardment moved on, the men from New South Wales swept into the valley, which was defended by a battalion of the 55th Infantry Regiment and one of the 15th. A German officer later reported: "It was too late for an orderly retirement of the two battalions. Incessantly chased by low flying aeroplanes, followed by the fire of the enemy infantry, machine guns, and tanks, the majority of the parties that managed in most parts to get away were scattered, and considerable bodies were completely surrounded and captured."[157]

This rather heroic picture was sheer romance. Those taken prisoner by the 13th Battalion were not taken fighting but sheltering in the valley or looting the canteens there. The ones who escaped did so long before they were outflanked, and were the "rabble" the 45th had seen fleeing towards Mericourt. Only one tank in fact supported the Diggers.

The 13th now re-formed to resume its advance. Captain Geary mounted one of the fine horses picketed there, and amid the cheers of his men galloped to the crest of the valley, in front of the columns advancing in "artillery formation." Dismounting with a flourish, Geary handed the reins to a soldier, and fell dead, shot through the head by a sniper. The 13th Battalion's immunity had ended. Snipers and machine gunners began a steady fire from the front, and Australian casualties mounted. Suddenly the left company came under heavy attack from the flank and rear! A bitter moment of panic ensued, but the men rallied and made the final rush to the crest of the ridge that was their portion of the Red Line. The final surge had cost the 13th over sixty casualties. Why were there still Germans on their left?

For the two battalions on the Australian flank, between the 13th and the River Somme, the situation was grave. Although the 15th Queensland was on the extreme left, the river's many meanders caused the 14th Victorians an equal share in the hell that ensued. Everything started off well enough. As the 4th Brigade battalions passed through the 41st back on the Green Line, the latter stood up and cheered them on. Ahead, in the trees bordering the Somme, lay the village of Cerisy. Behind it stood a ridge running southward from the river. The 15th, led by scouts and six tanks of the 8th Tank Battalion, set out for Cerisy. Low in the flats around the meanders, many patches of fog still persisted. Nevertheless, the tanks reached their objective without mishap. The first Mark V made straight for the mud-plaster building at the entrance to the town. Smashing through, it burst into Cerisy. Frightened Germans emerged with their hands up, and the Queenslanders rounded up several hundred prisoners before moving onto the flats to dig-in around the village.

Between them and the 13th, the 14th Victorians were making good progress despite strong opposition. This came in the form of German rifle and machine-gun fire — and the shells of one British howitzer, which regularly fell 1,500 yards short and caused thirteen casualties including the battalion medical officer. On the ridge half a mile ahead the men could see German officers confidently walking about. One was a survivor of the front line, Lieutenant Spengler of the 97th Infantry Regiment. Here Spengler had gathered various remnants, primarily from the 55th Infantry. Taking shelter in a gravel pit, Spengler's small party used its three machine guns to slow the Australian advance. But the tanks passed around to their rear, and one rushed the gallant defenders. At first the *feldgrau* put up stern resistance, but eventually Spengler, having already lost one eye, was mortally wounded through the other, and German resistance crumbled. The 14th swept up the last few yards to the crest of the ridge. The Red Line lay just ahead. But here the crisis feared by many began to unfold for the 4th Australian Brigade. III Corps on their left flank had failed to keep up. The Australian flank remained in German hands!

On the high ground on the other side of the Somme gunners of the 13th Foot Artillery Regiment gasped in astonishment as the fog lifted and a fantastic panorama suddenly appeared on their left. Their historian recorded:

> The southern slope of the Somme valley gradually rising to the commanding Roman Road was teeming with enemy columns which, hurrying forward under the protection of the slowly vanishing ground mist, had already passed the alignment of the German trenches on this side. The German line appeared to have been wiped away. On the far side of Cerisy ... half way up the slope crept four tanks in echelon.
>
> From about 2,000 metres range burst the first long shell ... into the march column of British [*sic* Australian] infantry which, after vain attempts to emplace its machine-guns behind the road hedges or in gardens of

Cerisy, sank out of sight in the meadow and hedges at the northern entrance of the village.

Now targets offered in confusing plenty. First came, in their turn, the tanks which in their clumsiness had not managed to get much further forward. After five or six shots all four flamed up, providing a dreadful end for their crews. Then the English [*sic* Australian] batteries brought into action on the same alignment as our batteries but with the front to the east, were taken over open sights....

The effect of the fire of the batteries was before long apparent.... The advance on the far side of the Somme, so far as lay within the range of the group, came to a stop and movement ceased.[158]

At the same moment the 14th Victorians had run into the most stubborn infantry resistance the Australian Corps was to encounter that day. They were about to descend into Morcourt Valley, the continuation of the German rest camp. This morning it housed two reserve companies of the 97th Infantry, one machine gun company of the 201st Reserve Infantry, plus Major Kuhlwein von Rathenow, CO of the 202nd Reserve Infantry Regiment, with his signalers and several machine-gun crews. Von Rathenow had just gathered his men from their dugouts where they had been sleeping. Now they met the 14th Victorians with a savage fire that killed several men. The advance of the 14th stopped abruptly as the sections dived for cover. Lewis gunners and men of the Australian Machine Gun Companies attempted to suppress the fire from the batteries across the Somme and von Rathenow's infantry to their front. The 4th Brigade's advance bogged down in confusion obscured by the last wisps of the fog and by smoke bombs dropped by the RAF. The men of the 4th Light Trench Mortar Battery were particularly frustrated. They had no shells to fire because theirs had gone up in the spectacular explosion of No. 1 Gun Carrier Company's tanks the evening before.

The next few minutes were described by a German historian:

Amid the burst of the heavy British shells, the first sign of the Australians' approach was the sound, coming from behind the Germans' right flank, of the first tank that pushed through Cerisy. The defenders at once faced to the rear. The mist was still too thick to see the monster, but they could hear it fighting a duel with two heavy machine-guns on the road below. Then the sound of its engine receded. The noise brought out the last sleepers. The steep bank was safe from the British shells most of which flung harmless geysers from the flats below. Aeroplanes flying very low now attacked, and then a tank came over the hill in front, firing its 6-pounder and machine-guns. The machine-guns could not stop it and panic began, but the officers were able to hold their men. The tank came on, to the edge of the cliff, the garrison with their guns having to press out of its way. Then its driver suddenly saw his danger and put his engine into reverse, and the monster slowly withdrew into the smoke.

Major von Rathenow now received a message from Lieutenant Spengler, who was valiantly defending the gravel pit, further to the south, against the 14th Australian Battalion. Von Rathenow sent two machine-gun sections to reinforce the one-eyed Spengler, and at the same time sent three scouts into the village of Cerisy to discover the situation there. The three NCOs, Dietrich, Anton, and Müller, were fired upon by two tanks but reported finding no Australians in the village.

A second tank now came over the spur. As it neared the bank its engine broke down. The crew could be heard trying to restart it. The German machine-gunners by intense fire tore open one of its embrasures; the Germans swarmed round, and it was eventually set on fire by an explosion [probably a trench mortar bomb]. Reserve-Lieutenant Imig saved the crew from some of his angry men. Another tank now appeared and moved parallel to the bank, firing, and receiving intense fire. Suddenly its crew left it and tried to take position behind it, but were over-powered and captured; their tank had burst into flames.

Shortly afterwards the Germans lining the bank were fired on by tanks which had got past on the southern flank, enfilading the position. Major von Rathenow decided to withdraw, and ordered the machine-gun company to retire first and cover him. "At 9:20," he says, "I ordered the withdrawal." The Australians came over the spur too late to prevent his crossing the flats below.[159]

At this juncture the former Jackaroo of "Boatman" and "Wellshot" stations in west Queensland galloped his guns across the exposed crest of the ridge south of Cerisy. At 1,300 yards range Captain A.O. Smith and his 39th Battery fired over one hundred shells into the German machine gunners, thus breaking the deadlock to enable the 14th and 16th battalions coming up behind it to move on. Many of the retreating Germans now attempted to cross the Somme by a bridge between Cerisy and Chipilly but Private J.P. Pringle of the 15th had already covered this escape route with his Lewis gun. None made it over, and the survivors made off southwards along the riverside road towards Morcourt.

Above on the ridge, Captain Wilson of the 14th saw these fugitives and decided to clear Morcourt without waiting for the allotted troops. Headed by one tank, the former bank clerk from East Malvern led his Victorians down the slope and into the village perched on the banks of the Somme. As they charged in, a German staff car made off, but two mounted officers trying to follow were shot down. The commanders of the 26th and 85th Brigades had made good their own escapes, but they had left behind three hundred weary *feldgrau*, who immediately surrendered to the Victorians.

Meanwhile the 15th Battalion was also completing its assignment. In its first attempt to reach its objective, its one remaining tank was driven off by accurate mortar fire. Captain Domeny then led a party around the flank, and, just in the nick of time, the Germans evacuated the crest of the ridge. A few moments later Corporal Knipe, who described himself as "a drover and kangaroo shooter," brought in fifty prisoners as well as the British tankmen whom the Germans had captured only minutes earlier. The last Australian battalion had reached the Red Line.

III CORPS

The Australian Corps had reached the Red Line on schedule, but prospects looked grim for a further advance on the left as long as the north bank of the Somme lay in German hands. Guns in Chipilly and in Celestine Wood still fired at everything in sight although they were situated in positions scheduled to have been taken hours earlier by III Corps. What had gone wrong?

The 58th London Division's 173rd Brigade had passed through the 174th more or less on schedule, but on leaving the shelter of Malard Wood it came under heavy fire. The men were forced to take cover, and within minutes were left far behind their own barrage. That was the extent of the advance. Fate, however, apparently allowed a few brave Londoners to penetrate the enemy position and reach their final objective on Chipilly Ridge. There they were spotted by a forward observing officer who reported at 8:45 to Divisional Headquarters that troops had reached the final objective. Air observation soon confirmed this with the result that III Corps Headquarters acted as though its troops were on the Red Line when in fact its main force was still over a mile away on the Green Line. What happened to these gallant souls on Chipilly Ridge — if indeed, they ever existed — has never been recorded.

Meanwhile, the 18th Eastern Division was in an almost similar situation although this division did record one success — temporary, as it turned out. It will be recalled that the 10th Battalion, the Essex Regiment had fought its way to the Green Line without tanks and without flank support. Realizing that there was no time for delay, the Essexmen continued on regardless. Owing to fog, the battalion became dispersed. One party, less than eighty strong, reached the objective without resistance and captured two batteries on the northwest edge of Gressaire Wood. The Germans had just settled down for breakfast when the Tommies materialized out of the mist. By 8:00 the 10th Essex reported that they were well dug-in on the Red Line.

Presently a roaring and clanking to the rear announced the arrival of the first tank. It was followed by three platoons of the 7th Royal West Kents. The remainder of that battalion had been driving off a heavy German attack from the north. Now the West Kents had linked up with the 10th Essex on the Red Line and with the Queen's who held the extreme left flank on the Green Line. This was as planned. The left flank of the Allied offensive seemed secure.

During this time the 8th Royal Berkshires, the other battalion of the 53rd Brigade, had arrived at the Green Line at 7:40 and pressed on without tanks. As they crossed the open area before Gressaire Wood the mist began to dissipate. Half a mile from the wood a withering blast of machine-gun fire burst upon them, and field guns opened up at point-blank range. After several vain attempts to reach the objective, the Berkshires fell back to the Green Line. The result was a gaping hole between the Australians and the 10th Essex.

The tank support provided for the 18th Eastern Division had certainly been a disappointment. By this time only two Mark Vs had caught up to the infantry they were supposed to have led. Of one company, four tanks had broken down before they reached the start line.

The second company had two breakdowns while another tank, having lost direction, joined the 12th Division further north.

By 10:30 the 10th Essex's position had become critical. Their two tanks were running short of petrol and no reinforcements were in evidence. Only five hundred yards to the front, two German batteries had set up at the edge of Gressaire Wood. Now they fired over open sights into the new British position. But worst of all, Germans had begun to filter through on the left between the Essex and the West Kents, while on their open right, infantry with machine guns outflanked them. Unknown to the beleaguered Tommies, the 5th Battalion, the Royal Berkshire Regiment was at that moment being ordered up from Divisional Reserve to support them. But it was already too late; at 10:30 the order was passed to retire. The Essexmen began their withdrawal in good order, but overwhelming fire from three sides caused their manoeuvre to lose all semblance of precision. The order was finally passed to scatter — each man for himself. The Red Line in III Corps' sector was once again in German hands.

The failure of III Corps to reach its second — and *final* — objective caused the Australian left flank to be enfiladed. Further advances would make it even more vulnerable. *The British Official History* is blunt about the failure: "Thus the main attack of III Corps ended on the first objective. With well trained troops and more experienced company leaders it should have gained complete success."[160] Left unasked were the questions, "Who was responsible for their training" and "Why were there no experienced company leaders left?" It is always easier for generals (and their historians) to ignore their own faulty planning and blame the dead.

THE FIRST FRENCH ARMY

The First French Army continued to come into action according to plan, each corps advancing in succession after its neighbour to the left had moved off. Immediately south of the Canadians General Toulorge's XXXI Corps continued in the wake of their assault. His 42nd Division, adjacent to the Canucks, was visible to the rearmost Canadian battalion. "We had a grandstand view of the First French Army on our immediate right," recalled Private Gad Neale of the 46th South Saskatchewan Battalion. "It was just like a picture show and only a mile or less away. There was a little village and the French 75s were shelling it. Then the *poilus* started out towards it and into the village they went — with their long coats with the corners turned back — and then out ran Heinie on the other side, and we had a wonderful view of the performance."

By 10:00 the 42nd and 37th divisions had reached the road from Moreuil to Villers aux Erbles. The latter was immediately enveloped in an encircling movement, and by 11:00 the town was liberated. Meanwhile, on General Toulorge's extreme right, his 66th Division's advance had gone like clockwork. In three phases, each one extending the attack further to the right, the division had advanced against light opposition.

Next in line and scheduled to move off at 8:20 was IX Corps. Right from the start things had not gone as well for IX Corps. Its 15th Colonial Division had come to a standstill in its attempts to cross the River Avre. However, the success of Toulorge's advance on the northern flank eventually produced a lessening of resistance in front of IX Corps, which by 11:40 was moving forward. Despite this hitch the French First Army was still on schedule.

THE CAVALRY CORPS

Now as the Canadian infantry reached the Red Line, cavalry appeared behind them. For most of the men of the British Cavalry Corps this would be their first significant taste of action since the early weeks of the war — almost four years ago. On the Western Front trench warfare had put cavalry on the shelf. Indeed, most of the belligerents had converted theirs to infantry. The British High Command, made up primarily of cavalry officers, had tenaciously clung to the fantasy that cavalry would once again come into its own. All that was needed was a "breakthrough." Reinforced by Whippet tanks — a fact that pleased neither horsemen nor tankers — two entire cavalry divisions would today be presented with the opportunity for which they had waited so long.

The sight of thousands of cavalry moving up caused astonishment among the infantry. Lieutenant-Colonel "Turkey" Ross of the 28th Nor'westers reflected the expectations of most as he watched the approach of the 8th King's Royal Irish Hussars, the "Fighting Fifteenth," and the 19th Hussars which made up the 9th Cavalry Brigade.

> One of the great sights of the war! Our troops had in
> other battles seen squadrons of horse employed, but never
> before had seen the Cavalry launched in the attack in
> such large formations. As they moved briskly forward

with horse-artillery, Whippet tanks, and all of their transport, they presented a magnificent sight. Trotting along in troops they would suddenly deploy in half-sections and disappear over the high ground east of Marcelcave to sweep into the enemy back areas, spreading consternation and confusion.[161]

Behind the Canadian centre the 7th Cavalry Brigade swept up to the Red Line — the 7th Dragoon Guards, the 6th Inniskillings, and the famous "Death or Glory Boys," the 17th Lancers. The most welcome sights to the Canucks however, cantered by on their right flank, overlapping into the French sector. These were three relatively unknown regiments that comprised the Canadian Cavalry Brigade, and for the first time they were going into action alongside the Canadian Corps. Every Canadian there felt a tremendous surge of pride as the Royal Canadian Dragoons, Lord Strathcona's Horse, and the Fort Garry Horse advanced into line. With them came two batteries of the Royal Canadian Horse Artillery, the Canadian Signal Troop, and the Canadian Cavalry Machine Gun Squadron.

Diggers of the 15th Australian Brigade had already watched the 1st Cavalry Brigade passing their flank near Bayonvillers. The Aussies had cheered as the famous regiments from the past had trotted by — The Queen's Bays, the 5th Dragoon Guards, and the famous "Cherrypickers," the 11th Hussars immortalized in Tennyson's "Charge of the Light Brigade." The 1st and 3rd Cavalry divisions had deployed behind the Canadian Corps with one brigade overlapping into the Australian sector. The cavalry had at last been given the "breakthrough" dreamed of by the generals. Thousands of horsemen would lead the assault to the Blue Line.

Morning, August 8. Sixty-pounders in action near Amiens.

German prisoners captured by Canadians on August 8.

PA 3668

Tanks going forward to the wood, August 9.

PA 40191

Typical field ambulance. These were situated in and around Amiens on the morning of August 8. By nightfall they were, in some cases, eleven miles behind the new front line.

Late morning, August 8. Troops dig in on their objective while a
Whippet tank passes through.

German prisoners captured by Canadians.

PA 2925

Canadian troops advance along the right flank. Note French soldiers
in the foreground.

Amiens: German prisoners prepare to be shipped further to the rear.

French artillery passing a tank.

Tank officers and men inspect a captured enemy anti-tank rifle.

Infantry and tanks move forward through undamaged fields.

A maple leaf crest is painted on the "bow" of a tank that was
in support of the Canadian infantry.

PA 2969

Tanks advance along the Amiens-Roye Road while German prisoners carry their wounded to an Allied field ambulance.

PA 3052

Canadian Corps Commander, General Sir Arthur Currie, and his staff inspect German artillery pieces captured during the Amiens battle.

Field Marshal Sir Douglas Haig congratulates mixed Canadian units after their victory at Amiens.

Cavalry resting in the wood — awaiting word of the elusive breakthrough.

PA 2985

German regimental officers captured during the
early hours of the battle.

Officers of the 5th Squadron, Royal Air Force.
This group flew in support of the Canadian Corps.

American infantrymen inspect captured German guns.

Canadian and French soldiers take a well-earned rest in the gun lines.

Allied soldiers take shelter behind an abandoned limber.

CHAPTER NINE

THE BLUE LINE —
A TRÉS BON STUNT

"It was a trés bon stunt. I wouldn't have missed it for worlds!"
Sergeant. F.F. Clausen, M.M.
59th Australian Infantry Battalion[162]

Incredibly, the Amiens offensive was still a secret to most of the world. Even at Canadian Corps Headquarters at "Molly-be-Damned" the three silent clerks were still being pumped by wheedling petitioners. Finally at noon one begged, "Come, Sergeant, tell us when the show is to open, that's a good fellow."

The clerk broke his long silence with obvious satisfaction. "The show opened at twenty minutes past four this morning, and by now we are six thousand yards inside the Boche lines."[163]

More exalted figures also remained in the dark. Basil Liddell-Hart relates that a general from a neighbouring army dropped into Rawlinson's headquarters on his way home on leave. He noted the rumblings from the front and inquired in passing why there was such heavy gunfire. In London the Prime Minister of Australia, William "Billy" Hughes, was speaking to the British Parliament. He vehemently demanded that the Australian Corps be taken out of the line for a well-deserved rest. As he spoke, a telegram arrived to inform the members that Hughes' compatriots were now miles inside the German lines.

Even on the front line a casual visitor arriving at noon on Thursday, August 8, might well have been deceived into thinking that nothing was afoot. In Bayonvillers he would have found L.G. Morrison and his fellow tankers pulling up for a break.

> Here we halted, shut off the engine to cool it, swung open the sponson doors, and chucked out the dixie, a pannikin of half-cooked rice, bread and corned beef.... Occasional shells fell at long intervals, buildings clattered, a rider galloped by, aeroplanes zoomed in the blue overhead. But the sun shone peacefully, the smoke from the wood fire drifted lazily upward, and we munched and champed like boys at a picnic. It didn't seem so bad after all.[164]

Five miles south on the Red Line beyond Hill 102 the 42nd Royal Highlanders of Canada too were dining. "Lunch that day was in the nature of a picnic, for the battle line by then was far ahead. The meal was made notable by the addition to the menu of cabbages and other vegetables salvaged from the garden of a nearby farm. Brigadier-General Dyer was the guest of Battalion Headquarters at lunch in the open.[165]

Such idyllic scenes were possible along the Red Line because the mobile components of Fourth Army had taken up the pursuit and were now far ahead. Cavalry, two divisions strong, were spread out across the entire Canadian front and the southern portion of the Australian. A swarm of Mark V* tanks, carrying their uneasy passengers — crews of Lewis and machine gunners — were clanking forward to seize the Blue Line.[166] On the Canadians' southern flank Brigadier Brutinel's Canadian Independent Force pressed along the Amiens-Roye Road well ahead of the infantry, while the 17th Armoured Car Battalion performed a similar function on the Australian front.

THE CANADIAN CORPS

The 4th Canadian Division's Sector

On the Canadian right the 4th Division had leapfrogged the 3rd at the Red Line. Their first problem centred around the village of Mézières in the French sector south of the road. It will be recalled that this village had been entered earlier by Lieutenant McKague's platoon of cyclists, who had been driven out by intense machine-gun fire. The French infantry that came up later halted, and the entire operation came to a standstill. At noon Brutinel and the CO of the French 94th Infantry Regiment had just completed plans to launch an attack on Mézières later in the afternoon when word arrived that the enemy had surrendered. Captain Trench's "C" Battery of Motor Machine Gunners, supported only by the lightly armed cyclists, had sped along the narrow road behind the village under heavy shelling and machine-gun fire to take the enemy from the rear. The Allied advance resumed at 12:30, when the Motor Machine Gunners turned Mézières over to the *poilus* of the 94th and 332nd regiments.

Further ahead, the Canadian Cavalry Brigade swept on, eager for action. Of this they received their share. The Strathconas advanced behind the Whippets astride the Amiens-Roye Road, which ran straight as an arrow from the Red Line to Roye twelve miles to the southeast. The advance had barely begun when machine-gun fire opened up from Beaucourt. The Strathconas, extremely vulnerable while moving at the speed of tanks, broke into a gallop and by-passed Beaucourt. They soon overran several German positions and took forty prisoners. This was what cavalry was all about!

Two troops now turned off into the French sector to seize Fresnoy-en-Chaussée while Major Torrance with the main body advanced on a small wood in front of Le Quesnel, which lay almost upon the final objective. The Strathconas charged, but were met by fire and only Major Torrance and a corporal reached the wood. There the two hung on, defending themselves for over eleven hours. Although the enemy threatened to surround them, the other survivors, pinned down in front of the wood, dug-in under heavy artillery fire.

Meanwhile the two troops dispatched to Fresnoy-en-Chaussée had taken another 125 prisoners. No sooner had these been sent back, however, than a large German force from the 1st Reserve Division, which had been resting nearby, advanced upon the village and commenced to encircle it. The Strathconas' small patrol was about to be cut off! The two isolated troops were recalled from impending annihilation just in time, and the Germans immediately occupied the village in force. Fresnoy-en-Chaussée provided an excellent position to enfilade the Canadian Corps' right flank, and proved to be a thorn in the side of both the 4th Canadian Division and the 42nd French Division for the remainder of the day.

While this was happening on the right flank the Royal Canadian Dragoons, with the assistance of the Royal Canadian Horse Artillery, had secured Beaucourt, and captured three hundred Germans trying to withdraw. Emerging on the eastern edge of the village, the RCD ran into murderous fire from Beaucourt Wood. "The mounted men dashed into the wood, directly at the waiting gunners. Killing began as if it were a grand movie scene," wrote Will Bird, now a spectator in the Red Line. "The Maxims opened fire and men and horses rolled among the shrubbery or fell in the open.... Several Huns were trodden to earth under the hoofs of the horses, which swept in on them like a stampede. It was whirlwind fighting, so fast and furious that the machine guns did not take half the toll we expected."[167] Nevertheless, German machine guns had, not surprisingly, proved to be more deadly than Canadian sabres, and Whippet tanks were called in. "One [German machine-gun] crew alone survived the cavalry charge. A tank headed straight for them. The Germans fired frantically, and we saw one of the men on the tank slide to the ground, but the tank went on and over gun and crew, so quickly that not a German escaped."[168] Although one Whippet, "Caliban 2," penetrated as far as the outskirts of Le Quesnel and sent back fifty prisoners, two other tanks were destroyed by shell fire and the Germans remained in control of Beaucourt Wood.

The unexpectedly heavy opposition at Beaucourt Wood was provided by three battalions of the 192nd Division, whose front was miles away in the French sector. On this day they were in residence at a "rest camp" under Major Bellmann. Their unexpected appearance had cost the Canadians dearly. Both forward regiments had suffered over sixty casualties each, but the loss in horses proved crippling — 125 for the Strathconas and 132 for the RCDs.

Meanwhile the Mark V*s of the 1st Tank Battalion had rolled onto the scene bearing their Lewis- and machine-gun crews. "It was a bit crowded but not too distressing considering there were no discernible springs," recalled Spencer Giffin, a "high-school drop-out" from Isaac's Harbour, Nova Scotia. "We heard plenty, but saw little. Bullets hitting our tank on the outside would send splinters flying off on the inside causing lots of bleeding — not too serious, but annoying." Other passengers were not as fortunate as Giffin. More than half were overcome with fumes and forced to walk behind. As the long Mark V*s lumbered past Beaucourt onto the open plain before Le Quesnel they met a sudden devastating fire. South of Beaucourt Wood two guns well-camouflaged with stooks of grain opened up at close range while the sharp barks of two more, well-protected in a sunken road, added to the surprise. In moments nine of the unwieldy monsters of "A" Company had been set alight. In desperation one charged straight at the guns, but was hit and exploded with its crew and thirteen passengers.

Now the survivors from these Mark V*s joined with the unhorsed Royal Canadian Dragoons to make some sort of line and await the arrival of the infantry to assault this unexpected strong point. Already advanced elements of the 11th Brigade, the 4th Canadian Division, had arrived — just in time to witness the disaster that had befallen the tanks and their comrades who had volunteered to serve with them.

The 4th Canadian Division had not begun to cross the Red Line till 12:40 p.m. — two hours behind the cavalry. To allow the Mark V*s to pass through them, at 1:30 a second pause became necessary. In the meantime Le Quesnel had become the focal point for German reserves rushing forward to fill the gaping hole in their line. Yet since 11:50 the village had been completely undisturbed by Allied artillery. By pre-arrangement the heavy artillery had ceased firing twenty minutes before the infantry had moved off. Consequently, Le Quesnel, basking peacefully in the warm sun, had been filling with German reinforcements. It was 3:00 p.m. when the 3rd Canadian Artillery Brigade arrived to open fire on Le Quesnel at five thousand yards range. But all attempts to call down a barrage by field telephones proved useless because of damage inflicted upon the cables by the passing cavalry and the tanks. In the meantime another battery arrived to reinforce the enemy.

The right wing of the Canadian infantry was provided by the 11th Canadian Brigade led by the 54th and 102nd, both central Ontario battalions. Lieutenant-Colonel Carey of the 54th found some of the dismounted cavalry pinned down in front of Beaucourt Wood and ordered them to attack. Their officer demanded written orders. As Carey commenced writing the order he glimpsed his own men coming up through the village of Beaucourt and informed the cavalry officer that he would do the job himself and with his own men. "We could see the C.O.'s pennant with the left company," recalled Bob Price, described by his platoon officer as "an incorrigible grouse." Now the diminutive Price volunteered to carry a message from his platoon to Lieutenant-Colonel Carey.

> The gap in between was about a hundred yards. I made my way over by quick jumps from cover to cover. Two machine gun bullets cut through my collar and through my iron-rations but I wasn't hit at all. I reached the Colonel and he scribbled out something and told me to watch myself on the way back. So off I went again and safely made it back to my Lewis gun and Lt. Preston. You know, it's a good thing that a person is scared because it adds little extra wings to your feet.

Led by their colonel, the two platoons of the 54th charged. Eighteen men were killed and a large number wounded but the little force reached Beaucourt Wood and began to ferret out the Germans. Carey then returned and brought up another company of his 54th, and one of the 102nd. To the north, the 102nd was joined by a pair of Whippets, and Beaucourt Wood was partially cleared of "Regiment Bellmann," although at heavy cost. Carey next commandeered a horse from the Dragoons and galloped back to report to Brigadier Odlum. The 54th had lost 151 men that afternoon. "That knocks a hell of a lot of Christianity out of you," observed Bob Price.

At this time the 75th Mississauga Battalion was crossing the open field in front of Beaucourt Ridge past the flaming wreckage of three burnt out Mark V*s where three of their Lewis-gun crews had been annihilated. Under fire from Le Quesnel in front and from Fresnoy-en-Chaussée to the south, the 75th faced an impossible task without heavy artillery support, and so it was decided to wait till dawn the next day to seize Le Quesnel.

In the meantime the British 7th and 6th Cavalry Brigades had enjoyed more success to the north. Leaving its Whippets behind, the 7th Brigade was ranging ahead. The 6th Inniskillings on the right had run into fire from the northern edge of Beaucourt Wood, and like their Canadian comrades had been forced to halt. However, on the left the 7th Dragoon Guards had charged Cayeux Wood, which had been conveniently cleared of brush by the enemy. Although they lost a large number of horses, the Dragoon Guards captured a field battery, twelve machine guns, and a large batch of prisoners. The 17th Lancers were then sent up with a battery of Royal Horse Artillery to hold the wood against a German counterattack.

The enemy beaten off, the 17th made a lightning thrust towards the Blue Line. They stopped, however, on a slope just short of the final objective. Finding the sector virtually undefended, the "Death or Glory Boys" spread out to secure the area assigned to their brigade. Patrols turned right, along the road from Caix to Le Quesnel, and, although no opposition was met, also stopped short. No attempt was made to take Le Quesnel in flank or in rear, nor was the opportunity accepted to advance further into the Germans' undefended rear areas.

Further north the 6th Cavalry Brigade also enjoyed a rapid advance against light opposition. Half of the Whippets had been detached to assist the infantry moving up to make the frontal attack on Le Quesnel. Taking advantage of the rolling country and the valley of the Luce, which meandered eastward here, the 3rd Prince of Wales Dragoon Guards, the 1st

Royal Dragoons and the 10th Prince of Wales' Royal Hussars rapidly cleared the south bank by 2:30. Although it would be another hour before the 12th Canadian Infantry Brigade would arrive with the tanks, no Germans had appeared to fill the gap. The deserted countryside basked in the warm afternoon sun, silent except for the droning of flies and the distant popping of guns. Like the 7th, the 6th Cavalry Brigade made no attempt to "sweep into the enemy back areas, spreading consternation and confusion," as "Turkey" Ross and so many others had expected.

Next to approach the Blue Line were some of the Mark V*'s and their passengers. Lieutenant F.M. MacDonald of the Canadian Machine Gun Corps was in a Mark V* just north of Beaucourt Wood. Two of his crew had already been left behind having been almost asphyxiated; and the rest had only been revived by doses of anti-gas tablets.

> We met with fire from anti-tank rifles, and a few bullets from these penetrated our tanks. Slight casualties were also caused from splinters from the inside of the tank. By continued concentrated fire on the revolver loop holes in the tank, the enemy succeeded in breaking the loophole frames and causing casualties.... After a direct hit on our tank it stalled a couple of times, and on one of these occasions, about 2 p.m. ... one thousand yards in the rear of the Blue Line ... the enemy began to rush from the woods near by. Machine gun and rifle bullets were rapping on our tanks from all sides and our only hope was to keep all our guns firing and get the tank started if possible. After a great deal of difficulty in cranking the engine, we succeeded in starting the tank again and with our machine guns we wiped out groups of the retreating enemy. We pushed forward about 1,000 yards farther on until we reached our final objective, where we unloaded our guns and took up positions on some level ground. Our tank was hit and destroyed by a shell before we got all our ammunition and rations out of it. We remained there and held our position against enemy fire until the 72nd Battalion reached us about 6:30 p.m.[169]

Spencer Giffin, the "high-school drop-out," was more fortunate. The Mark V* in which he had been riding eventually stopped on the Blue Line and the half-dead infantry stumbled out into the sunshine and fresh air, "We appeared to be in a salient as we had guns pointing front and right and left. We did not dig in other than to position the Vickers and Lewis guns, and I cannot recall us firing one shot." Giffin and his comrades were soon ordered to board their tank and withdraw 1,500 yards to a less isolated position. Of the 34 Mark V*s that began the attack only eleven reached the Blue Line. Of these, seven were ordered to load their passengers and pull back.

Advancing well behind the cavalry and Mark V*s, the 12th Canadian Infantry Brigade met little opposition. Only from the northern edge of Beaucourt Wood did they meet stiff resistance. There the 78th Winnipeg Grenadiers detached a company under Lieutenant James Tait, a native of Dumfries, Scotland. This veteran led his company with great skill, but was stopped by a hidden machine gun. Taking a rifle, he charged the gun and killed the gunner. Led by Tait, the company then rushed the position and captured eleven more machine guns and over twenty prisoners. Tait was recommended for the Victorian Cross, but it was awarded posthumously as he was mortally wounded three days later.

Overcoming enemy fire emanating from a large tented hospital, the 78th reached its objective alongside the 38th Ottawa Battalion and was leapfrogged by the 72nd Seaforth Highlanders of Canada and the 85th Nova Scotia Highlanders. These two battalions established themselves along the Blue Line, which they shared with the 6th Cavalry Brigade. The 72nd on the right was forced to form a defensive flank to the north of Le Quesnel which was now strongly held by German reserves. The 4th Canadian Division was in possession of the Blue Line — except for their open right flank where Le Quesnel was still filling with German troops.

The 1st Canadian Division's Sector

For the men of the 1st Canadian Division, the advance to the Blue Line was almost a pleasant stroll. On a narrow front only two battalions wide, Brigadier Loomis's 2nd Brigade advanced on Caix preceded by the 2nd Cavalry Brigade made up of the 4th Royal Irish Dragoon Guards (the first British unit to fire upon the Germans back in August, 1914), the 5th Royal Irish Lancers, and the 18th Queen Mary's Own Hussars. These regiments swept the area almost clear of Germans in their dash forward through the village of Caix. Behind them on the right the 7th British Columbia Battalion reached the Blue Line by 2:35.

Even this early hour paled when compared to the 7th's neighbour, the 10th from Calgary. The Albertans were on the Blue Line by 1:15. There had been little excitement. "We just kind of strolled along over the rolling ground, though we were held up once," admitted Stan Carr, a former trail-guide from Banff. "There was a clump of woods just ahead of us, and one of our big heavy guns behind us evidently thought there was something there. They were throwing over these great heavies — 'digging basements' — so we just lay doggo until they stopped firing."

Although only scattered individuals could be seen ahead, almost out of rifle range, both infantry and cavalry settled down to consolidate their position on the Blue Line. There they passed the sunny afternoon chatting, sniping at the occasional German, and comparing souvenirs. Again the cavalry did not push on to exploit the almost deserted enemy back areas.

The 2nd Canadian Division's Sector

For the 2nd Canadian Division's 6th Brigade the assault on the final objective was pretty much an anti-climax. Theirs was to be a very short bound due to the great forward curve of the Red Line in this sector. The advance of the 31st Albertans and the 29th Vancouver Battalion began well behind schedule — 2:30 that afternoon — due to the late arrival of the 9th Cavalry Brigade. An American, Art Spencer, from St. George, Utah, was a member of the 31st. "Now excitement took over. The wings of victory rustled over our shoulders. On we went, long files of tanks swept by on our left. A great mass of cavalry rode slowly across the plains. I have always felt I was privileged to be there that day and see the might of the British Empire going to victory."

The War Diary of the 29th, which was on the extreme left of the Canadian Corps, contained only one short note for August 8, 1918: "No opposition was offered and this Battalion occupied this line at 4:55 taking over from the cavalry who had already garrisoned the line."

The cavalry mentioned were members of the 9th Cavalry Brigade. They too had made an uneventful advance. Three Hussar regiments — the 8th Royal Irish, the 15th King's, and the 19th Queen Alexandra's Own — had arrived on the Blue Line sometime earlier after meeting negligible resistance. They too remained where they were.

AMIENS:
Dawn of Victory
THE AUSTRALIAN CORPS

The Australian advance to the Blue Line was made by the 5th Division (next to the Canadians) and the 4th. The former employed four battalions — two each from the 15th and 8th brigades, while the 4th Division on a narrower frontage advanced with only two battalions leading. The 5th Australian Division followed the British 1st Cavalry Brigade, and both Australian divisions had a quota of Mark V*s full of machine-gun crews, but these fell far behind the remainder of the attackers and took little part in the action on August 8. These formations had already been preceded by the 17th Armoured Car Battalion which had hours ago disappeared along the Roman Road. No more would be heard of them for many hours.

At the same time as the Australian advance began, near the Canadian-Australian boundary a lone Whippet tank was playing out one of the great dramas of the day. "Musical Box," commanded by Lieutenant Arnold, continued its trail of devastation, shooting up defended positions, hundreds of fugitives, and several disciplined formations. First the young Welshman and his two-man crew came to the aid of two cavalry patrols:

> The first patrol was receiving casualties from a party of enemy in a field of corn. I dealt with this, killing three or four, the remainder escaping out of sight into the corn. Proceeding further east, I saw the second patrol pursuing six enemy. The leading horse was so tired that he was not gaining appreciably on the rearmost Hun. Some of the leading fugitives turned about and fired at the cavalry man when his sword was stretched out and practically touching the back of the last Hun. Horse and rider were brought down on the left of the road. The remainder of the cavalry deployed to the right, coming in close under the railway embankment. There they dismounted and came under fire from the enemy, who had now taken up a position on the railway bridge, and were firing over the parapet, inflicting one or two casualties. I ran the machine up until we had a clear view of the bridge, and killed four of the enemy with one long burst, the other two running across the bridge and so down the opposite slope out of sight.[170]

Next Arnold headed for a valley he knew to be full of German hutments. Here he surprised a large number of enemy packing their kits. "Musical Box" rampaged through these huts spewing destruction. Within moments the place was deserted, and when Gunner Ribbans climbed out to investigate he counted sixty German dead. Next the lone Whippet ran left from the railway line and came across long lines of German troops retiring through fields of standing wheat. Arnold attacked at once, cruising up and down for at least an hour. Many more casualties were inflicted here, but eventually the survivors slipped away through the high stands of wheat.

By this time Arnold and his crew were suffering severe discomfort. Against Tank Corps Standing Orders, "Musical Box" had been ordered to carry nine tins of petrol on the roof,

> for refilling purposes when well into the enemy lines (should the opportunity occur). The perforated tins allowed the petrol to run all over the cab. These fumes, combined with the intense bullet splash and the great heat after being in action (by this time) nine to ten hours, made it necessary at this point to breathe through the mouthpiece of the box respirator, without actually wearing the mask.[171]

At 2:00 p.m., heading east once again, parallel to the railway but one hundred yards north of it, "Musical Box" intruded upon a stunning panorama.

> I could see a large aerodrome and also an observation balloon at a height of about 200 ft. I could also see great quantities of motor and horse transport moving in all directions.... I could see a long line of men retiring on both sides of the railway, and fired at these at ranges of 400 yards to 500 yrds, inflicting heavy casualties.... We now crossed a small road which crossed the main railway, and came in view of a large horse and wagon lines ... gunner Ribbans ... fired continuously into motor and horse transport moving on three roads.... I turned quarter left towards a small copse, where there were more horses and men, about 200 yards away. On the way across we met the most intense rifle and machine gun fire imaginable, from all sides. When at all possible we

returned the fire, until the left hand revolver port cover
was shot away. I withdrew the forward gun, locked the
mounting, and held the body of the gun against the hole.
Petrol was still running down the inside of the back
door.... We were still moving forward, and I was shouting
to driver Carney to turn about as it was impossible to
continue the action, when two heavy concussions closely
followed one another and the cab burst into flames.
Carney and Ribbans got to the door and collapsed. I was
almost overcome, but managed to get the door open and
fell out on the ground, and was able to drag out the other
two men. Burning petrol was running onto the ground
where we were lying. The fresh air revived us and we all
got up and made a short rush to get away from the
burning petrol. We were all on fire. In this rush Carney
was shot in the stomach and killed. We rolled over and
over to try to extinguish the flames. I saw numbers of the
enemy approaching from all round. The first arrival came
for me with a rifle and bayonet. I got hold of this and the
point of the bayonet entered my right forearm. The
second man struck at my head with the butt end of his
rifle, hit my shoulder and neck, and knocked me down.
When I came to, there were dozens all around me, and
anyone who could reach me did so, and I was well kicked;
they were furious.[172]

While "Musical Box" burned brightly — the holed petrol tins
feeding the flames — the outraged Germans argued about disposing of
the survivors. Sergeant Carney's scorched body already lay huddled beside
his Whippet. A similar fate appeared inevitable for Arnold and Ribbans,
but the German captain won the argument with his *feldgrau*, and the two
burned and beaten prisoners were marched off into captivity.

The 5th Australian Division's Sector

In the meantime the 1st Cavalry Brigade had been advancing ahead of
the 5th Australian Division. The Queen's Bays south of Harbonnières
provided the advance guard. To the north of the town the 5th Princess
Charlotte of Wales' Dragoon Guards had been ordered to exploit

Framerville, which had already been "shot up" by one of the 17th Armoured Car patrols.

Running parallel to the Red and Blue lines and almost midway between them were several German railway tracks, both regular and narrow gauge. From the Red Line the Australian infantry and the 5th Dragoon Guards could see three trains under steam but at rest. One included a huge, hump-backed car, which had erupted three or four times producing large clouds of tawny-coloured smoke. As the 5th Dragoon Guards raced across the plateau in long lines they realized that this was one of the Germans' giant railway guns on a standard-gauge track. Above, two pilots of 201 Squadron also spotted the trains as they began to move. The Sopwith Camels swooped to attack, each dropping four twenty-five-pound bombs from a scant one hundred feet. As they came out of their dive both glimpsed an enemy two-seater, which they engaged and eventually forced to land. Meanwhile below them the two narrow-gauge trains had begun to chug southeast towards Vauvillers. The train bearing the large gun had been badly damaged by the bombs and appeared disabled.

A few random shots were fired from the carriage windows as the 5th Dragoon Guards galloped up, and then it was all over. They found the engine stalled and the engineer severely burned while several cars at the rear were in flames. The giant gun was undamaged and its crew and a large number of passengers, just returning from leave, "went into the bag." Men of the 8th Field Company, Australian Engineers later uncoupled the burning cars, raised steam, and brought the gun into the new Australian lines. (At the request of Marshal Foch this trophy was eventually displayed in Paris, the city that had suffered over the past months from this gun's much larger sister, "the Paris gun.")

Leaving the prisoners for the approaching Diggers, the 5th Dragoon Guards continued eastward. The right-hand squadron swept around Vauvillers and captured three batteries of field guns retiring along the road, but were then stopped cold by a party of Germans south of the village. Major Mitchell's force was now reduced to twenty men, and seeing this, the swarms of fugitives now began to recover. The squadron found itself in danger of being cut off, so Mitchell disabled the guns as best he could and herded his prisoners back under heavy fire. At a hospital camp north of Vauvillers he made contact with the centre squadron, which had lost one man to a British armoured car firing from Harbonnières. At the same time the third squadron farther north had suffered several casualties from machine guns. So Colonel Terrot, himself wounded, withdrew the 5th Dragoon Guards, who had lost fifty-eight men and 122 horses.

AMIENS:
DAWN OF VICTORY

By this time the Australians, not waiting for their passenger-carrying Mark V*s, had started for the Blue Line. On their right, the Canadian sector was still unoccupied by the 6th Canadian Brigade which, because of the delayed arrival of the cavalry, did not get under way till 2:30. The 57th and 59th Victorian battalions of the 15th Brigade set out on what looked to be an easy approach. However, after passing through Harbonnières, they came up against the old 1916 trench system. On the right flank, the Queen's Bays had already been halted by heavy fire from a resting half-battalion of the 148th Infantry Regiment under Major Picht. Their division's last reserve, the 148th, had been ordered towards Bayonvillers, but shelling, strafing from the air, flank fire from tanks, and swarms of cavalry had combined to force them back into the old trench system. Here they were determined to stay.

Brigadier "Pompey" Elliott, who had just come up, "pointed out" to the CO of the 59th that his battalion was not yet on the Blue Line and ordered it to attack. A Mark V was located in Harbonnières, its weary crew fast asleep, and they volunteered to assist. The advance recommenced but resulted in the annihilation of one platoon. The Mark V developed engine trouble as it reached the enemy, and barely made it back, surrounded part of the way by enraged *feldgrau* trying to find a chink in its armour.

The 57th Victorian Battalion had had no better luck than the 59th and had also stopped short of the Blue Line. Here a defensive flank was formed facing onto the Canadian sector using the machine-gun teams brought up by the tanks. It was several hours before the Canadians came up, but when they did, they swept on to their section of the Blue Line with almost no opposition. Nevertheless, the battalions of the 15th Australian Brigade had been stopped in their attempt to reach the Blue Line, and remained where they were, less than half a mile from their objective.

On the northern side of Harbonnières the 8th Brigade advanced to the Blue Line unscathed. The front battalions, the 30th and 31st, found the old trench system deserted, and by 11:00 reported themselves on their objective. Thus the 5th Australian Division could report partial success, with only its right wing halted short of the final objective.

The 4th Australian Division's Sector

The left of the Australian sector was the responsibility of the 4th Australian Division whose assaulting force, consisting of two understrength battalions totalling one thousand men, was much weaker than that of the other divisions. Its right brigade, the 12th, made up of only three battalions, was only able to use one, the 48th, for its final drive. On the left the 4th Brigade, having employed three of its battalions in the advance through Morcourt and Cerisy, had only the 16th available to take the Blue Line.

Prior to launching their attack the Australians received messages from the 58th London Division, III Corps, and Fourth Army, all stating that the 58th Division had secured its second objective. These reports were treated with justifiable scorn, for if they had been true, the Diggers would not have been under the heavy enfilade fire from now fell all around them from German artillery clearly visible on the other side of the Somme.

The 48th was originally made up of West Australians, but now included a sizeable number from South Australia. Simply reaching the Red Line had cost them several casualties including their CO, Lieutenant-Colonel Perry, slightly wounded. What was worse, they had seen three of the six tanks that had managed to keep up with them destroyed by German artillery fire. Their first glimpse of their attack zone was not likely to hearten them either — "a long field of growing crops sloping on the left front into a deep valley.... Germans could be seen at the Old Amiens line a mile away on the left. Several opposing machine guns opened up. A field gun fired at three Mark V tanks that had covered the second phase.... All three were hit."[173] Fortunately the German battery commander caught sight of a British armoured car to his rear near Proyart. Seeing his limbers thus threatened, he ordered the battery to retire.

Consequently, when Perry's men left their start-line at 10:55, the right company met little opposition. Two Mark V*s from the 15th Tank Battalion accompanied them, and one, "Optimist," was even able to make two trips, thereby bringing up machine-gun crews from one of the damaged tanks. On the left and centre what at first appeared to be a critical set-back was overcome by the courage of a handful of machine gunners. "Orpheus," the remaining Mark V*, ran into concentrated machine gun fire one hundred yards beyond the Amiens line when it almost overran the headquarters of a composite German unit, "Regiment Dultz." Orpheus was hit by several mortar bombs and burst into flames. The crews attempting to escape the inferno were met by deadly fire from close range. Somehow Lieutenant King, who hailed from Tonga, was able to set up a machine gun. King was killed, but corporals Pritchard and Prentice opened up such devastating fire that they swept away the horde of Germans swarming around Orpheus. The advance then resumed as planned but without tank support, and the Blue Line was seized at a cost to the 48th Battalion of only sixty casualties.

On the left flank the 16th Western Australians had been given the unenviable task of seizing Mericourt on the banks of the Somme where it swung northwards. This involved passing around and beneath the higher tongue of land on the north side, which was still held by the enemy. It also meant that once the battalion approached its objective it could be fired upon from three sides — front, left, and rear. This was due to the failure of III Corps' advance north of the Somme, which here curled around behind the 16th. The Australian Official History describes the 16th Battalion's task as "by far the hardest task of the day on the Australian front."[174]

The 16th had already lost several men while moving up to the Red Line. There they waited for their eight Mark V*s which would be commanded by Captain W.D. Lynas, described by the Official History as "one of the finest fighting leaders that Australia produced."[175] At 10:25 four tanks arrived, and Captain Lynas ordered them forward towards the Old Amiens Line.

> The banging of the engines and clangour of metal inside the moving tanks was so great that Lynas could only see, not hear, the bursts. He and his officers sat by the drivers, looking through the slits and directing by touching the drivers on right or left...In a sunken road here they found 70 Germans who surrendered without firing a shot. A number of others in holes and shelters, finding (as Lynas afterwards said) 'that prisoners were not massacred,' came out and gave themselves up. The tanks drove them before them down the valley, quickly delivering them to the outposts of the 13th on top of the Red Line spur...This was done by opening the doors in front of the tank and waving them on, firing a threatening burst from the Hotchkiss machine-guns if any strayed from the road.[176]

Resuming the advance once again, Lynas discovered that the under-powered Mark V*s were too huge to climb the ridge, so he led them along a riverside road towards Mericourt. After a third of a mile they came upon open ground, and there three of the tanks charged the slope in front of the Old Amiens Defence Line, which lay five hundred yards away. The first tank succeeded in disembarking its unhappy passengers before being set afire. A second was destroyed part way up and several of its passengers burned to death.

Lynas's tank was struck as soon as it emerged from the cover of the trees along the road. The shell was a dud and did not penetrate, but the splash killed two and wounded ten inside the shuddering giant. Hot noxious fumes from a damaged exhaust pipe now filled the interior, but onward crawled the "Star." Lynas ordered his teams to disembark at intervals and assumed that all was proceeding well. Then the gas tank was blown off! Miraculously the monster did not catch fire, but rolled on to the shelter of a bank on the rear slope of the ridge. There Lynas discovered his crews were still aboard the tank. Every one had collapsed from the fumes, none having the strength to push open the iron doors. Lynas managed to climb out the top of the tank, and with the assistance of some infantry, rescued his half-asphyxiated comrades.

The three tanks had been knocked out from the "captured" side of the Somme by Lieutenant Burchardi's howitzer in Chipilly. The fourth Mark V* had turned to find an alternate route and was sheltered by trees from Burchardi's gun. However, it was in clear view from Mericourt where Reserve Lieutenant Schroer brought his gun into position. After three shots the last of Lynas's tanks burst into flames.

The 16th Battalion's advance was a difficult one, made as it was, under heavy fire from three sides. The companies had not been ready to start when the four tanks plunged forward, and only reached their objective at 12:30, by advancing in short rushes. They captured two hundred prisoners and twelve machine guns. Fortunately, the old trenches gave good shelter, and the 16th — now down to two-thirds of its strength — spread out to hold the Blue Line.

One eight-man outpost was startled to discover two hundred or so Germans approaching the 1916 trenches nearby. They seemed oblivious to the Diggers and filed into the old trenches. If the enemy discovered the true situation it would be "curtains" for the eight West Australians, so they decided upon a bluff. Opening rapid fire upon the enemy, they ordered them to surrender or die. Fifty of the demoralized Germans came forward with their hands up. There was no one available to escort them. "They were simply booted off to the rear," explained one of their captors.[177]

By this time the German artillery fire from the left and rear had begun to slacken noticeably. For most of the day eight and a half German batteries had been enfilading the Australians. However, they had not been having it all their own way. The 11th Australian Field Artillery Brigade had, as early as 8:45, requested permission to fire on Malard Wood. This had been denied because of the reports that the 58th London Division held the wood. By noon, regardless of orders, the 111th Australian Howitzer Battery had opened up on Malard Wood. Soon sections of three field batteries also joined in, although they received such savage reprisals that two guns had to be temporarily abandoned. Nevertheless, the Australian artillery had dampened the German fire somewhat, and by 12:30 when the 16th West Australians got under way, it had begun to falter. Fifteen minutes later two of the German batteries withdrew, and men of the 58th London Division occupied their positions immediately.

Back on the Red Line two Australian sappers had just repaired a bridge across the river in the rear of Cerisy. A former carpenter from Hobart, Sapper Dean, and his mate, Sapper Campbell, a saddler from Daylesford, Victoria, found a vantage point from which they could see a company of the 3rd City of London halted southwest of Malard Wood. This was half a mile in rear of the 15th Australians' flank, and well short of the day's second objective the Tommies were being held up by a nest of machine guns at the foot of a cliff. The two Sappers ended the deadlock by charging across a wide meadow. The Germans saw them coming, but evidently assuming that they were the first of many, surrendered by raising a white flag. When the Londoners came up the two Aussie Sappers turned over their prisoners and went back to their work. The stalled 58th Division was now able to advance to a point north of Cerisy, in line with the Australians' *first* objective.

On the Blue Line patrols from the 16th Battalion discovered that the Germans were preparing to flee Mericourt. But with the 16th spread so thinly, and enfilade fire from the other side of the Somme — which lay in rear of the Australians — it was decided to shorten the line by holding on south and east of the village of Mericourt. With this exception and that of Harbonnières on the 5th Division's right flank, the Australians were now in possession of the Blue Line.

THE FRENCH FIRST ARMY

The French plan to advance as far as Hangert was proving to be overly optimistic. Although Mézières had finally been taken with the assistance of the Canadian Independent Force, the advance had bogged down beyond that point. By now the artillery barrage had ceased, and the 42nd and the 153rd divisions encountered German resistance from Fresnoy-en-Chaussée and from Plessier, two miles to the south. The leading troops went to ground and stalemate ensued. Farther south, IX Corps also came to a halt by early afternoon. Evidently a pause to regroup would be necessary if the French First Army was to reach the Blue Line by nightfall.

THE BLACK DAY
The Blue Line — A Trés Bon Stunt
Beyond the Blue Line — The 17th Armoured Car Battalion

First to reach the Blue Line was the 17th Armoured Car Battalion attached to the Australian Corps. Racing along the old Roman Road well before noon, the cars passed through the last of the Allied barrage, miraculously suffering no casualties. At the Blue Line the unit split, two sections wheeling south by separate roads towards Framerville, two swinging northwards in the direction of Proyart, and two staying on the Roman Road. Now hidden beyond a long swell of land the 17th virtually vanished for the remainder of the day.

The southern group under Major W.E. Boucher sped to Framerville, one of an almost untouched row of villages extending across the plateau which made up the Blue Line. Two cars led by Lieutenant Herd tore apart a column of transport wagons heading north out of the town. Into the streets scrambled German soldiers to discover the cause of the uproar, only to be killed or scattered in confusion. At the southern edge of Framerville three artillery limbers were stampeded and a lorry then swerved into this chaos after its driver was killed. Framerville was in bedlam.

Two other cars under Lieutenant Rollings tore through the town from west to east breaking every traffic law. This must have appealed perversely to Rollings, a former policeman from Knighton in Wales. Next he added theft to his crimes. Coming upon a headquarters of some sort on the eastern side of the town, Rollings raced upstairs, revolver in hand, to discover the offices abandoned only minutes before. Documents were everywhere. Hastily jamming great wads of them into sandbags, he rushed back into the street at the same moment that four German staff officers rode up. These were immediately shot down and their papers added to the sandbags.

At 11:05 Rollings released a pigeon bearing his report, but it was not till 1:23 p.m. that the bird arrived at headquarters. "Enemy infantry surrendering very freely," reported Rollings. "Have sent scores back and killed scores, others running away. Enemy artillery nil. Have toured round Framerville and upset all their transport etc." By 11:15 he had nailed above the door of a German Headquarters a small Australian flag given him by General Monash.

"The cars then ran down to the east side of Harbonnières, on the southeast road to Vauvillers, and met there a number of steam wagons. Fired into their boilers causing an impassable block," Lieutenant-Colonel Carter later reported. "Had lot of good shooting around Vauvillers. Then came back to main road."[178]

179

The two sections that had kept to the Roman Road shot up the huge roadside dumps at La Flaque, then rolled on to spread panic among the transport and reserves five minutes down the road. The chaos was appalling. The Germans evidently mistook the 17th's red, white, and blue pennons for the red, white, and black of their own flag, and made no move to seek cover. At one stage the armoured cars were able to cruise along behind German transport firing into lorries packed with troops.

Straight as an arrow the old Roman Road stretched to Foucaucourt, four miles beyond the Blue Line. Here the cars ran into their first serious opposition — a tangle of German transport that effectively blocked their route. All at once shells began to burst around the intruders — shells fired from close range! Every car was hit, one going out of control into a tree. Its guns were retrieved under fire, and the patrol commanders, lieutenants A.C. Wood and J.T. Yeoman, ordered a withdrawal.

Certainly one of the great adventures of August 8 was that of the four cars that turned north towards Proyart. Here they found German troops at dinner. These unfortunates were machine-gunned until the survivors dispersed in panic east of the town. Next the section commander spotted in the fields west of the town swarms of fugitives driven from their trenches by the advancing Australians. On the outskirts of Proyart the cars took cover to await their chance. The mob was only fifty yards distant when the cars roared out, cutting down scores. Two adventurous crews now headed north toward the River Somme. Here they once again dispersed the same swarm of Germans, now sadly depleted. Near Chuignolles a lorry full of unfortunate *feldgrau* raced the cars and lost. Onward the armoured cars sped, down the valley towards the river near Froissy. Returning, they met a German staff car, which they shot up. Finding the driver, terrified but unharmed, they ordered him to turn his car about and accompany them back to the Australian lines.

The 17th Armoured Cars' escapade was carried out well beyond the Blue Line and in areas invisible to the infantry. Thus it had little direct bearing on the outcome of the battle. However, the terror they spread and the disorganization they caused probably prevented a much stiffer opposition from solidifying against the Australian infantry. Having been fortunate enough to hit a particularly "soft" area, the 17th's response had been to take the initiative, resulting in far greater impact than their numbers warranted. Their exploits revealed to what extent the enemy line had been torn asunder. "I saw no sign of any wired system anywhere," Carter would later report. "Old overgrown trenches but no organized trench system.... Saw no trace of any organized system of defence of any kind and no troops. My people saw no formed bodies of troops of any kind during the day coming towards us, but very large numbers of fugitives hastening in the opposite direction.... I saw from the hill, open country."[179] But did anyone else know it was open?

CHAPTER TEN
THE ACCOMPLISHED FACT

"When darkness fell on the 8th of August over the battle-field
of the Second Army, the heaviest defeat suffered by the
German Army since the beginning of the war had become an
accomplished fact."
     Schlachten des Weltkrieges 1914–1918:
     Die Katastrophe des 8 August, 1918, p. 196.

AFTERNOON, THURSDAY, AUGUST 8

Most of the day's objectives had been achieved shortly after noon, and there appeared to be no reason why all objectives could not be reached by late afternoon. Of course, there were several places — particularly on the flanks — where the advance had fallen behind schedule, but in the centre only three small sectors had not been taken: Le Quesnel in the Canadian zone and two small German salients in the Australian sector. However, over most of the front an air of tranquillity had already descended as though the front line had been transformed into a rear area.

"Rations came up and were distributed; mail and parcels arrived; billets were taken over; and more or less normal day-to-day duties resumed," noted G.B Key of the 7th Canadian Brigade Signals. "Even the Salvation Army, which had somehow managed to provide hot cocoa and biscuits to the troops during the advance, were operating a canteen. It was even possible for impromptu football games to be organized."

In his illicit journal Bert Hart, one of Winnipeg's "Little Black Devils," recorded, "We dug-in on the outskirts of Caix, not a regular trench, just isolated holes a few yards apart. Just room enough to accommodate two men for the night, a little precaution taken in case of a counter-attack or shell fire. Corporal Nichols and I shared a hole we dug in no time, and then lit a smoke and looked over the souvenirs we had collected on the way."

Further back, streams of field-gray prisoners eventually pooled to form lakes in the Corps cages. Some were merry and cheerful, some slouched dejectedly, and a few were bitter. One officer summed up the feelings of many. "You Canadians have no business down here. We were told you were in Flanders; how I would like to hang our fools of Intelligence officers!"[180]

On the Australian front the men worked in almost unbroken silence. Wire and stakes taken from German dumps provided the material to consolidate the Red and Blue lines while captured weapons served to strengthen the defences. When they had finished, the Diggers napped, or talked of the day's adventures under a warm, drowsy sun. Meanwhile Australian Engineers were busy shunting the huge German railway gun across no man's land into Australian territory.

At 4:30 an unarmed staff car from Fourth Army drove along the Roman Road, beyond the front line into no man's land. It was not impeded in any way until it reached the village of La Flaque a mile east of the dug-in Australians. Silence reigned, and only solitary *feldgrau* could be spotted heading eastward. Indeed, there seemed to be no opposition in front of the Australian centre at all. But as sunset approached, the plateau ahead began to show signs of movement. Everywhere small groups of Germans began to appear, and it became evident that the enemy was plugging the gap.

North of the Somme, III Corps continued its attempts to capture Chipilly. Since 12:30 a steadily increasing bombardment had fallen on that village. Germans could be seen fleeing to the rear. Once again, however, an air reconnaissance report was received at 58th Division Headquarters stating that British troops were already on Chipilly Spur. Consequently, the bombardment was called off, and the 2nd City of London Battalion was ordered to advance at 3:00. The Londoners were received by heavy fire in front and by a crossfire from the village and from Gressaire Wood to the north. Their advance stalled and they were driven back to Malard Wood.

On the extreme northern end of the offensive, despite the many difficulties encountered, a subsidiary attack by III Corps' 12th Division had been totally successful. Brigadier Vincent, whose 35th Brigade carried out the assault, had been almost blinded by gas, yet like his men, he refused to quit. By 12:25 they had completed a thousand-yard advance southeast of Morlancourt against stiff opposition. With only forty-three field guns and one tank — "Ju Ju," a stray from the 18th Division — the 1st Cambridgeshire Regiment, the 7th Norfolks, and the 9th Essex had captured well over six hundred Germans. This minor, subsidiary action would turn out to be III Corps' major success of the day.

On the right flank the French First Army still lagged behind the Canadians. Mézières had just been taken, but movement had ground to a halt in front of Fresnoy-en-Chaussée. Situated on the extreme north of the French sector, this hold-up caused a chain reaction southward. General Debeney had already inserted the 153rd Division between the 42nd and the 37th. This fresh formation with its two battalions of light Renault tanks would, it was felt, give a renewed impetus to the fading attack. However, the infantry had already taken cover, and everyone was waiting for the artillery to come up. At 3:30 Debeney issued orders for XXXI Corps to resume the advance with Arvillers as the objective for the evening. At the same time he ordered his reserves forward. By 4:30 a bombardment opened up on the German positions in front of Fresnoy-en-Chaussée and further southwest in front of Plessier. The 42nd, 153rd, and 37th divisions were ordered to attack in an hour, at 5:30.

All day the ground support squadrons of the RAF had been welcomed enthusiastically by the troops. "Our planes seemed like things possessed," recorded the War Diary of the 5th (Western Cavalry) Battalion, CEF. "A plane would streak down from behind to within a few yards of our heads, and with a roar, shoot up almost perpendicularly, the cheers of our men following it. Kilometres ahead they could be seen diving at the retreating enemy, and the merry rattle of their machine guns was heard continuously. The air was thick with them, and never an enemy plane to be seen."

By noon numerous reports had stressed the fact that all roads leading eastward were crowded with retreating German troops and transport. An enormous, unforeseen opportunity seemed to be presenting itself. The Somme meanders eastward from Amiens to the town of Peronne, almost twenty-five miles away. There it suddenly turns at right angles, and runs south, *directly behind the German front line*. This meant that a continued retreat would force the Germans to cross the Somme by a series of bridges only eight miles behind the Blue Line. If these bridges could be destroyed in time it would not only prevent reinforcements from arriving, but would isolate the German Second Army in front of Amiens.

Major-General J.M. Salmond, General Officer Commanding the RAF in the field, "presumably on the instructions of General Headquarters, canceled, by telephone, all the existing arrangements for bombing in the afternoon of the 8th of August, and ordered, instead, attacks upon the Somme bridges, which were to be bombed 'as long as weather and light permits': the fighter squadrons were to take part by dropping bombs of 25-lb. weight."[181] The last laconic statement masked the enormity of the gamble involved: fighters carrying bombs would not be able to perform their normal escort role for the vulnerable bombers.

This decision resulted in a total of 205 daylight bombing attacks on the bridges at Peronne, Brie, Bethencourt, Voyennes, Pithon, and Offay. Many of the pilots made three flights before darkness forced them to cease operations. Despite these impressive figures only twelve tons of bombs were actually dropped — "payloads" were still light in 1918.

These bombing missions ran into unexpectedly fierce German resistance. A surprising number of enemy fighters appeared, as the Germans' normally cautious tactics were discarded. At Bethencourt, for instance, German fighters attacked with reckless courage at a height of one thousand feet — just as the RAF planes were diving at their targets. Consequently, few bombs were aimed with precision, and several planes were prevented from launching their attacks at all. Only a single 112-pounder hit the bridge at Bethencourt.

This abrupt change in German tactics was also the result of a midday decision. At noon Army Command had ordered its fighters to leave the upper levels and come down to support their artillery spotters and contact patrol aircraft at lower levels. The latter had suffered severely in the morning, and further losses would destroy any chance of artillery support or reconnaissance for the ground forces. As it happened, this order brought the fighters to the right level to intercept British bombers. Reinforcements had also been promised, including the famous "Flying Circus." Indeed, two flights of the "Circus" did arrive after mid-day in time to join the fray.

During the afternoon the French Air Service, still hampered by mist, sent out only several light patrols. Later, more fighters were able to get up and join in the fighting while 49 bombers hit the railway terminals at Hombleux, Ham, Fransart, and Roye.

Afternoon was the opportunity for the Commander-in-Chief to visit his subordinates. First, Sir Douglas visited Rawlinson's Fourth Army Headquarters at Flixecourt. There he learned of III Corps' difficulties, but was assured that Lieutenant-General Butler had ample reserves to handle the problem. Rawlinson was instructed to continue operations in accordance with existing orders. First, the left flank had to be extended as far north as Albert and pushed forward to Bray, a full five miles beyond III Corps' final objective; Secondly, the main thrust would continue in the Canadian sector to a line from Roye to Chaulnes — five miles forward of the current Canadian-Australian junction, and ten miles forward of the Canadian-French junction, which was still short of the Blue Line at Le Quesnel; Thirdly, a special effort was to be made in the latter area to assist the French; Fourthly, the cavalry was to be immediately pushed forward — even as far as the proposed Roye-Chaulnes line. Formal orders detailing those ambitious plans were issued by late afternoon.

Haig then motored south to visit the French First Army Headquarters. There he found a very distressed General Debeney, "almost in tears because three battalions of his Colonial infantry had bolted before a German machine gun."[182] Although Sir Douglas overstated his point, the fact was that Debeney's vehement orders to attack "with but one preoccupation, to achieve the greatest rapidity in a succession of forward bounds," was being ignored by his troops. Sir Douglas remained calm although he had earlier in the day received another jolt from Debeney. At 11:30 that morning, Haig had sent an officer to the French Army Commander outlining the situation and instructing him to send forward all the French cavalry to operate in rear of the Germans holding Montdidier. General Debeney's reply shattered some of the ex-cavalryman's illusions; French cavalry could not be in position for another twenty-four hours!

In the meantime "Rawly the Fox" had been taking steps to keep the advance rolling. Three reserve divisions were ordered forward: the 63rd Royal Naval Division to reinforce III Corps, the 17th (Northern) behind the Australians, and the 32nd Imperial to join the Canadian Corps. Then accompanied by a single ADC, he motored to Advanced Canadian Headquarters at Gentelles. Arriving at 4:00 p.m., he found that Currie was forward visiting his divisional headquarters. Rawlinson was effusively grateful. "He would, I think, have given Currie anything he asked for, so pleased was he," noted one of his officers.[183] Rawlinson discussed the next day's plans with Currie's senior staff officer, Brigadier-General Webber. They agreed that the advance would be resumed by the 1st and the 2nd Canadian divisions and by the British 32nd, which would pass through the 4th Canadian Division as soon as the latter had taken Le Quesnel. The 32nd Division was placed under command of the Canadian Corps. Upon Currie's return he began drawing up the necessary orders as evening stole across the battlefield. Zero hour was set for 5:00 next morning.

Evening, Thursday, August 8

Dusk saw the final attempts to complete the day's tasks. In front of Plessier the French First Army's 153rd Division recommenced operations at 5:30 as ordered. Advancing with a company of nineteen Renault tanks, the troops ran into stiff resistance. Thirteen of the tanks were knocked out, and it was not until 7:00 that the village was taken. On the immediate right of the Canadians the 42nd Division resumed its offensive in front of Fresnoy-en-Chaussée at 7:30 but with little result. Finally, assisted by the 153rd, several light tank companies, and heavy artillery support, an enveloping movement was tried at 9:15. Fifteen minutes later Fresnoy-en-Chaussée was at last taken with negligible casualties — seven hours after it had first been seized by two troops of Lord Strathcona's Horse.

On the Canadian front only rare clashes in the outpost lines disturbed the evening quiet, although a German air attack provided some excitement. Lieutenant-Colonel "Turkey" Ross of the 28th wrote:

> At dusk our unit was treated to the first real sign of enemy activity when a formation of enemy aircraft coming in out of the east flying line-abreast, fiercely fired at our infantry. At the same time some of the British planes appeared and a dog-fight followed with one of the enemy's planes being dropped to the earth in flames. One unfortunate Hun pilot fell out of his plane about five-hundred feet up, crashing to his death within our Battalion lines. The remainder of the enemy craft speedily disappeared to be seen no more, and conditions settled back to normal.

As darkness descended, Will Bird of the 42nd thought of his two chums who that morning had told him of their premonitions. Sergeant

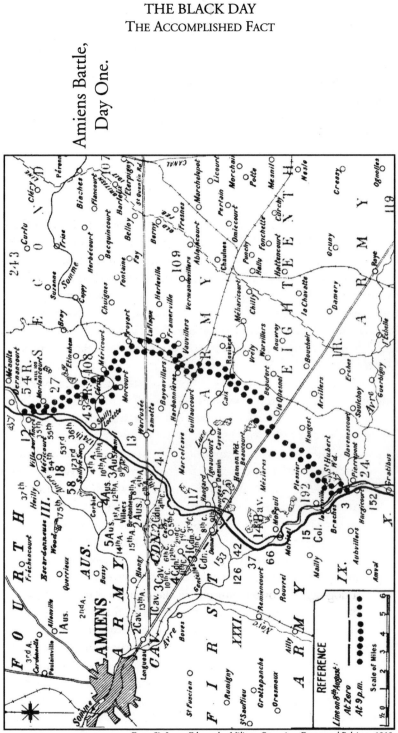

From Sir James Edmonds, *Military Operations France and Belgium, 1918.*
London, HM Stationary Office, 1947, sketch #2

Eddie Cuvilier had been the first 42nd Highlander killed, while Bob Christensen had "got a blighty" and was carried out on one of his stretchers. Now the Sergeant-Major came over to Bird. "Too bad about Christensen," he remarked.

"What about him?" asked Bird.

"He had a nice blighty and was well on his way out when he was killed by a shell. Tough luck."[184]

Evening was a time to be philosophical. "It was a beautiful summer evening, and the little river Luce was beautiful. It was like a little river in England and the flowers growing at the water's edge where my horses were drinking, were English flowers," noted Lieutenant P.J. Campbell, the one-time mathematics student. "The water was so clean, the field in front of me looked utterly peaceful, but only fifty yards away there was that trench, full of dead Germans,... the grey faces, the poor twisted bodies. They had been bayoneted by the Canadians in the morning — you can't take prisoners in a front-line trench in an attack. Wives, mothers, sweethearts, would not know yet; they would still be writing letters, but the letters would never be read." Then recalling his own experiences on March 21st, he added, "It might have been us."[185]

In the Australian sector Lieutenant Williams of the 56th New South Wales had forgotten his earlier premonition. He was safe and sound, full of bully-beef and biscuits, and fast asleep in German blankets.

> Sleep was soon interrupted by the unmistakable drone of German bombing-planes. Nearer they came — and then the swish of the descending aerial bombs, followed by the crash of their explosion.... Bomb after bomb was dropped between our position and Harbonnières, and pandemonium reigned in the packed horse-lines just to the rear of the village. We could hear horses kicking and plunging at their tethers, some neighing, and one poor brute screaming.... The near explosion of an aerial bomb of any size seemed to tie one's intestines into knots.[186]

On the northern flank III Corps launched its final effort at 7:30. A barrage opened up to cover the renewed attack on Chipilly Spur. The main infantry component, the 175th Brigade, was farther back than had been supposed, however, and nothing was accomplished. Another battalion, ordered to co-operate with the 175th, did advance from in front of Sailly Lorette. Here the 10th London (Hackney) attacked with the same courage that had enabled them to seize their own objective fifteen hours earlier. This time however, their barrage fell 1,500 yards in front of them, and they were met by furious machine-gun fire from front and flank. Nevertheless, the Cockneys carried on to the bend in the road northwest of the village. There they hung on till midnight when the exhausted battalion was ordered to withdraw after spending a very long day under fire and in isolation. Chipilly Spur remained in German hands.

Midnight, August 8/9

While the weary Hackneys were withdrawing from their isolated position, just behind the line elements of the United States 33rd Division were being roused from their slumbers. The 131st Infantry Regiment had been placed under orders of the 58th London Division at 4:30 that afternoon. Made up of National Guardsmen from Illinois, this division had been attached to III Corps only three weeks earlier. As part of Corps Reserve, the 131st — minus its machine-gun company, supports, and its transport — had arrived in position at 8:42. Now telephone orders had been received from the 58th London Division to move up to a jumping-off line astride the Bray-Corbie Road. The "Doughboys" were to attack at dawn!

A hurried conference was convened with General Butler commanding the 58th Division. "Due to the fact that the troops had been marching the greater portion of the day and night, were without supports, ground had never been reconnoitred, no provisions made for supplies, etc., it was decided ... it was inadvisable to make the attack," records the 131st's Report of Operations. Nevertheless, the regiment was ordered forward into a valley east of Sailly le Sec, and the 131st trudged off into the inky blackness on another wearying march.

The land battle had died out, but in the darkened sky miles behind the new German line the air war raged on. The noon decision to bomb the Somme bridges now involved the night-bombing squadrons. Forty-five FE2b's and five Camels of the RAF dropped a total of six tons of bombs in attempts to knock out the bridges. The French Air Service also took a major role in the battle. Their targets were railway stations at Ham, Hombleux, Roye, Fresnoy-les-Roye, and Fransart. In the front lines the night was made eerie by the sounds of flights of large airplanes passing overhead and fading into the distance and with German Taubes going in the opposite direction.

The first monkey-wrenches were thrown into the plans for the next day at 6:30, when Brigadier-General Webber (the Canadian Corps staff officer who had conferred with Rawlinson in Currie's absence) received a wire. It came from Major-General Montgomery, Rawlinson's senior staff officer, and it sizzled. First it canceled Rawlinson's order committing the 32nd Division to Currie's command, and second, it had instructed Webber to travel eight miles to Dury to receive further instructions by telephone. The road back to Dury was packed with on-coming transport and the battalions of the 32nd Division; consequently, Webber did not reach the telephone till 8:30. Here he was informed by Montgomery that the latter was "very irate with the Army Commander for daring to give away the 32nd Division and with myself for aiding and abetting."[187] Montgomery's demonstration of pique had wasted hours of critical planning time, for Webber now had to struggle back to Currie's advance Headquarters at Gentelles to carry out the countermanded orders. The 32nd Division would have to be turned about to push its way back through the Canadian transport moving up, while the tired 3rd Canadian Division, relieved at noon, would have to be brought forward. Currie and his staff now worked through the night to jury-rig a new attack and send out make-shift orders. Meanwhile, all unknowing, the 32nd Division continued to march toward the front while the men of the 3rd Division slept the sleep of victors.

Currie was not the only Allied commander keeping a late night. Another was General Toulorge of XXXI Corps. After a relatively easy advance of eight miles his 42nd Division had at last taken Fresnoy-en-Chaussée and over 2,000 prisoners, 70 artillery pieces, 26 "minenwerfers," and 200 machine guns. The 42nd Division's own casualties totaled only 141 killed and 400 wounded. But now, at 11:30, Toulorge was just receiving the following report from the 42nd's divisional commander, General Deville:

> The effort made during the three preceding nights by untrained troops and throughout today during an uninterrupted advance of a dozen kilometers over difficult ground is considerable. It would not be wise, in case of an enemy counterattack, to count upon an unlimited fighting capacity.[188]

Undoubtedly the relief of this division would delay tomorrow's attack. Nevertheless, Toulorge had little choice; he ordered the 126th Division to relieve the 42nd before dawn. Meanwhile his superior, General Debeney, had already sent out his orders for Friday morning. This time there was no talk of seizing opportunities and exploiting success. The orders were simply to cover the Canadians' right, with Hangert, Arvillers, and Erches to be the successive objectives. South of Montdidier, XXXV Corps, originally ordered to attack, was now to wait for orders. Again the French cavalry were to take no part, being ordered to remain where they were, over twenty miles from the junction with their allies at Le Quesnel.

August 8 had been a banner day for the Allies, producing their largest advance of the war. On a front of over fifteen miles the German line had been torn asunder, and had been penetrated eight miles in the Canadian and Australian sectors, an average of five miles in the French, and two miles in the British. The Allied prisoner of war cages were swamped with 15,000 men, while over 400 artillery pieces had been taken. The staggering number of captured mortars and machine guns remained uncounted. Clearly the German Army had suffered its greatest defeat ever. To achieve this astonishing success the Allies had paid a comparatively small price — approximately 8,000 casualties:

Canadian Corps	3,868(actual)
Australian Corps	2,000(estimate)
III Corps,	700(estimate)
Cavalry Corps	600(estimate)
Tank Corps	400(estimate)
TOTAL	**8,568**[189]

French First Army casualties are not recorded for the day, but as already noted, the most heavily engaged French division, the 42nd, suffered less than 550. Thus it seems likely that there were fewer than two thousand French casualties on August 8.

Although the first day of the Amiens offensive had been a great success, there were disappointments. The fog, a mixed blessing to the infantry, had been decidedly bad for the RAF's battle plan. Its prime target had been the German aerodromes. A knockout strike delivered at dawn on every major German air field would have almost destroyed the enemy's air power in this sector. As it was, only three aerodromes were bombed, and with little effect.

The fog did not hamper the German Air Service. That morning as Lothar von Richthofen and his wingman, Lieutenant Erich Loewenhardt, fought their way back to Puisieux Farm — the base about to be abandoned by their Flying Circus — they proved to be a formidable pair. Lothar shot down his 33rd, 34th, and 35th Allied planes, while Loewenhardt, Germany's top surviving Ace, destroyed his 49th, 50th, and 51st adversaries. That afternoon, they led two flights as the Flying Circus entered the fray to the detriment of the Allies' new plan of attack.

The bridge-bombing operations since noon had cost the RAF dearly. That and the day's normal operations claimed 4 fliers killed, 19 wounded, and 57 missing — plus 13 percent of the committed planes. The attacks on the Somme bridges claimed 70 of these planes — 23 percent of the attacking force. Realizing the importance of the bridges, the Germans fought desperately to shield them. Without fighter cover the bombers were savaged by swarms of German fighters, including numerous *jagdstaffeln* (squadrons) which had not been expected to arrive till the next day. Certainly the decision to arm the RAF fighters with bombs had not produced the result expected for not one bridge had been put out of service. Consequently orders for Friday absolved the fighters from serving as bombers, and allowed them to revert to their escort role.

Artillery support too had become a problem. The opening barrage had been one of the best executed operations of the war, and the counter-battery fire had in many areas completely stopped German fire. However, the follow-up was not an equal success. Batteries moving up behind the infantry found it difficult to keep pace with the rapid advance, and in many cases these batteries, when they did arrive, were employed overly cautiously or not at all. "Andy" McNaughton, the Canadian specialist, was disappointed in the use made of his heavy artillery, which had moved up under the control of the infantry divisions. McNaughton found them sitting ready but silent, without fire orders. Divisional commanders had been too wrapped up in their infantry advance to envision the terrible effect these heavies could have produced in the rear areas on the roads packed with retreating enemy and later with their reserves pressing forward. "I vowed then that never again would I not have guns under [my] command at all phases of an attack."[190]

Communications had proven to be the artillery's biggest problem due to its reliance upon field telephones. Even when the cable-layers were able to do their job effectively, the cavalry galloped over the lines, then the tanks churned across them, making spaghetti of these vital communication links. Consequently batteries in position and ready to fire were not advised of targets that had halted an entire stage of the advance.

The Mark V tanks played their role marvelously. In many sectors the infantry suffered almost no casualties due to the presence of tanks. However, as had been feared, the Allied tank force became sadly depleted in this first day of battle. Only 145 tanks remained fit for action, and their crews were completely exhausted from the tension, the long approach, the day-long fighting, and the fumes. The 5th Tank Brigade south of the Somme lost 40 Mark Vs alone, mostly from the guns on Chipilly Spur.

The Mark V*s proved to be tragic failures. Their imaginative role as "passenger tanks" was unproductive. The "Star's" extra length made it a larger target for the well-hidden German guns, and the loss of life was multiplied by the presence of passengers. In areas where the Mark V*s reached their objectives, circumstances beyond their control forced their withdrawal or employment as mere flank guards. The passengers, unfortunately, nearly all became ill or chose to walk behind, a fault of the vehicle rather than the concept. Nevertheless, this visionary plan was not to be employed again during the war.

Another failure was the "supply tank." Owing to the weak cables employed, most of their sledges broke free during the long advance, with the result that grenades, small arms ammunition, and drinking water were in short supply among many forward units.

The armoured cars proved successful up to a point. Certainly, along the Roman Road where resistance had collapsed, the 17th's performance was spectacular. Yet when nightfall halted their operations over 50 percent of the cars were out of action. Incredibly, there were no casualties among personnel, but the unit still had to be withdrawn to make repairs. The Canadian Independent Force was not, strictly speaking, an armoured car unit, being a very polyglot force, yet its role was essentially the same. However, in their operational zone along the Amiens-Roye Road enemy resistance was much more determined, especially at Mézières, Fresnoy-en-Chaussée, and Le Quesnel. Here the Independent Force performed several incredible feats, and was ready to go into action again the next day, yet the limitations of a force restricted to road travel had been made glaringly obvious.

The Whippet tanks were seriously handicapped by being attached to the cavalry. In the early going the cavalry complained of being held up by the slower tanks, but once machine-gun fire was encountered, it was the cavalry that was in the way. Neither tank officers nor cavalry officers had wanted this "team approach," but it had been ordered by higher authority. The tank officers had anticipated a powerful, concentrated thrust that would swing south and ravage the German rear areas ahead of the French First Army. Tied to the vulnerable cavalry, however, the Whippets were spread out over a wide front, which reduced their impact and eliminated the possibility of a concerted swing southward.

Casualties among the Whippets were light compared to the other tank forces. The 3rd Battalion, which had been engaged on the right around Le Quesnel, had two breakdowns and five knocked out, two of whose crews were wounded without the tank being disabled. This left thirty-nine of the Canadians' Whippets fit for action. The 6th Battalion on the left at the junction with the Australian Corps had lost eight for various reasons, including "Musical Box," now reported missing. For tomorrow's operations thirty-four Whippets would be fit for duty with the Australians.

The glaring failure of the day was the performance of the cavalry. Although problems had plagued the flanks of the Fourth Army, the centre of the advance had provided the long-awaited breakthrough. The Cavalry Corps, preserved so long for just this moment, failed to exploit this success. Communications, stretched over exceptional distances, had broken down, it is true. Cable layers had been unable to keep up to the two cavalry divisions, but such a development should have been anticipated. Orders to press on beyond the Blue Line issued shortly after noon by Fourth Army did not reach the 1st Cavalry Division till 4:30. But surely such orders were not required! Contrary to the training and traditions of cavalry, mounted units that had reached the Blue Line almost unopposed, dug in and consolidated to await the infantry while ahead of them lay vistas of open country. Only late in the afternoon did they send out small patrols, which encountered the steadily increasing German resistance. It was too little too late. Had nearly four years of waiting in the wings robbed the cavalry of its initiative? Had lack of battlefield experience deprived their officers of the will to lead? Had four years of caring for their horses made the troopers too attached and careful of their mounts' safety? There are many theories to explain the hesitancy, but the reason may simply have been a belated realization that they were in way beyond their depth — anachronisms from a previous century.

THE ACCOMPLISHED FACT

Despite the overwhelming success of August 8, one critical factor must have staggered the more astute Allied generals. This was the lack of enthusiasm and enterprise on the part of their troops. True, the tankers, the Canadians, and the Australians displayed their traditional élan and initiative; but III Corps' performance, after all the extenuating circumstances are considered, showed a distinct lack of "push." "That very night I was to hear the old Australian sneer again," wrote C.E. Montague. "The Canadians were all right, of course, but the Tommies! Well, we might have known!"[191] For a patriot like Montague this was a heart-wrenching moment. The British Official Historian noted, "there was not only a shortage of experienced officers and non-commissioned officers, but the ranks of the infantry units had been filled up with young recruits from home. These convalescent divisions had not entered with great enthusiasm on the hard task of preparing a field of battle ... the willing co-operation usually exhibited before an attack was absent."[192]

The French First Army showed even less enthusiasm. Despite Debeney's vehement instructions to press the attack and strive for deep penetration, the French advance was very cautious. Although XXXI Corps started three-quarters of an hour after the Canadians (its own flank totally cleared as a result) it was five hours before the *poilus* again drew abreast of the Canucks. The village of Mézières held up a French division until a handful of men from the Canadian Independent Force cleared it. Later that afternoon a patrol of Lord Strathcona's Horse seized Fresnoy-en-Chaussée in the French sector, but the snail-like advance of their allies prevented them from holding on when threatened with encirclement. French élan had been squandered on too many senseless operations in the past; now at the moment when overwhelming victory was within their grasp, the *poilus's* will to win became a will to survive.

THE GERMANS

General Erich Ludendorff wrote in his memoirs, "August 8 was the black day of the German Army in the history of the war." Losses were enormous — according to "the Automatic Boiler," the Second Army's General von der Marwitz, "about 700 officers and 27,000 men, over 400 guns and a great mass of machine guns and trench mortars."[193]

After the war a German investigating committee in a report titled, "The Catastrophe of 8 August, 1918" made the following points:

The position divisions between the Avre and the Somme which had been struck by the enemy attack were nearly completely annihilated. The troops in the front line north of the Somme had also suffered seriously, as also the reserve divisions thrown into the battle in the course of the day.... Except for a local fight at Mézières, the fate of the 225th Division [which had faced the 3rd Canadian Division along the Amiens-Roye Road] was settled about 10 a.m. The entire position artillery was lost; of the front line and support battalions practically nothing had come back; and the resting battalions, thrown in piecemeal, had either been thrown back or had not gone into action at all. Only two fragments were still in being, the already shaken Krause group [two companies of engineers] southeast of Cayeux and three companies of Reserve Regiment No. 18 just north of Beaucourt. Between these yawned a gap, completely unoccupied.[194]

The fresh and highly touted 117th Division which had faced the 1st Canadian Division, was described as "shrunk to nothing, barely any infantry left."[195] The 41st Division astride the junction of the 2nd Canadian Division and the 2nd Australian Division lost all its front-line and support infantry and its artillery except for "trifling remnants" (three guns). "Of the reserves only seven infantry companies and three machine gun companies remained."[196] The woefully weak 13th Division in its "paper defences" was gobbled up piecemeal by the 3rd Australian Division and lost all of its artillery. On both flanks, opposite French and British troops, losses were also heavy although not nearly as crippling as the unfortunate divisions in the centre.

For the German High Command even this enormous casualty total was not the worst consequence of August 8. What most depressed Ludendorff was the state of German morale and discipline. "The report of the staff officer I had sent to the battlefield [Mertz von Quirnheim] as to the condition of those divisions which had met the first shock of the attack on the 8th, perturbed me deeply," wrote Ludendorff after the war.

I was told of deeds of glorious valour but also of behaviour which, I openly confess, I should not have thought possible in the German army; whole bodies of men had surrendered to single troopers, or isolated squadrons.

> Retiring troops, meeting a fresh division going bravely into
> action, had shouted out things like "Blackleg", and "You're
> prolonging the war".... The officers in many places had lost
> their influence and allowed themselves to be swept along
> with the rest.[197]

"Everything was affected by the fearful impression that the fire-vomiting iron dragons had made on artillery and infantry," wrote the historian of the 119th Infantry Regiment (26th Reserve Division) which had come up that afternoon. "A true tank-panic had seized on everything, and where any dark shapes moved, men saw the black monster. 'Everything is lost' was the cry that met the incoming battalions."[198]

Fortunately for von der Marwitz and his Second Army, six reserve divisions lay within striking distance of the gaping hole. Three were able to make it through the congestion and confusion to take part in the battle that day. Misled by the slowness of the French advance, General von Hofacker of LI Corps moved two reserve divisions, the 119th and the 1st Reserve, into the area around Le Quesnel, Fresnoy-en-Chassée, and Beaucourt. It was their advance battalions plus several resting battalions that met in order the Canadian Independent Force, then the Canadian Cavalry Brigade, and finally the 4th Canadian Division.

The 109th Division, which had only the night before been relieved by the well-rested 117th, reassembled near Harbonnières in front of the Australian right. Instead of the craved-for rest, this exhausted formation was again stretched thinly over three miles of front. Fortunately for the 109th, their line was not challenged by the 5th Australian Division, which had stopped on the Blue Line in front of them.

It was early evening before the 107th Division arrived near Proyart, thus closing the wide gap which had lain open before the 4th Australian Division for most of the afternoon. This was the area through which the 17th Armoured Car Battalion had rampaged without opposition for much of the day. On the north bank of the Somme in front of III Corps, von der Marwitz's fifth available reserve division was being deployed. The 243rd was first ordered to Cappy and Bray, but would soon move south towards Proyart. The sixth available division, the 26th Reserve, was broken into battalions and batteries to be spread among the other reinforcements.

The result of these frantic efforts on the part of von der Marwitz and his Corps Commanders was the establishment of a defensive line across the entire front. It was a thin line, to be sure, and in many places it consisted of mere remnants of yesterday's front line divisions, but it was a line where hours before there had been none, and help was on the way. OHL was frantically searching for more units to stop the Allies' most successful offensive.

At home the facts had not yet become known. German newspapers labeled the Allied offensive "a failure" due to "the heroic resistance of the trench garrisons which at many points held on in a hurricane of fire until surrounded on all sides."[199] Meanwhile, the Kaiser and his entourage received an inkling of the true situation and were sunk in gloom. "Disastrous day on the Somme," wrote Admiral von Müller. "The French, British, and Canadians have broken through our front to a depth of 12 kilometres. The Kaiser was very low in spirits this evening. He said: 'It's very strange that our men cannot get used to tanks.'"[200]

While the Kaiser was soul-searching, Lieutenant-Colonel Carter of the 17th Armoured Car Battalion was reporting at Australian Headquarters in Bertangles. "They were scarcely recognizable, covered as they were from head to foot with grime and grease," noted Monash.[201] Since assisting the Australians at Morcourt Valley around 9:30 that morning nothing more had been seen of the 17th by their friends. Carter and one staff officer had just arrived — in style, having employed a large party of German prisoners to tow back his disabled car. Carter's report was given verbally with excitement and pride. It should have aroused great interest with its description of the undefended countryside. "But of any notion of occupying the ground ahead of the Australian infantry while it was almost vacant the records contain no trace," states the Australian Official History. "Monash was apparently preoccupied with two determinations — to consolidate the position taken, and to safeguard his left flank against possible counterattack from across the Somme."[202] Years of experience had shown that savage counterattacks had to be expected, and that failure to consolidate would lead inevitably to disaster. Thus the needless labour continued throughout the night.

Nevertheless, the orders had been explicit — exploit every success by pushing farther. At 12:45 that afternoon "Rawly the Fox" had repeated Haig's order to press on and take advantage of the enemy's confusion. Yet it is evident that few, if any, from Foch down to the lowliest private, understood the extent of the German catastrophe. There would be — there could be — no German counterattack on August 8, the "black day of the German Army."

PART IV
THE WAR MUST BE BROUGHT TO AN END

"We are at the limit of our powers. The war must be brought to an end."
Kaiser Wilhelm II, 11 August, 1918[203]

CHAPTER ELEVEN
ORDER, COUNTER-ORDER, DISORDER

*"The day furnishes another example of the old saying,
'Order, counter-order, disorder.'"*
The British Official History, 1918[204]

Lieutenant Jim Pedley of the "Mad Fourth" perused several German newspapers while his morning tea, reeking of rum, fumed away in a captured green mug. The dawn sky was clear, and the warm sun promised a glorious Friday, August 9. From the adjoining kitchen came the aroma of braised meat. Outside someone voiced the belief that Fritz was "bitched, buggered and bewildered."[205] Pedley and his mates were not alone in their certainty. All along the front cocky Australians and Canadians shared the conviction and were anxious to "get going while the going was good," in the words of General Currie. Yet from the first moment, Friday's operations seemed to go wrong.

As a preliminary, the 4th Canadian Division had to seize the right corner of the Blue Line not captured yesterday. Although two battalions jumped off at zero hour, 4:30, to take Le Quesnel, the attack almost broke down before it started. A desperate dispatch rider bearing the artillery fire-orders arrived late after hours of wandering about. "At about 4:35 a.m. [five minutes late] a shoot was placed on Le Quesnel by a few guns," reported the 75th Mississauga Battalion. "The shoot was too light to take any great effect, many of the shells falling short into our advancing troops."

Supported by Brutinel's Canadian Independent Force on the Amiens-Roye Road, the Mississaugas pressed on under murderous machine-gun fire into Le Quesnel, which they found almost undamaged. By 5:30 the village was in Canadian hands, and the 75th occupied a German divisional headquarters packed with documents and maps. The village now came under very heavy shelling from German batteries, and serious casualties occurred as the town was pounded into rubble. The Mississaugas made the best of it, enjoying a large cache of cigars and cigarettes left by the enemy. Other booty included two searchlights, three completely equipped hospitals, and a field kitchen.

The second attacking battalion, the 87th Canadian Grenadier Guards, also began badly, the troops having been delayed crossing Beaucourt Wood in the dark. Nevertheless, they occupied the Blue Line north of Le Quesnel with only light casualties, and by 12:30 the Canadian Corps held every foot of the Blue Line.

On the northern flank, III Corps had been ordered to press on and seize yesterday's objective, Chipilly Spur. It was considered imperative that this flank be secured before the Australian Corps advance further. To this end, General Butler had issued orders for a dawn attack, but upon learning that the 131st Illinois would not be able to take up its position till much later countermanded his order to attack at 5:30. Ironically, the greatest success of the day was one of these postponed advances. The 6th Buffs of the 12th Eastern Division did not receive the orders cancelling its 5:30 attack. The battalion proceeded to take its objective without loss, capturing one exhausted *feldgrau*. The Buffs had shown what could have been achieved, but they were withdrawn. The stage was now set — belatedly — for the main attack.

The muddles that followed are mostly traceable to General Montgomery's removal of the 32nd Division from the Canadian command the night before. The switch from trench warfare to open warfare was making impossible demands upon the normal field-telephone system. That fact had been proven yesterday. Consequently, orders were now being sent by mounted dispatch riders because motorcycles, restricted to road travel, were being caught up in the miles-long traffic congestion. Fourth Army had become the victim of a colossal communications snarl. Now the truth of the old army adage was to be proven — "Order, counter-order, disorder."

The Canadian Corps had been given the day's principal task, the push to Roye, nine miles away. Monash's Australians would be advised to move only after Butler and Currie had set the time. Currie had planned to employ the 32nd Division on his extreme right, but its removal from his command had thrown the whole plan into confusion. His new orders did not reach the various divisions till dawn, necessitating postponement of the attack till 10:00. Thus the precious cover of darkness had been squandered. A side-stepping manoeuvre to the south by his divisions was now necessary to cover the Corps' frontage with the troops available. Consequently, the infantry spent most of the morning moving sideways under fire. Regrouping the artillery was even more complicated and caused a second postponement, then a third, and finally a fourth. What resulted was a series of individual attacks, invariably hours late and totally lacking in co-ordination.

The cavalry were the first off the mark, and did get a reasonably early start after a plethora of confusing orders and counter-orders had sent them from one rendezvous to another. Hours late the first patrols trotted into the seemingly deserted countryside. There they were ambushed by German infantry who let them approach within a few yards before emptying a few saddles. It suddenly became clear that German reinforcements had closed the gaps created yesterday. The cavalry's great opportunity so eagerly anticipated for so long had been missed. What was not realized was that the defenders had become numerically equal to the attackers. For the infantry the fighting on Friday, August 9, would be deadly, as was attested to by the six Victoria Crosses awarded.

THE CANADIAN CORPS

The Canadian Corps, having been delayed at least five hours, and in the case of the 3rd Division by almost ten hours, found itself facing stiff resistance. During the night three German reserve divisions had been brought in, and by afternoon elements of a fourth had arrived to face the Canucks. The 2nd Division, on the left flank where it had been less affected by the side-stepping manoeuvre, started first. Led by the 29th and 31st battalions, the 6th Brigade set off at 11:00. Forty-five minutes later its neighbour, the 5th Brigade (22e and 25th battalions) got under way. It was not till 1:00 p.m. that elements of the 1st Division began their attack — the 2nd Brigade followed by the 1st Brigade a quarter of an hour later. The weary 3rd Division, employing only its 8th Brigade, did not get under way till 2:00 (4th CMRs) and 2:50 (5th CMRs). The effect of these long postponements and the ensuing unco-ordinated advances was that each unit bogged down once its flanks were enfiladed. Thus the earlier attacking forces were forced to take cover and wait till the formations on their flanks came up.

"At 11 a.m. our troops started forward, our artillery having already opened fire, but the shells fell far behind our front line," reported Lieutenant

L.S. McGill, Scout Officer of the 29th Vancouver Battalion, the first to begin the advance.

> Enemy machine guns opened heavy fire as soon as our men started, and German artillery also put down a barrage of all calibres. Our tanks had failed to arrive, but infantry, with 31st Battalion in close touch, pushed on.... Meantime our men were dropping in considerable numbers all down the line, though no hesitation was shown. On the left flank ... particularly heavy machine gun fire was thinning our ranks, and Australians had not kept abreast of us.

Led by their Lewis gunners firing from the hip, the two battalions pressed through Rosières-en-Santerre towards the road that was their objective. The 31st Alberta Battalion being forced to veer right, Lieutenant "Turkey" Ross seized the opportunity to insert his 28th into the gap. The road was taken and held, but the victory had been costly. The 28th lost 124, the 29th 159, and the 31st estimated that "little more than one half of the Battalion strength was present at this time to hold the captured line."[206]

The greatest advance of the day was by the 5th Brigade whose *22e bataillon canadien-français* and 25th Nova Scotia Rifles pushed 3 1/2 miles through Vrély and into Meharicourt where they established a salient around the town by 5:00 after a long day of heavy fighting. Lieutenant Jean Brillant of *le 22e*, or "Van Doos" as it was better known, led "B" Company. Yesterday he had been wounded in the arm while rushing a machine gun. With his arm in a sling Brillant reconnoitred the ground himself before leading a charge on a nest of machine guns. A short savage fight with grenades and bayonets resulted in the capture of fifteen machine guns and 150 prisoners. During this action the lieutenant killed five Germans with his pistol, but was wounded in the head. While being bandaged he supervised the use of these captured guns. In this manner Vrély was taken.

Shortly after 3:00 the tanks finally arrived and the advance continued to Meharicourt. At this time a German shell landed on 5th Brigade Headquarters killing the Brigade-Major and the divisional liaison officer and badly wounding Brigadier Ross. Lieutenant-Colonel Tremblay of the "Van Doos" assumed command and turned the *22e* over to Major Georges Vanier, a future governor general of Canada.

At this time Lieutenant Brillant ran into a "whizz-bang" firing over open sights at his men. Calling for volunteers he rushed the gun and covered several hundred yards when it fired. The bursting shell riddled Brillant, but again he got up and advanced two hundred yards doubled over to prevent his intestines from pouring out. He collapsed before his second-in-command. "I am finished. Take charge of the company for I know that I cannot last long." Jean Brillant, a twenty-eight-year-old lieutenant from Assametquaghan, Quebec, died the next day and became the second "Van Doo" to be awarded the Victoria Cross.

Although the Canadians all found "the going hard," none had a tougher time than the 2nd Brigade, which finally moved off at 1:00 in the afternoon and fought its way through Warvillers, then beyond to the Meharicourt-Rouvroy-en-Santerre Road. "When the whistle blew," wrote Bert Hart of the 8th Winnipeg Battalion, "we charged out of the wood into the open only to be met with a hail of machine gun bullets." "The Little Black Devils" had run into serious opposition from Hatchet Wood, but this was overcome by the example of men like Corporal Fred Coppins and Lance Corporal Alex Brereton, who both won VCs storming machine guns. Now the shoe was on the other foot. "Out in the open, the German machine gunners were fleeing with their guns over their shoulders, running for cover," noted Hart. "but we potted at them and bowled them over on the run. My rifle became very hot from incessant firing."

The advance continued and once more the Canadians were under heavy fire. Hart saw the mess-tin shot off a comrade's back and the rifle shot out of the hand of another. "All of a sudden my left leg went useless. I felt no pain, but I knew I had been hit. So I fell to my knees, dropped my rifle, pulled off my equipment, salvaged a few knick-nacks out of my haversack and started the crawl back." When Hart reached the captured trench he found every other man of his section lying wounded. By nightfall only eight men of his company were left in action.

The 5th Western Cavalry Battalion found the country great for sectional rushes — flat, but masked by growing crops. In the advance Sergeant Raphael Zengel, a Minnesota-born veteran, charged a machine gun on the battalion's flank. He destroyed its crew and saved the lives of many of his comrades. Zengel survived to wear his Victoria Cross.

By mid-afternoon the Mark Vs had come up accompanied by several Whippets. These greatly alleviated the infantry's burden. By dusk both 2nd Brigade battalions were in position along the road south of Meharicourt. It had cost the plainsmen dearly; the 5th alone had suffered 306 casualties.

Next off the mark at 1:15 was the 1st Brigade. The advance of the 1st and 2nd battalions had been rapid at first, but typical of the day, the 1st Western Ontario had been forced to veer right into Folies, thus leaving the 4th to carry on up the centre. During the latter stages of this advance Lieutenant Jim Pedley was shot through the leg while leading his men. He was just one of 285 casualties suffered by the "Mad Fourth" in two days of fighting.

On the right flank the 4th CMR moved off at 2:00 accompanied by three tanks. "The big lumbering, awkward machines followed their officers out of the town at 2:00 p.m. ambling along like faithful prehistoric monsters. One of the Tanks was knocked out at the outset by an anti-tank gun firing at almost point-blank range. Another was put out of action later, but the third fought all day and assisted in clearing the town of Folies."[207] Led with "absolute disregard for his personal safety" by Major Sifton, the 4th CMR advanced by sectional rushes until the objective was taken. One of their eighty-one casualties was their padre, Captain W.H. Davis.

On the extreme right flank where the 5th Canadian Mounted Rifles advanced along the Amiens-Roye Road there occurred an incident, insignificant strategically but typical in many ways of the events of Friday, August 9. The 5th had by-passed Arvillers, a town to their right in the French sector, and assisted by four tanks had pressed on to take their own objective, Bouchoir.

The French south of the road had been stopped in front of Arvillers despite the support of Brutinel's Independent Force. Around 5:00 the men of the two motor machine gun batteries fought their way into Arvillers and captured twenty-five prisoners. Of these fifteen were captured single-handedly by Private Harry McCorkell. The 5th CMRs, looking over their right shoulder and seeing groups of the enemy retreating from Arvillers in the French sector, dispatched a platoon and one tank to occupy and mop up the village at 5:30.

At 5:40 p.m., in the words of the War Diary of the 5th CMR,

> A considerable number of enemy vehicles [a German ammunition convoy, as it turned out] were noticed retiring South eastwards from Southern outskirts of Arvillers. This was pointed out to a Squadron of Imperial Cavalry who had just moved up in close proximity to our H.Q., and we suggested that they could with very little difficulty, make a good capture, but they were either unable or unwilling to seize the opportunity.

Instead, five volunteers from the Canadian Light Horse offered to tackle the ammunition convoy. Lieutenant F.A. Taylor and his men had been sent forward from Brigade Headquarters to deliver a message. Now Taylor, Sergeant Duncan, and privates Dudgeon, Grisdale, and Hastie mounted and galloped to a line of old trenches south of the road. There they dismounted and worked their way along the trenches.

"I decided to rush the convoy and left the trenches," reported Lieutenant Taylor.

> Some resistance was offered so I opened fire and shot the Officer and 12 or 15 men. The remainder, about 20 men, surrendered. Heavy rifle and M.G. fire was opened on us from the trenches so we seized the lead horses and rushed them toward our own lines. The enemy advanced some machine guns within 400 yards and as I realized there was no chance of getting the convoy clear, I shot some of the horses and rushed my prisoners into the trench ... as a body of the enemy were advancing with the intention of cutting us off.

Meanwhile another platoon of the 5th CMR and a tank had been dispatched to help the five Light Horsemen bring in the captured ammunition convoy. But while they were on their way the French put down a belated rolling barrage on Arvillers where the CMRs first platoon was mopping up with the aid of a tank. Both platoons and both tanks were hastily recalled. Taylor and his four men were split up and forced to abandon their prisoners. When they reached Canadian lines, two were missing — Hastie and Grisdale. It is believed that Grisdale stayed with his wounded comrade. That night a search was carried out and the body of Private Hastie was found having apparently died of wounds. There was no trace of Grisdale.

THE AUSTRALIAN CORPS

The Australian Corps had had an easy time on the first day, and as far as they were concerned, the real fighting began on the second day. The Diggers' was to be a subsidiary attack and its objectives and even its zero hour depended on events on either flank. The basic plan was for the 1st Australian Division to pass through the 5th on the right and act as a flank guard for the Canadians. In the centre the 2nd Australian Division would side-step south a short distance and then advance as a flank guard for the 1st Division. The 4th, next to the River Somme, was ordered to stay in place till the British on the north bank advanced as far as Bray.

Muddles, so typical of the second day, plagued the Australian advance. Zero hour was postponed time and time again by the Canadians. Then it transpired that the 1st Australian Division was not where it was thought to be, and it was obvious that it would be unable to get into position even for the 11:00 zero hour. This was a great concern for the Canadian staff, so at 9:30 an officer arrived at the Australians' 15th Brigade Headquarters at the junction of the two sectors. He asked Brigadier "Pompey" Elliott for help covering the Canadian flank. This the Australian agreed to provide, and the tired 15th (Victorian) Brigade prepared to advance in place of the missing 1st Division. The move involved leapfrogging the brigade's two support battalions, the 60th (next to the Canadians) and the 58th. Both missed the originally scheduled zero hour of 10:00, but arrived just as the Canucks' 6th Brigade set off at 11:00. The 1st Division had elected to dispense with a barrage, and the weary 15th Brigade inherited the consequences when they set off ten minutes later.

The Canadians had advanced to the Blue Line yesterday, whereas the Australians had been held up short before Harbonnières. Thus the Diggers would remain several hundred yards to the left rear of the Canadians throughout the day. "The troops of the 15th Brigade leapt to their task without question. It was unthinkable that the Canadians should be let down. But the undertaking was no easy one. The brigade was given no objective — it was simply to go on till the 1st Division came up."[208]

Almost immediately both battalions ran into heavy artillery and machine-gun fire which swept the open ground. A long series of sectional rushes and outflanking movements therefore continued all morning. The fact that the Germans on the right had now been outflanked by the Canadians helped considerably. So did the tanks loaned by them, one Mark V and several Whippets. The latter were soon knocked out, but the Victorians' progress was steady despite this.

On their left flank the 29th Battalion (8th Brigade) had been rushed forward to cover their flank. The 29th was an hour too late to take advantage of the scant barrage put down, and the six tanks that supported them were soon knocked out in the open country. Although the 29th suffered severe casualties including twelve officers, with help from the 31st Battalion, Vauvillers was taken.

At 1:45 troops of the 1st Division at last began to pass through their weary comrades of the 15th Brigade.

The efforts of the "stand ins" were certainly appreciated by the Canadians. Major-General Burstall, commanding the 2nd Canadian

Division wrote, "It is difficult to express the appreciation which I, and all units under my command, have for the unselfish spirit with which this decision to advance was made and for the very gallant co-operation which was thus given us."[209]

The 1st Division was led by two Victorian battalions, the 7th and 8th. Following in the wake of the Canadian advance, the 8th had a somewhat easier time than the 7th. The latter's Mark Vs were hit one after another by guns on Lihons Hill — at the foot of which five hulks soon burned — but the infantry pressed on. "While the front line kept on charging forward in its little rushes, with rifle grasped in both hands across the chest, and bayonets flashing every now and then against the darker grey or green of the hill, the second line walked very quietly," wrote an unknown Digger. "We watched the brave little advance up that hill for ever so long ... it seemed to be that the last rushes became shorter and numbers fewer."[210] The scene reminded veterans of the brigade of their famous attack at Krithia in Gallipoli on May 8, 1915.

The 7th pressed on through heavy fire that eventually claimed fourteen officers, including every company commander. This fire came mainly from the northern flank, where the 2nd Division had not yet come up.

On many occasions it was necessary to storm machine guns over open ground to prevent the advance from petering out. One man who repeatedly led these charges was a former labourer from Geelong. Despite being wounded on his first attack, Private R.M. Beatham and his chum, Lance Corporal Nottingham, captured four machine guns and ten prisoners after killing another ten. During Beatham's fifth attempt he was riddled with bullets, although he managed to silence the gun with bombs before he died. Private Beatham was awarded the Victoria Cross posthumously.

By evening the 1st Australian Division's advance had run down. Opposition had been greatly increased by the arrival of strong German reserves. At the same time, the Diggers, who had been on the march all day loaded with extra rations and ammunition as well as greatcoats and waterproof sheets, were falling prey to exhaustion. The line nevertheless had been advanced almost four miles.

The 2nd Division had been given no fixed starting time for its attack. Because the units had to side-step so they could advance through the left flank of the 5th on the Blue Line, it had been decided to delay the attack till

4:30. However, they were in position before 4:00 p.m. Their promptness resulted in a short strafing by German planes while they waited to jump off.

Sharp at 4:30 the four battalions rose and advanced at a quick walk led by their scouts and thirteen enormous Mark V*s. The Germans at first fled before this advance and neither side put down a barrage although "targets of opportunity" were taken on. For the German gunners these were mainly the lumbering Mark V*s. Before Framerville had been taken and three hundred prisoners "put in the bag," only two tanks remained unhit. One of these next fell victim to its own crankshaft, leaving a lone survivor.

"For their part even the southernmost troops of the 2nd Division never knew throughout this attack whether the 1st Division had already advanced or was still to start: actually it had moved three hours before and its flank was two miles ahead, a full mile beyond the alignment of Vauvillers, the last point at which it had been protected by the 8th Brigade's advance."[211] Like the 1st Division, the 2nd's heaviest opposition came from its open left flank. Deadly fire rained from across the Roman Road where the 18th New South Wales Battalion suffered severely from machine guns and even from artillery, which galloped out to fire over open sights at them. But the Germans did not have it all their own way. Twenty-one *feldgrau* and their officer were captured when Sergeant J.J. Luck led an assault on a mortar post. The officer demanded that the former coal-lumper stand at attention and salute him. Luck's salute was to flatten his punctilious prisoner with a haymaker to the chin. When the officer was able to regain his feet he stood docilely at attention himself before obeying the Sergeant's orders to march to the rear.

The main German resistance centred on a red-brick factory in the village of La Flaque. Suddenly out of the dust lumbered the division's one remaining Mark V* under Lieutenant Craig, its young Scots commander. The tank charged the factory, and shell after shell hammered into the red bricks sheltering the Germans. At last they scuttled out, and Craig circled the area before taking his Mark V* to the rear.

The 2nd Division had almost achieved its objective and lay along a line that slanted from the Blue Line north of the Roman Road to Framerville thence across the slopes of Knoll 91, two thousand yards east of Vauvillers. The slopes were held by the 25th Queensland Battalion. In order to the northwest were the 27th South Australians, and the 17th and 18th New South Wales battalions. Like the 1st Division troops on their right, the 25th and 27th assumed they had reached their objectives, but were in fact well west of them. They also did not know it, but they had encountered newly arrived reinforcements from the 5th Bavarian Division.

THE WAR MUST BE BROUGHT TO AN END
Order, Counter-order, Disorder
III CORPS

North of the Somme the troops of III Corps, worn and "thin on the ground," had been ordered to attack at 5:30 that afternoon. At first it had been planned to advance at dawn, but as it soon became evident that the 131st U.S. Regiment would never be able to get into position in time, subsequent orders were sent postponing the advance. Eventually, the delays consumed over twelve hours.

The plan was for elements from three brigades of the 58th London Division to be thrown into another attempt to take Chipilly. At the same time, a mish-mash of battalions from three brigades, assisted by the 131st Illinois, was to attack Gressaire Wood, Tailles Wood, and the Old Amiens Outer Defence Line which extended north to Dernancourt. This was classified as the "main operation." To the north the 12th Eastern Division was to pinch out Morlancourt and occupy the Old Amiens Outer Defence Line. Twenty Mark Vs of the 10th Tank Battalion supported the two divisions — twelve with the 58th and eight with the 12th. Artillery had been pounding away throughout the afternoon on the southern part of the Chipilly Spur, but the major barrage would begin at zero.

What was in Chipilly? Various patrols and sightseers had entered the village early that morning, and each had made a different report. The most unusual penetration was carried out by two Australian souvenir-hunters, Company Quartermaster Sergeant Hayes and Sergeant Andrews of the 1st New South Wales Battalion. Incredibly enough, the former railway man and the farmer from Wauchope approached a Somme footbridge unarmed! Not being fired upon, the two crossed and entered the village, which had provided such stiff resistance the day before. Belatedly cautious, the two then armed themselves with abandoned German rifles. A suspicious chalk pit next caught their attention, and this they stalked. Leaping into the position they found only a silent machine gun which they appropriated. As Chipilly was obviously deserted, Hayes and Andrews started back towards the Somme, then were startled by shouts in English. There, almost half a mile to the west, was a British post, so the two tourists visited it to exchange news and pleasantries. Hayes and Andrews then ambled back to the bridge with their souvenirs, crossed the Somme, and reported to their company commander that Chipilly was deserted.

Theirs was merely one of several confusing reports on the village of Chipilly. Earlier that morning a patrol from the 1st New South Wales

Battalion had met Germans in its darkened streets and had been fired upon by a machine gun. A British patrol had also entered, as had the war correspondent, H.W. Nevinson of *The Guardian*. Later, the OC of the 6th City of London Rifles, Lieutenant-Colonel Benson, personally reconnoitred and reported both Chipilly and the heights "fairly strongly held," It seems probable that there were no Germans stationed in the village itself although they commanded it from the spur above and sent patrols through at intervals.

The first move against Chipilly came at 4:15 p.m. when the 6th City of London Rifles advanced. So depleted was this unit that only six officers and ninety men were available. Nevertheless, with a small patrol from the 7th Londons to protect their flank, this handful of Londoners advanced until met by severe fire from the high Chipilly Spur to their front and enfilade fire from Les Celestins Wood to their north. These remnants of the 6th London were pinned to the ground and the attack squelched.

At this moment two companies of the 10th Hackneys materialized out of Malard Wood. They had been ordered to advance by their OC who, unaware of the latest postponement, had decided to attack even though his men had been detailed only as supports to another brigade. Skillfully using covering fire, the Hackneys worked southeastward towards Chipilly until the German machine-gun nests just north of the village pinned them down, and artillery assistance was called for.

At this moment a second body of rescuers appeared on the scene — six Australians from the 1st New South Wales. It was 6:00 p.m. The two souvenir-hunting NCOs had been sent back with four privates to penetrate Chipilly again. Once across the foot bridge west of Chipilly they encountered one company of the Hackneys and were advised to go no farther. But Chipilly proved too enticing, and the six, with twelve pace intervals between them, rushed the village and entered unscathed. Here they split into two parties and searched the abandoned buildings and located the German posts on the spur. These they attacked with the assistance of the Hackneys. Each post was captured in turn by Hayes, Andrews, and their men — privates G.A. Stevens, (a carter from Young), J.R. Turpin (a former Cootamundra labourer), W.H. Kane (the sleeper-cutter from Macksville), and A. Fuller (a former tailor from Alexandria). Two-hundred prisoners and twelve machine guns were captured in this way, with the Diggers personally claiming eighty prisoners and three guns. Not yet finished, they pushed on to engage the enemy on the ridge above them.

By now, "K" Company, 3rd Battalion, 131st Illinois National Guard, had been dispatched from the north to help, and they appeared on Chipilly

Spur. The first thing the Yanks spied was the mass of prisoners, and they opened fire. The six cursing Aussies and their captives took cover until the Hackneys came up, forcing the Germans on the ridge to break and run. The Yanks then ceased fire and the Australians resumed their private war. With Andrews firing his captured machine gun, the others captured another thirty *feldgrau* and led the British advance till nightfall when they returned to their battalion. Chipilly was at last in Allied hands.

Meanwhile the main attack by III Corps went in at 5:30 that afternoon. This was the assault on Gressaire Wood, Tailes Wood, and the old trench line, which extended north to Dernancourt. It would be a difficult task as Gressaire Wood was full of German field guns well covered by machine guns in concrete emplacements. These and the spur from Chipilly northwards to the wood provided an excellent defensive position for the enemy.

The right flank of the main advance was made by the remnants of the 3rd, 4th, and 2nd London Regiments in line from Chipilly Spur northwards. Advancing behind a heavy but ineffective barrage, the three tiny battalions emerged from Malard Wood and covered the first five-hundred yards, but upon crossing the Chipilly-Morlancourt Road descended into ravines swept by crossfire from Chipilly and from Gressaire Wood. There they stayed pinned down until Chipilly was taken. Still taking severe casualties the three battalions continued the advance at 8:00 p.m., and shortly before midnight were on their objective.

In the centre of the main attack was the 131st Illinois, whose three battalions made it numerically the equivalent of a British brigade. The men were keen for a fight and in splendid physical condition. Fearing they would be late, the entire column covered the last mile at the double. There on the start-line they met their sixty-year-old commanding officer, Colonel Joseph B. Sanborn, who had run ahead to reconnoitre. Through Malard Wood doubled the 131st and were directed to positions for their first attack, 1st and 2nd battalions in front and 3rd in support. At zero, still breathing hard, they swarmed forward as the enemy counter-barrage hit their line.

"Colonel Sanborn conducted the first one hundred men through the hostile barrage himself, in order to establish the line and to be sure that the men would get the right direction," reported the 33rd Illinois Division's historian.

On his way back he was knocked over by a hostile shell, but luckily for himself and the U.S. Government, the shell did not explode. Sanborn shook himself free of the dust and debris, and continued his way to the command post bareheaded. As soon as the barrage lifted, which was at 5:38 p.m., nine companies of the 131st Infantry advanced....

They had hardly come out of the woods when they were met by a terrific hostile machine gun fire from the right. The Boche machine gunners had infiltrated down a ravine and had dug themselves in on the opposite side and camouflaged their positions. Before the action was over, at least 500 of these machine gunners were run out of their positions.... It had been understood that the flanks would be covered by other troops, but apparently this was not done completely.... Our men continued on into the Gressaire Woods, but half way through were held up by machine gun nests.... Assistance was asked for from the tanks ... but they were "hors de combat".... The only thing left to do was to push on through with rifle, bayonet and nerve. The British Division commander, turned to the Chief of Staff, 33rd Division, who was with him at the Battle Station, and asked him if he thought that the 131st could go through the woods. Being assured that there was no question about it ... the order was given.... At about midnight, Sanborn's second attack started, and by sheer nerve, and nothing else, pushed on through, isolated and wiped out the machine gun nests, and finally arrived at its ultimate objective.[212]

"The Americans swept everything before them, and the German resistance collapsed," wrote Major-General Montgomery, Rawlinson's senior staff officer. "So precipitate was the retreat of the enemy that a German battalion commander fled from his dug-out, abandoning his orders, maps, and telephone switchboard. The Americans were so impetuous that they outstripped the British on the left, and it was due to them that the objective was so quickly and rapidly gained on the front of the 58th Division."[213]

The price of success had been heavy, however; forty-five men killed and 255 wounded in the 131st's baptism of fire, but paled in comparison with those suffered by their allies. The 131st had been supported in the final stages by the 7th London Regiment which went into action with seventeen officers and 360 other ranks, and emerged from the day with three officers and sixty other ranks. "Other battalions suffered similarly," is the laconic comment of the British Official History.[214]

On the left of the Americans the 12th London (The Rangers) and 8th London (Post Office Rifles) advanced at 5:30 after having been withdrawn from the line during the day for a brief period of rest. They were supported by the 5th Royal Berkshire Regiment with the 9th London (Queen Victoria's) in reserve. Progress was slow, but by 9:00 p.m. The Rangers were on their objective and the 8th almost there.

On the extreme left flank of the Allied offensive the 12th Eastern Division had been ready to attack for well over twelve hours. In fact, one brigade had begun its attack at 5:30 that morning before being recalled by III Corps. The 6th Buffs, it will be remembered, had penetrated to their objective without a casualty before the counter-order reached them. Now twelve frustrating hours later they had to do it again against heavy resistance. The second time would be costly.

The enemy had been alerted a quarter of an hour before the 37th Brigade's attack by the early arrival of a tank — the only one to arrive in time. It had shown itself just in rear of the 1st Cambridgeshires waiting in front of Morlancourt. "There was a metallic clang and a flash of flame,"[215] and the 12th Division's tank support went up in a plume of smoke.

Only one battalion was immediately successful in its attack. The 6th Royal West Kent Regiment was inspired by the example of Sergeant Tom Harris of Lower Halling, Kent. Harris attacked three machine-gun posts in turn. The first two crews he killed single-handedly, but the third managed to shoot the indomitable sergeant. Harris's example made the Kentish men irresistible and they swept into their objective, suffering only light casualties. Tom Harris was posthumously awarded the Victoria Cross.

Speed and confidence like that shown by the West Kents were vital to success. Units that allowed themselves to slow down were blasted mercilessly and suffered high casualties; those that pressed on rapidly were relatively unscathed. The 1st Cambridgeshires attacking Morlancourt, the key to the German line, rushed across three hundred yards of completely open ground swept by fire. Through Morlancourt they stormed and seized their objective. The cost — two officers and ten other ranks.

THE FRENCH FIRST ARMY

The French First Army had resumed the offensive on Friday, the first formation to advance being General Toulorge's XXXI Corps. In reality the "offensive" was simply a cautious advance to yesterday's Blue Line already held by the Canadians on the left. The advance, which began at 8:00, moved at such a snail's pace that Hangert, two miles away, was not reached till 11:00 by the fresh 126th Division, which had relieved the 42nd during the night. Further south IX and X Corps made similar advances and connected up with the old line southwest of the Avre.

This cautious attitude did not escape the supreme commander, Marshal Foch, who on two occasions that morning reminded General Debeney of the necessity of speed. "It must be quite understood that the French First Army should reach Roye as soon as possible and stretch out its hand to the Third," Foch informed Debeney during his first call.

> With this object in view Divisions should not at any cost be withdrawn. [Toulorge had already allowed the 42nd to be withdrawn, a manoeuvre which had delayed his advance by 3 1/2 hours.] Those which cannot advance should be leapfrogged, should join the second line and be used in support until the result desired by High Command has been obtained.... Therefore push on quickly, march in force ... send up supports in rear with every man you have until achievement of the results.[216]

The Supreme Commander's orders had no impact on the plodding pace of the advance. Infantry-artillery co-ordination had vanished. For a start, at 4:30 a.m. the barrage had begun on schedule although the infantry attack had been delayed; then at 8:00 when the infantry set off they did so without any artillery support. Throughout the day the Germans made several counterattacks, which, though beaten off, were effective in slowing the advance of XXXI Corps still further.

Foch became more and more upset by the crawling pace of the French First Army. Finally, at 10:35 he telephoned Debeney's headquarters exhorting him to strengthen his left wing next to the Canadians. Speaking to one of the general's aides, Foch thundered, "It is in that direction above all that he must act, and therefore push forward the XXXI Corps, drums beating, on Roye, without losing a moment and prevent any delay or hesitation."[217]

But XXXI Corps had no drums to beat today, for after capturing Hangert at 11:00 it waited till 1:15 to get moving again. On its right, Contoire was not taken till 1:30 although it entailed an even shorter advance. Later that afternoon, in the understated words of the official report, "progress slowed down."

It had been decided that the XXXV Corps south of Montdidier would attack at 4:00 if an air offensive could be launched to knock down the German observation balloons in the area. As a result, a hastily planned attack was staged by three divisions. Two, the 169th and 133rd — enjoying reasonable success considering the late hour and the lack of preparation — advanced two and a half miles. The third, on the left of the 169th and bordering the inactive X Corps, had little success. There the 46th Division had, like the others, been unprepared. But the 46th also lacked spirit, and its commander proved to be ultra-cautious. The result: a very inferior performance and a slowing of the advance of the entire corps. The hoped-for breakthrough on the French sector did not materialize, and the II Cavalry Corps, which had been following XXXV Corps, was given no chance for glory on Friday.

On the whole, the French First Army had not performed well on the second day. Field Marshal Haig was dissatisfied, and at 4:00 in an interview with Debeney, said so. Debeney could only reply that he had visited all his corps commanders in an attempt to hasten them. The French historian, Commandant Dialle, delicately summed up Friday's unpalatable truth: "Without striking the least blow to the merit and the glory of those involved, we must state that on this day the offensive lacked spirit."[218]

THE AIR OFFENSIVE

The Royal Air Force had begun Friday with a series of widely scattered bombing raids. At 5:00 a.m. the first thirty bombers had taken off with orders to bomb the Somme bridges from five hundred feet or lower. H.F. Taylor of 205 Squadron had been a rookie observer a day earlier. On this day he was a rookie pilot flying one of the Rolls-Royce DH4s.

> Nothing happened as we crossed the lines and neared our objective. Then suddenly, a dirty yellow cloud unrolled itself about 20 yards on my right, and a hoarse "Woof" followed. It was "Archie", an anti-aircraft battery....
>
> Over the target we dropped our cargo, then as we turned, we met the enemy scouts [as fighters were often called].... Our observers opened fire. Streams of tracer bullets shot out from each gun, and our machines began to

sway from side to side, and up and down, yet still keeping in the V shape, which it would have been fatal to lose.

For fifteen minutes it went on. Above the roar of the engine could be heard the sharp rattle of machine guns. Little rags of fabric would spring up in the wings as bullets tore them....

We reached the lines, and our attackers vanished. We could fly steadily now, and I had time to look behind. My observer was leaning on the side, white-faced, and gazing longingly at the ground below. I realized he had been wounded, and the awful thought flashed through my head that he might fall across the controls, setting the machine into a dive from which I might be unable to pull out.[219]

Taylor and his observer were lucky; they both reached the aerodrome. Four of 205 Squadron's other planes never returned. Other squadrons also lost heavily, having run into stiff German resistance. Fifty fighter planes were to have accompanied the bombers, plus another seventy-four on patrol higher up. Yet in most cases the fighters returned having failed to rendezvous with the bombers. The result was that more than half of the bombs were dropped towards targets other than the bridges. Very few, if any, hit their marks, and no damage was done to the Somme bridges.

Due to the failure of the morning's widely scattered bombing attacks it was decided to launch one massive simultaneous assault in the afternoon. Every available plane was to be employed, and each formation was to arrive over its target at 5:00 p.m. exactly. A new tactic was also to be employed. "All available machines of both Wings [Ninth and Fifty-First] will be detailed to afford close protection of the bombers," advised IX Brigade's orders.

> By close protection is meant that scout machines are to fly at about the same level as bombing machines, and to remain in their immediate vicinity till completion of the operation.... Four squadrons of the I Brigade [specially brought down from the north for this operation] will be patrolling from 4:30 to 6:00.... Each of these patrols will be of approximately squadron strength, and they will fly just above the clouds. Our scout machines are therefore free to escort the bombers closely.[220]

Four squadrons took off around 4:00 p.m. to bomb four of the bridges. Cloud had developed between two thousand and three thousand feet. Once again, the escorting fighters or "scouts" failed to make contact with the bombers, and the results were minimal. Only thirty-five bombs were dropped in the vicinity of the bridges with no definite hits registered, although bursts had reportedly been seen at both ends of the Bethencourt bridge. This was the meager result achieved by thirty bombers, escorted by fifty fighters, and supported by another seventy-four immediately above the clouds — a total of 154 planes.

The French Air Service was also active on Friday. The railway stations that had been last night's targets received return visits during the day; Man, Hombleux, Roye, Fresnoy-les-Roye, and Fransart were bombed again. The cantonments at Tilloloy, Beuvraignes, and Bus were also attacked by French bombers. The fighters had been ordered to maintain control over the French battlefield as far south as Rollot with enemy observation balloons coming in for special attention.

The enemy's Flying Circus had another successful day as Lothar von Richthofen in his "Red Bird" scored victories number 36 and 37, both Airco DH9 bombers. At the same time his partner, Erich Loewenhardt, in his famous yellow Fokker D VII, knocked down two Sopwith Camels to add numbers 52 and 53 to his total.

All through the night the air war continued. An RAF force of 106 planes dropped a total of 16 1/2 tons of bombs. Again, the targets were the bridges over the Somme. Two hits on the bridge at Voyennes were the only claims made. The French Air Service continued its attacks on the rail centres of Ham, Hombleux, and Guiscard. At the same time German night bombers were trying to knock out bridges on the Allied side. The vital Domart Bridge over the Luce attracted particular attention. No hits were registered, but one stray bomb landed among the horse-lines of the 32nd Imperial Division causing unexpected repercussions for the morrow.

THE GERMANS

During the day the Germans had brought another four divisions (the 21st, 79th Reserve, 5th Bavarian, and 82nd Reserve) to be thrown into the vortex along with the six divisions brought in the previous night. Most of these reinforcements arrived in the afternoon just in time to be used against the Allies' belated and disjointed attacks. The remains of five of the divisions that had been overwhelmed in the initial attack were now being gradually withdrawn. The 13th, 41st, 43rd Reserve, and the 225th had been in need of this long before the offensive. The fifth of these divisions, however, revealed the true situation to anyone who could read between the lines. The 117th, called "one of the freshest and most battle-worthy divisions of the German Army" at dawn on the 8th was withdrawn on the evening of the 9th after being all but destroyed by the 1st Canadian Division.

At home OHL's blunt communiqué hinted at the magnitude of the disaster; "The enemy has broken in south of the Somme on a broad front." Panic seared the Fatherland, and the news spread into eastern Europe. General von Cramon, the German military plenipotentiary in Austria phoned Ludendorff and begged him to consider "the harmful effect that a short bleak admission of disaster had on our Allies, who saw in Germany their only salvation. Such admissions did not help; they must be 'beautified', if not on account of the German public, then for the sake of our Allies."[221]

Nevertheless, the situation, at least when judged by maps, did not look that critical for the Germans. North of the Somme the four original divisions still faced a British III Corps composed of four equally tired divisions supported by one partially trained American division; the forces facing the French First Army were still intact and had in fact been reinforced by the 82nd Reserve Division; facing the Allies' main attacking force of ten Australian and Canadian divisions (including the 32nd Imperial Division) were nine German divisions, six of whom were fresh while the other three had seen action only since the previous afternoon. On paper the problems facing OHL did not seem as serious as it had on August 8, "the black day."

All day Ludendorff opposed any suggestion to withdraw. He had once more immersed himself in detail and spoke repeatedly on the telephone, giving instructions even to the extent of placing individual battalions. "Ludendorff is continually insisting on having a say in all the particulars," wrote General von Kuhl, the Chief of Staff of Army Group Rupprecht, "talking to all the armies and their chiefs, arranging details often quite contrary to his orders to me. Then when one talks to the army commanders, one hears they are doing something entirely different from what we ordered. This makes everything terribly difficult. At the same time he is extremely restless and does not listen to a single suggestion."[222]

There was no shortage of suggestions to withdraw. Tschischwitz (Chief of Staff, Second Army) phoned to recommend that the Second Army retire behind the Somme. Next on the line was Marwitz, "the Automatic Boiler," to say the same. Mertz von Quirnheim then returned from the front to report that both Tschischwitz and Marwitz "were finished." This report resulted in the replacement of the former, but suggestions to withdraw continued to pour in.

THE WAR MUST BE BROUGHT TO AN END
ORDER, COUNTER-ORDER, DISORDER

Throughout the day von Kuhl argued in frustration and anguish that the time for Lossberg's strategy of a withdrawal to the Siegfried Line had now arrived. Holding on to the present front at all costs only exposed Germany to danger in every sector, it left her naked and it gobbled up the slim resources still available. But Ludendorff remained adamant; all positions must be held. The maps and reports from his staff officers had combined with his stubborn nature to convince him that this was the only possible reaction to the Allies' Amiens offensive.

In front of Amiens, however, many of the men Ludendorff counted on to stop the offensive were ready to drop from exhaustion. Survivors of the original divisions had endured two days of incredible pounding and catastrophic losses. These men were at the very end of their tethers. The newcomers who were rushed in to retrieve the situation had endured hours of forced marching then hours of confused fighting, usually under the threat of being overrun by tanks or outflanked by the Allies' finest infantry. Many had gone for two days without sleep, and almost as long without food. Their demoralization was revealed by numerous small incidents. The history of the 2nd Grenadiers reports that during the quiet of the night one post "must have seen ghosts" for it fled en masse in sudden panic. The 5th Australian Battalion reported, "Lt. T.S. Parker's platoon rushed [a] post — eight Germans, with two machine guns, under an N.C.O. These men had just committed the vilest of military crimes — their N.C.O. lay in the trench dead, his skull cracked by a blow from behind."[223]

The reserve divisions, brought up in haste, had been thrown into the line piecemeal. Those sent in whole, often suffered such losses or were immediately attacked with such violence that plans, where they existed, were worthless. Replacements reached the front without their transport or any heavy equipment such as artillery. The staff too arrived without transport or horses, making it impossible to transmit orders to the front line. For all these reasons counterattacks seldom materialized.

North of the Somme four "original" divisions still possessed the staff and communications to carry on the battle, but they had by now suffered severe losses in fighting men and equipment. At Gressaire Wood alone seventy artillery pieces had been lost. Infantry casualties had been appalling; for instance, the two front line battalions of the 123rd Infantry Regiment had been reduced to forty-four men in total.

As evening fell Ludendorff was reluctantly forced to face these realities. From far to the south in the French sector had come more alarming reports. Indications of imminent attacks had been detected on the southern face of the German salient, which extended from

Montdidier in the west almost eighteen miles east to Noyon. At last the "Iron Man" agreed to a withdrawal in the French sector. The right flank of the Eighteenth Army under General Hutier was ordered to drop back approximately four miles in front of the French First and

Day Two — August 9

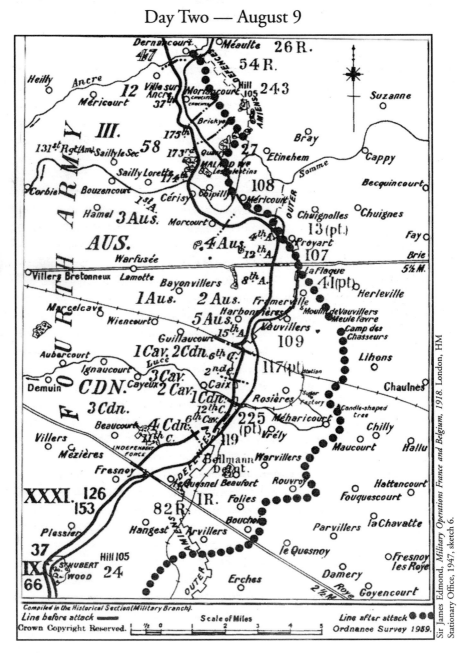

Sir James Edmond, *Military Operations France and Belgium, 1918.* London, HM Stationary Office, 1947, sketch 6.

Third Armies. To conform, von der Marwitz's Second Army also began to withdraw north of Montdidier.

THE ALLIES — MIDNIGHT, AUGUST 9/10

That night strong patrols were sent out north of the Somme by the 131st Illinois and the 175th Brigade. They returned with the astounding news that the enemy was withdrawing. So despite opposition from artillery, machine guns, and snipers the Doughboys and the Tommies pushed on. The German withdrawal was giving several units a second chance to reach their objectives. Thus the Blue Line was belatedly occupied by III Corps around midnight. Although it had failed to reach the old Outer Defence Line, the 58th Division that night achieved all of the objectives set for it for the previous day.

Friday, August 9, was a day of disappointments. Although substantial territorial gains resulted from the day's offensive, it was not as much as had been hoped for. German resistance stiffened and casualties increased. The tanks, in particular, suffered severe losses. Only 145 survived the previous day; now a further thirty-nine were destroyed. This left 106 to carry on — not only tomorrow, but well into the future until more vehicles could be delivered and more crews assembled from the survivors. There were many depressing examples of their new-found vulnerability. In front of Vauvillers only one out of seven survived. The 2nd Australian Division lost twelve of its thirteen Mark V*s. Even the Whippets, which had survived yesterday's action, proved to be easy marks on this day. The tank crews themselves fought magnificently, however. One crew, whose tank had been destroyed leading the 2nd Canadian Division, bailed out. Led by their young officer, they charged a German machine-gun position. The officer was killed, but his men in their anger wiped out the post. In the Australian sector a tank battled its way to the top of Knoll 91 before being hit. Its crew then fought to the last man vainly trying to hold the position until the Diggers got there. Although today the Allies' "ace in the hole" had suffered a further 30 percent loss, no one could fault the courage of the British tank crews.

Artillery support was disappointing. Many of the barrages were so thin as to belie the word; others fell short, causing casualties among the infantry. On several occasions barrages were fired according to orders that had been canceled. The only result, of course, was to alert the enemy. These problems were typical of the second day of an offensive during which the infantry out-distanced not only their artillery, but their supplies and communications.

Aircraft losses were also heavy. Today cost the RAF another forty-five planes, mainly in the bridge-bombing raids, and achieved no noticeable result. The ground-support planes, on the other hand, suffered fewer losses — in a role considered the most costly — and achieved spectacular results. Since the battle opened on Thursday, V Brigade's nine squadrons had dropped 1,536 of their twenty-five-pound bombs and had fired 122,150 rounds on ground targets.

The number of prisoners taken by Rawlinson's Fourth Army now totaled 387 officers and 15,516 men while the French First Army held 150 officers and 4,300 men. The Germans also lost heavily in guns — over two hundred to the Fourth Army and one hundred to the French. By far the largest concentration of these was in Gressaire Wood, which proved such an obstacle to the 58th London Division. In this one small wood no less than seventy guns were captured. All of these were now being removed, a precaution that must have suggested a lack of optimism to some. At Cambrai, nine months earlier, after a brilliant advance by the British, the Germans had counterattacked and recaptured all of the guns they had lost. Is this what was expected tomorrow?

As the fighting died down plans were being formulated for the third day, Saturday, August 10. During his 4:00 p.m. meeting with Debeney, Haig requested that the French First Army extend its frontage northward three miles. Debeney declined, but in a compromise agreed to take over as far north as Roye. At corps level, Currie ordered his reserves up for zero hour at 8:00 a.m. Two fresh brigades of the 4th Canadian Division would attack on the left, while the 32nd Division, belatedly made available to him, would attack on the right adjacent to the French. In the meantime Monash convinced Rawlinson to give his Australian Corps control of a portion of III Corps' sector north of the Somme. Because Lieutenant-General Butler had been ordered home on sick leave it was felt that this move could be arranged diplomatically with his temporary replacement, General Godley.

As Friday became Saturday, at headquarters all along the front, staffs burned the midnight oil. Plans and orders for tomorrow were being drawn up. Those who laboured prayed that the results would be more dramatic than those produced by today's disorganized, disjointed operation. In the words of the British Official History, "The second day of the battle was a day of wasted opportunities."[224]

CHAPTER TWELVE
THE CLASSIC EXAMPLE

*"The operation will probably furnish a classic example of
how not to follow up a great attack."*
*The Official History of Australia in the
War of 1914-1918*[225]

Saturday, August 10, began with an attack by the 3rd Canadian
Division on Le Quesnoy which lay two thousand yards ahead of
Bouchoir and just off the Amiens-Roye Road. The attacking force
was made up of three companies of the 2nd Canadian Mounted Rifles.
These British Columbians had been ferried up at midnight by Brutinel's
Canadian Independent Force. Sharp at 4:20 a.m. they jumped off,
supported by machine-gun fire and four tanks on each flank. German fire
was heavy and half of the tanks were knocked out in short order.
Nevertheless, the Canucks entered Le Quesnoy, and by 6:30 had cleared
it. An hour later they occupied the eastern edge of the 1916 trench line.
The 1st CMR from Saskatchewan now came up and extended the
Canadian line northwards facing the town of Parvillers. Like Friday, the
morning had started off with a successful attack on the Canadian right.

The Allies' main attack was once again to be delivered by the Canadian
Corps. With their own 4th Division on the left and the 32nd Imperial
Division on the right, the objectives were the same as yesterday. General

Currie was once again given freedom to set zero hour and to communicate this decision to his neighbours. Currie chose 8:00 a.m. in hopes that all preparations could be completed before the day was too far advanced.

The 3rd Cavalry Division had been directed to operate on the right, and despite yesterday's experience, it was instructed to "gain the objectives allotted to the Canadian Corps and to facilitate the advance of the French First Army." With that in mind, cavalry patrols were sent forward to report on "the suitability of the ground up to and beyond the objective for the employment of cavalry moving fast and in large numbers."[226]

To support the main attack the 13th Tank Battalion had been ordered forward from reserve. However, this unit had not received word of its role till shortly after midnight, and then without details of the attack or of the infantry's positions. It was 6:30 before these essential facts were ascertained and the tanks ordered to Rosières-en-Santerre. Currie had been frustrated once again; he was forced to send out orders delaying the attack till 10:00.

Meanwhile the infantry moved up to their start lines and began the long, unexpected wait. By now reports from the cavalry patrols had started to come in. They were not encouraging; "the country was unsuitable, even impassable, for cavalry — unless dismounted — and also for Whippet tanks."[227] So the frustrated cavalry stood-fast throughout the morning. For some, like the Fort Garry Horse, now in reserve, the chance for action and glory seemed to have vanished forever. After two and a half days of cavalry action they were still in reserve, and future prospects appeared very dim.

Three infantry divisions were to be employed in Fourth Army's advance: the 32nd Division beside the Amiens-Roye Road, the 4th Canadian beside them, and the 1st Australian on the left. The earliest to advance was the 1st Australian Division, which had not received word of the postponement. At 6:30 a.m. when Currie had discovered that his tanks could not be brought forward in time he had sent a telegram to warn the Australians. The telegram was addressed to "Australian Division on our flank." Someone evidently believed this to be the 5th Australian Division, and the message duly arrived there. Assuming it was merely a duplicate, the 5th did not forward it to the 1st, now in the front line.

The 1st Australian Division

A few minutes before 8:00 a heavy ground mist covered the land and the Diggers were anxious to move off before it dissipated. Then just before the barrage was to commence, the roar of an aircraft was heard. Swooping low over the assembled Australians came a lone plane bearing the ominous black crosses on its wings. Its machine guns chattered and a man leaned over the side and fired two white flares. Lewis gunners opened fire, but it was too late, and the lone scout vanished leaving the tell-tale flares to mark the concentration. The enemy had been forewarned. Moments later the Australian barrage burst on schedule at 7:45 — unfortunately, well beyond the German line.

The two Victorian battalions, the 5th and the 6th (2nd Brigade), encountered severe fire and soon discovered to their dismay that the Canadians were not advancing with them. Farther north two 3rd Brigade battalions, the 9th and 11th, lost direction in the mist, and veered southwards, passing Crepey Wood on their left instead of their right. This would cost them some of the heaviest casualties of the day.

South of Crepey Wood the 5th and 6th Victorians had been squeezed south by the veering 3rd Brigade. Heavy fire and open country combined to make progress slow. Numerous enemy machine-gun nests overshot by the barrage posed special problems, as did the open flank on the Canadian side of the railway. Casualties were mounting and the attack was losing momentum when the commander of the 6th Canadian Brigade, Brigadier A.H. Bell, ordered the 27th City of Winnipeg Battalion to advance and clear the Victorians' flank. The Winnipegers — who had taken part in the "Ypres ruse" — pushed on under heavy fire alongside their dominion allies. Later (shortly after 10:15) the 4th Canadian Division would pass through the 27th, and a solitary tank, "Mudsplasher," would cross the railway to assist the Aussies.

Meanwhile the 9th Queensland and 11th West Australian battalions were suffering heavily as they passed Crepey Wood on the wrong side. "Crepey Wood" was the name given to a tangle of underbrush huddled beneath the skeletal remains of the towering trees that had once crested Lihons Hill. This difficult obstacle, which extended for five hundred yards along the crest, was the hiding place for numerous enemy machine guns. The Diggers attempted to set up outposts around the wood, but were soon driven out by fire from the crest. The fiercest fighting of the day for the Australian Corps involved taking Crepey Wood. Tremendous Lewis-gun fire and individual heroism enabled the 9th to assault from the south and penetrate the wood. "Lieutenant Gower leading one party, worked from shell-hole to shell-hole, finding and outflanking German machine-gun posts and killing or capturing the gunners," recorded the official historian. "He is said to have finally rushed one machine-gun crew with only a Lewis gun rod in his hand, bluffing its members into surrender. While seeking the best site for a post beyond the wood, he was badly wounded, but his N.C.O. [Sergeant D.H. Brown of Warwick, Queensland] took charge and a chain of posts was for a time established around the woods."[228]

Reinforcements had by then arrived in the shape of a company of the 10th South Australian Battalion, and two Stokes mortars of the 3rd Light Trench Mortar Battery. The latter under Sergeant McSweeney, a one-time "timber-hewer" from Bunbury, knocked out a battery of German guns. The fighting for Crepey Wood was savage and confused, with both sides making several attacks to capture or recapture posts or sections of trench. Both Australians and Bavarians lost heavily.

The 32nd Imperial Division

The 32nd Division jumped off at zero hour, 10:00, without their own artillery support. The accidental bombing of their horse lines near the Domart Bridge had made it impossible to move their artillery up in time. Fortunately, the 5th Canadian Divisional Artillery was available to give fire support. At first the troops moved forward with little problem. With Le Quesnoy in the hands of the 2nd Canadian Mounted Rifles and Erches taken by the French, the 96th Brigade had nothing to fear from the right or left for the first thousand yards. After that they encountered the infamous trench system of the 1916 Battles of the Somme. The battlefield, scene of some of the greatest carnage in history, was still a formidable obstacle. Long stretches of rusted wire, several feet in breadth, stretched as far as the eye could see, overgrown and partially hidden by two years' growth of weeds. Craters and old trenches — shallow and indistinct, but trenches all the same — spread everywhere in an incredible maze. They too were hidden from view by the knee-high overgrowth.

By 9:30 the 96th Brigade, led by the 15th and 16th battalions of the Lancashire Fusiliers, reached the point where the old German front line crossed the Amiens-Roye Road. Already four tanks working ahead of the infantry had been destroyed by anti-tank gun fire. The Fusiliers, supported by the 2nd Battalion of the Manchester Regiment, rushed and captured a German pill-box, the famous "Tour de Defiance," on the edge of "Square Wood" and pressed on to take the wood itself. The enemy counterattacked, but the Tommies clung to the pill-box and the western edge of the wood. Around 2:00 p.m. four more tanks arrived, and the advance resumed. But within ten minutes of crossing the 1916 German line all four were knocked out. The battle for control of Square Wood would surge back and forth throughout the afternoon.

The 97th Brigade had very similar experiences. With the 10th Argyll and Sutherland Highlanders on the right and the 5th Battalion, the Border Regiment on the left, the advance at first went smoothly. Against steadily stiffening resistance, the Borderers reached the 1916 British front line at about 10:00, making contact with the 1st Canadian Mounted Rifles. By 11:00 the Argylls too reached the old front line where the advance ground to a halt after gains of approximately two thousand yards. Ahead lay the ominous 1916 no man's land, the site of one of history's greatest slaughters.

The 4th Canadian Division

The 4th Canadian Division, the spearhead of the entire Allied attack, had been instructed to wait for tank support, and consequently lay in long rows in the fields as the sun dissipated the protective mist. Eventually at 10:15, a quarter of an hour after zero, the men were given the order to move off behind the Mark Vs that had just arrived. Nineteen-year-old Gad Neale of the 46th South Saskatchewan Battalion would always remember the sight: "We were in extended order. It was a beautiful day, warm with the sun shining when we started up that long slope with Heinie's whizz-bangs at the top and our tanks ahead. I looked along the line both ways and it was straight as a ruler, not a man out of place."

The 10th Brigade beside the 32nd Imperial Division employed two battalions in the initial advance — the 44th New Brunswick and 46th South Saskatchewan. The advance began well, but as the line reached the overgrown trenches all hell broke loose. "Suddenly Fritz landed a wall of bursting shells in front of us, and I do mean a *wall*," recalled Curry Spidell, a rangy, raw-boned farmer from Mortlach, Saskatchewan. "A gap appeared right in front of Sergeant Jack Scott and me, and we made a dash for it.... Just as we got there, it closed.... A small shell splinter came through my right cheek, cut off two teeth, and went out through my mouth. Along with that I got three others in my right shoulder."[229] Spidell tumbled into an overgrown trench. A typical Canadian, he had carried along with his regular equipment two water-bottles full of rum and a half-gallon can of strawberry jam. Before starting back to enjoy his "blighty," Spidell "disposed of" these treasures despite being somewhat handicapped by his paralyzed jaw.

All along the 4th Division front the story was the same; point-blank artillery fire and desperate resistance from greenish-clad German infantry, the famous Alpine Corps. At one point just west of Maucourt, a German battery kept up a hot fire over open sights. The 46th advanced by sectional rushes. "When the first wave got within a hundred yards of the guns the Germans fetched their teams out to limber them up," recalled the one-time ranch-hand, Gad Neale. "One of our Lewis gunners started to run, and as he ran he opened up with his gun which they carried at their hips on a sling over the shoulder. And he stopped them cold." The South Saskatchewans captured the battery and one decrepit old nag, which one of the runners appropriated. Riding bareback and wild as any cowboy, he could be seen galloping back and forth through the fierce barrage. Incredibly, both horse and rider survived the day.

On the left, the 12th Brigade's casualties were mounting, the 85th Nova Scotia Highlanders losing two commanding officers in minutes. The village of Chilly was taken, and the line passed through into the no man's land of 1916. Both Highland battalions reached their objectives, and the 72nd Seaforth Highlanders from Vancouver pushed a salient into the German lines. Here where the old trenches veered eastward, was the furthest forward point in the Allied advance.

The 78th Winnipeg Grenadiers arrived at Chilly and pushed on through the Seaforths to deepen the salient another 1,500 yards. "The advance towards Hallu from Chilly proceeded without incident, with the exception of some long range machine gun fire and field guns," reported the Grenadiers' War Diary. "The ground was reported by Major Linnell to be very difficult to advance over, this at 2:10 p.m." Communications with the forward companies became intermittent, although by late afternoon it was learned that they had penetrated well into the old German position and into Hallu itself. This village lay alongside a railway track running north and south from Roye to join the main line from Amiens which formed the boundary between the Australian and Canadian Corps. Here the 78th clung to their fragile salient in deceptive calm.

Despite abundant evidence to the contrary, in the rear areas a persistent rumour began to circulate — "The enemy is on the run!" The rumour was two days late. Possibly because of such wishful thinking, the Cavalry Corps sent forward its reserve, the Canadian Cavalry Brigade. Along the Amiens-Roye Road they trotted with the Fort Garry Horse in the lead. One squadron under Major Strachan galloped through a barrage, then over trenches and several belts of wire to cross into the French sector and seize the town of Andechy. Here the Manitobans hung on after capturing a large supply dump and a number of prisoners. When French infantry appeared around 4:00 Strachan turned Andechy over to the *poilus* and retired after a further advance had proven impossible.

In the meantime the remainder of the Fort Garrys had advanced down the Amiens-Roye Road past La Cambuse towards "Z Wood." This tiny wood was strongly held by German infantry and machine gunners. Nevertheless, the squadron broke into a gallop and charged the wood. Due to the trenches, wire, and other obstacles, the horses were soon funneled along the narrow road. Only one trooper managed to get within a hundred yards of Z Wood before being shot down. This incredible charge claimed forty-five men and 112 horses within a matter of seconds. The Fort Garrys, desperately courageous, were preparing for a second mad attempt when an unidentified infantry brigadier intervened. Such action, he rightly judged, would be suicidal. Once again, German machine guns had proven superior to Canadian sabres.

North of the Somme

North of the River Somme most of the skirmishing had been verbal. As ordered by Fourth Army, the 4th Australian Division had taken over the sector as far as the Bray-Corbie Road. The divisional commander, General MacLagan, had also been ordered to take command of the 131st Illinois Regiment and several units of the 18th and 58th divisions located a mile or so behind the lines. However, III Corps had instructed its 58th Division to retain command over these troops, and a hitch had occurred that brought barely hidden ill-feelings to the surface. The ostensible reason for III Corps' contradictory order was that the units in question were reserves. MacLagan had refused to complete the operation until Monash's orders had been complied with. A call to Rawlinson had quickly clarified matters, and the 13th Australian Brigade had moved into position behind the Yanks by early morning.

Meanwhile patrols from the 58th London Division and its American comrades had been pushing forward against lessening opposition, the result being that by 2:10 that afternoon they had occupied the Old Amiens Defence Line. The 1916 trenches were still in fair condition, and the enemy had left behind huge dumps of stores including wire, which was used to strengthen the existing belts facing the enemy.

To the north the obstacles facing the 12th Eastern Division were not so easily surmounted. Enemy resistance continued, and it would take a full-scale attack later in the day to dislodge them.

The French Sector

Throughout the day the British commanders had operated as if in pursuit of a beaten enemy. Their continued determination to employ cavalry and their unrealistic assessment of possible gains show that they had not as yet grasped that the enemy now outnumbered their own troops, particularly in the Canadian sector. French generals, on the other hand, found themselves in pursuit of an enemy who was withdrawing, but they continued to operate as though they were conducting a set-piece offensive against strongly held positions.

In the French sector the most important development of the day was the extension of the offensive another ten miles to the south. Promptly at 4:20 that morning six divisions of General Humbert's Third Army had advanced into no man's land without a bombardment only to discover that, except for small rearguards, "*les Boches*" had vanished. Nevertheless, Third Army kept its right-hand division in place while the others swung ponderously forward in an arc, keeping roughly in line with Debeney's First Army.

On the French left, the First Army had jumped off somewhat later (5:30 a.m.) after half an hour of artillery preparation. Here too the *poilus* found the enemy had withdrawn leaving only rearguards behind them. Both French armies continued their cautious advance, and the city of Montdidier, now almost completely destroyed, was reoccupied without a fight. However, when the 1916 trenches were encountered all forward movement ceased. Although the offensive had been extended to a length of thirty-five miles that morning, by evening the French role had petered out.

The First German Counterattack

In late afternoon a disturbing development occurred. For the first time since the Amiens offensive began the Germans launched a strong counterattack. It fell on Crepey Wood in the Australian sector. There outposts of the 9th Queensland and 10th South Australians had occupied the far edges of the undergrowth. At 5:30 a terrific bombardment hit the crest of the hill crowned with the skeletal remains of tall trees and a tangle of low scrub.

"The whole wood simply oozed with dun-coloured shell-smoke," wrote an eyewitness, "oozing out between the trees as the soup-coloured water might ooze between a man's fingers if he gripped a dirty sponge."[230] This German barrage was laid down by one field battery which, because of the shortage of ammunition, could only manage five minutes rapid-fire before lifting to the centre of the wood for another three minutes. Finally the battery lay down a curtain of fire on the western edge to prevent Australian reinforcements from coming up. Meanwhile at 5:35 German infantry assaulted the Aussies from three sides. The attackers were men of the 19th and 21st Bavarian Infantry Regiments. The Australians had three Lewis guns destroyed in the bombardment and were forced to abandon their most advanced posts. Thirty casualties severely reduced the Australian force, but they gave better than they got. The 21st Bavarian's historian wrote, "Sharp enemy machine gun fire soon dampened the ardour; the companies fell back to their starting point."[231] The 19th Bavarian's also lost heavily. "The enemy opposition was so strong that a farther advance was considered impossible. August 10 will generally be held in sad memory by all who took part — fearful artillery fire, no visibility, many losses, no combination in carrying out orders, and confusion were its characteristics. The regiment lost ... 250 men."[232] All in all, it had been a bad afternoon for the Bavarians, one platoon of whom abandoned their positions in the night and vanished to the rear.

The 12th Eastern Division

On the northern flank of the offensive the 12th Eastern Division launched its attack late in the day, having found that the German withdrawal had not extended to its sector. At 6:00 that evening the 37th Brigade attacked with six tanks of the 10th Tank Battalion and special artillery support. Across the flat top of the main ridge three battalions advanced — the 6th Buffs, the 9th Essex, and the 6th Queen's Royal West Surrey Regiment. A battery of howitzers was captured and the objective taken and held, except for Hill 105, a knoll cleared by the tanks and the Buffs, but retaken by the enemy. Nevertheless, III Corps now occupied the Old Amiens Defence Line.

The Second German Counterattack

At 7:30 that evening the Germans launched a second determined counterattack, this time against the most forward Allied position, the tiny

Canadian salient at Hallu. Here the 78th Winnipeg Grenadiers had occupied the western outskirts of the hamlet, in the middle of the 1916 German defensive line. On their right was the 50th Calgary Battalion. Two battalions of the Alpine Corps attacked from the north against the left flank of the 78th. While his forward companies in the salient were under heavy attack, the 78th's commanding officer found his headquarters in Chilly about to be overrun by swarms of Germans only 150 yards away. "I immediately organized my battalion Headquarters staff and engaged the enemy from then until dusk when he was forced to withdraw," reported the War Diary in colourless prose. "Lieutenant Kilborn carried out a successful flanking attack during which time the enemy was being checked in front by drummers, runners, signalers, pioneers, and scouts, etc." After this counterattack had been beaten off night descended, the stillness broken by sporadic rifle-fire and the explosions of grenades. Still no word had been heard from the companies holding the salient. Finally at 10:00 that night the long-awaited message arrived from Major Linnell: "I have taken all precautions possible to protect the flanks of my positions.... Everyone here have their tails up and on no account shall we retire from our present positions."

THE AIR OFFENSIVE

On Saturday, the third day of the offensive, the RAF threw ninety additional planes into the fray. This brought the total concentration of British single-seater fighters to 480 — an incredible 70 percent of RAF fighter strength on the Western Front. Nevertheless, the attacks on the Somme bridges tapered off. Only two raids were launched, both by one squadron, which attempted to hit the bridges at St. Christ from twelve thousand feet. For the first time in the offensive the RAF turned to German rail communications. This morning the stations at Peronne and Equancourt were attacked. Few hits were registered as the bombs were dropped from twelve thousand feet and German fighters resisted fiercely. A savage dogfight ensued above Peronne, where once again the Fokker proved to be the superior plane. Here the Germans lost one aircraft while the RAF suffered one bomber and four fighters shot down in German territory and another fighter written off after it had limped back to its base.

During the day ground support squadrons kept up a wearying succession of patrols. At 1:15 p.m. Bill Lambert, an American serving with "C" Flight, 24 Squadron, was flying his third patrol of the day in his fighter, "Number 8395." Along with eleven other S.E.5s, Lambert was jumped by eighteen German fighters.

> Most of them overshoot us in their first dive. The members of "C" Flight separate and so do the Germans. It is a question now of every man for himself.... Nose down and swing right to get behind that golden D.VII. He is leaving me. More throttle, nose down more and we close the gap. I try to fix him in my Aldis [gunsight] and push the stick farther forward. About 100 yards between us. I push the throttle full forward. We are closing; almost ready now.... My thumb presses the button. Both guns fire and what they threw out was enough. The D.VII goes into the craziest manoeuvre, its nose well down with the tail waving up and down ... he heads for the ground with tail still waving....
>
> The others are 3,000 or 4,000 feet above me and scattered all around in a terrific fight.... I climb as fast as possible.... A smoking Albatross suddenly dives past me about 20 yards away... I reach the scrap above which is hectic. The Germans are everywhere, in some cases, two after one S.E.5.
>
> Something hits me from the rear. I turn in my seat and am looking at the red nose of an Albatross at about 100 yards. Down goes 8395 as I ram my throttle full front preparatory to pulling up for a climbing right turn to get above and behind him. He does the same but ends up off my tail and two other S.E.5's are after him like hawks....
>
> A Hannover is busy with an S.E.5 above and to the left front of him. I push my nose up to get above and to his right as the other S.E. dives from the top left with both guns flaming. The Hannover observer and his pilot are both concentrating on that S.E. and do not see me.... My range is about 30 yards.... I press the button and fire about 50 rounds from each gun. The observer jerks up in his cockpit, drops his gun and falls down out of sight. The aircraft falls to the left in a side-slip for a few hundred feet then into a spin to the ground. It hits with a terrific burst of flame and smoke. A second later I see

two sets of black crosses falling through the sky with
heavy smoke trailing behind. They, too, hit the ground.
Someone is doing a good job.[233]

The Germans received the worst of this dogfight. Lambert and his
eleven comrades headed home only slightly the worse for wear; the
German Air Service was now seven fewer.

Number 8 Squadron, the Tank Support Force, had an active day
once again despite the shortage of tanks. Captain Ferdinand Maurice
Felix West, formerly of the Royal Munster Fusiliers, flew one such tank
contact patrol over Rosières. West and his observer, Lieutenant Haslam,
had already shared several adventures. On the 8th, their plane was one of
the first up to fly through the fog and return to report. Unfortunately,
they had crash-landed at their fog-bound aerodrome and both suffered
minor injuries. Then yesterday they scattered a force of enemy infantry
surrounding four tanks. Again West and Haslam suffered the
consequences when their engine was put out of commission by ground
fire, and they had barely made it back into the front lines.

Now West spotted movement near Roye, a good eight thousand
yards away in German-held territory. Without a pause he swooped in and
shot up the enemy convoy he had discovered. As he turned the lone
Armstrong-Whitworth it was attacked by seven enemy aircraft. Their first
bursts hit West in the left leg above the knee with an explosive bullet. The
leg flopped down around the control lever while blood spurted from the
severed femoral artery. West was forced to reach down and remove his leg
from the controls. Meanwhile Lieutenant Haslam, also wounded, kept up
a steady fire on their pursuers. Now West suffered a second wound, in his
right foot, but managed to retain consciousness and manoeuvre adroitly
enough for Haslam to drive off their assailants. Somehow West contrived
to fly his battered machine back to the British lines where he safely
landed before passing out. On regaining consciousness Captain West
insisted on writing his own report. He was awarded a well-deserved
Victoria Cross for his devotion, courage, and endurance.

That evening Bill Lambert and the rest of 24 Squadron's "C" Flight
took off on their fourth patrol of the day. Not an enemy aircraft was to be
seen. Their "joy-ride" ended at 8:30, and the tired but jubilant pilots at
last found time to celebrate their seven victories.

While "C" Flight celebrated, other planes were taking off. These were
the night bombers. The areas around the Somme bridges were to receive
another scattering of bombs, although the intensity was beginning to wane.

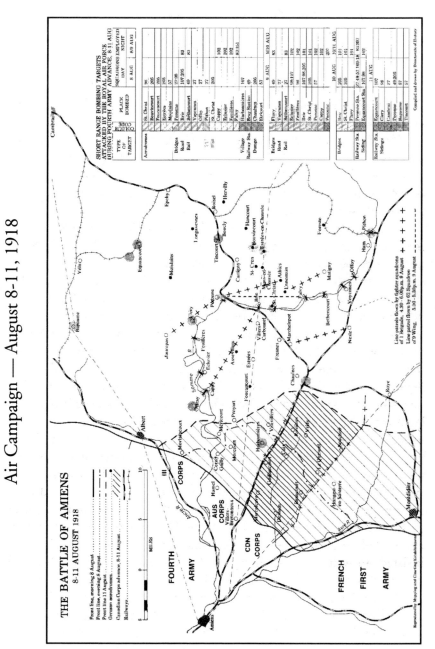

S.F. Wise, *Canadian Airmen and the First World War. The Official History of the Royal Canadian Air Force*, vol. 1, Toronto, University of Toronto Press, Department of National Defence and Canadian Government Publishing Centre, Supply and Services Canada, 1980. Courtesy of Minister of Public Works and Government Services

The railway station at Peronne was the target of two hundred bombs, mostly 112-pounders. These were dropped from six thousand feet, and, in some cases, from as low as one thousand feet, but there were few hits.

Today, August 10, was a red-letter day for the German Air Service as the news of Loewenhardt's recent victories was trumpeted in the press to encourage the flagging patriotism of the masses. Meanwhile he and Lothar von Richthofen took ten beginners up to gain experience. They managed to avoid a formation of S.E.5s and eventually found a lone Sopwith Camel piloted by Lieutenant M.A. Toomey of their old rivals, 209 Squadron, RAF. Loewenhardt signaled the others to follow him down and "watch the master at work." They did so and observed as the lone Camel started to smoke and go into a steep dive. From above, Lothar von Richthofen realized that one of the beginners was following too close. "At about the same moment — what's that! Loewenhardt is no longer flying behind the falling Englishman; instead there is a wild confusion of thousands of splinters!" reported von Richthofen. "It is immediately clear — Loewenhardt has been rammed!"[234] From the falling planes two figures dropped at the end of parachutes, but one failed to open and its wearer plummeted towards earth. Toomey slipped away to fly his battered Camel home. Loewenhardt was not so lucky, for it had been the beginner's parachute that had opened. The ace fell near Chaulnes where heavy ground fighting was taking place. His body was not recovered for a week.

The Australian Night-Attack

Saturday, August 10, saw the first nighttime operation carried out by either side. On this night a truly remarkable manoeuvre was to be attempted by the Australians. "The German," General Monash declared, "is in a condition of great confusion, and we have only to hit him without warning and roll him up." The plan was for infantry, preceded by tanks, to cut through the enemy line in two places — one either side of the Somme — and advance along parallel roads almost eight thousand yards apart. Then each column would wheel inwards and advance to meet on opposite banks of the river. A square would thus be cut out of the German line astride the Somme. The 13th Brigade north of the Somme was to penetrate along the Bray-Corbie Road. South of the Somme the 10th Brigade would advance along the Roman Road towards La Flaque. The Diggers were not enthused. "Someone's confidence had overreached itself," the War Diary of the 37th Victorians noted acidly.

Their battalion had been chosen to lead the infantry along the Roman Road. "The opinion of the front line soldier was that the enterprise was ridiculous and stupid."

Captain Hickey of the 8th Tanks was to head the advance along the Roman Road. He too was astounded. "Zero hour was fixed for half-past nine that night.... This meant that the tanks had to do the 'Approach March' in broad daylight, a breach of the first principles of tank warfare."[235] To make matters worse, a cursory inspection of the ground ruled out the instructions issued for the tanks to proceed with one on the road and one on each side in the fields. The "fields" were crisscrossed with old trenches and earthworks and dotted with huts and supply dumps. There was even a railway spur to cross. The tanks would have to advance in single file along the Roman Road devoid of cover. "As far as I could see, the only way to get over this difficulty was to adopt the method used in night 'Approach Marches,'" observed Hickey. "On such occasions a man walked in front picking out the way and guiding the tank by the glow of a cigarette. But this suggestion was greeted with the remark, 'Who would supply the cigarettes?'"[236]

The purpose of the tanks was later explained by Monash: "It was thought that the effect of the noise they made would lead to the speedy collapse of the defence."[237] The officers of the 10th Brigade, however, viewed the tanks' involvement differently, being extremely anxious lest their clamour warn the enemy and bring fire down on the unprotected infantry advancing along the arrow-straight road behind them.

North of the Somme where the advance would start off from the cover of Gressaire Wood there was less apprehension. Brigadier Herring ordered that the tanks "were only to go up and down the road and make a noise and overawe the Germans — they could fire a few grape-shot down the road on the first trip." There were actually two parallel roads to be used north of the Somme. The 49th Queensland was to advance only after two tanks from the 2nd Tank Battalion had set off on their decoy run up the Bray-Corbie Road. Approximately half a mile south, on a minor road nearly parallel to the former, the 50th South Australian Battalion would advance — also with a tank, it was hoped. The 50th would be supported by one company of the 51st. Both battalions would hook south after advancing approximately two thousand yards, and the 50th would press on to occupy the heights above the Somme where it curled south between Etinehem and Bray.

The advance north of the Somme began sharp at 9:30 along the Bray-Corbie Road, but the two Mark Vs soon left the Diggers behind. In the distance they could be heard shooting up the German defenders, mainly young replacements of the 119th Reserve Infantry Regiment (26th Reserve Division). The 119th's War Diary records what happened:

> The black monsters slowly rolled along the road towards us, spewing fire to front and flank. Out of the loophole and slits broke the bands of light from the electric lights inside, and gave the machine guns good targets. The tanks were taken under fire with steel bullets by two heavy and several light machine guns of the 2nd Battalion. The impact of their bullets struck bright sparks from the armour, which was strong enough to resist them, but the crew was uncannily able to overcome this sinister drumming on the steel walls, and extinguished the lights to make the aim more difficult. As the tanks came ever nearer and did not allow themselves to be held up, a small part of the 7th Company was seized by tank-panic and ran back. Only one platoon maintained its valiant stand in common with the 8th Company.... The troops crept away, as the monsters approached their shelter pits, and let them drive by.... The two tanks drove on to Bray, one right up to the eastern edge of the little town; but when they found no opposition anywhere and marked their separation from the infantry they turned round and drove back.[238]

A golden opportunity had presented itself. The two tanks, playing only the role of decoys, had succeeded far beyond anyone's wildest dreams. In the words of the historian of the German 27th Division charged with defending the road, "in the dark our anti-tank gunners could not fire, and panic overcame the troops — for the sake of truth it must be plainly said — and the road through Bray lay open to the enemy."[239] Divisional Headquarters at Curlu, five miles east of Bray, prepared for a last-ditch stand against an Allied attack. But the Bray-Corbie Road again lay deserted in the pale moonlight.

Meanwhile the two Australian infantry battalions had carried out their manoeuvres with little opposition from the fleeing Germans. One post was captured single-handedly by Private A.V. Hockey, of Toowoomba. He killed two and captured five quaking teenagers, terrified on learning their captors were Australian. By midnight the Australians were digging in on the Etinehem Spur. Now the 49th and 50th lay in position facing parallel to the former front line, which was almost two thousand yards behind. The company of the 51st had dug in across the roads leading east out of Etinehem. At dawn it would sweep down on the village, now cut off by the new line, and bag its entire three hundred-man garrison. Everyone hoped that the amazing operation had been equally successful south of the Somme.

Shortly after nightfall three Mark Vs of the 8th Tanks and the men of the 37th Victorian Battalion had begun their advance along the Roman Road towards La Flaque. A former school teacher, Lieutenant N.G. McNicol, now the Intelligence Officer of the 37th, led the way with several scouts and the only map. They were followed by three roaring Mark Vs making a tremendous din as they clattered along the cobblestones. Then in a twenty-five yard gap before the 37th, which was advancing in single file, came Lieutenant-Colonel Knox-Knight of the 37th and the twenty-three-year old Captain Hickey, student turned tank officer. The Australian colonel grimly remarked, "There will be a train-load of V.C.'s waiting for us when we get back if it's a success." Then he added, "but we won't want them — if we get through with our lives."[240]

Wrote Hickey:

> When we got to La Flaque darkness had fallen. We were all keyed up, expecting opposition at this point. But, to our surprise, we met with none. The colonel and I wondered if the enemy had withdrawn his line to a point further back, or if the tanks had been observed moving up in the daylight, and he was laying a trap for us. The night sky in front looked peaceful and calm. If the enemy were holding a line at this point is seemed impossible that he should be unaware of our presence, for the clatter of the tanks on the hard road rent the stillness of the night. About a quarter of a mile beyond La Flaque we heard above the noise of the tanks the roar of a plane overhead. Suddenly there was a downward whizz, a blinding flash and then a terrific explosion. The unditching-beam of the rear tank — about ten yards away — flew up into the air and crashed back.... The bomb had exploded on impact, and the unditching beam, resting loosely on top of the tank, had taken the force of the explosion....

As luck would have it, this was exactly the spot where the enemy was holding his line and had a strong-point in a large dump at the side of the road. Other bombs fell. The noise of the bombing-plane had up to this moment drowned the clatter of the tanks, but now the enemy was alarmed. He at once put up flares that made the night as bright as day. In the ghastly light we could see the poplars and the hedges along the road. Then hell was let loose! A withering machine gun fire was opened on the tanks. The infantry following close behind, being swept by it, took cover in the ditch on the south side of the road. The tanks replied with their six-pounders and machine guns, but without effect, for no targets could be seen.... In short rushes the infantry continued to advance. The enemy had now got his artillery to bear on us, and shells began to explode in the road and on either side of it. The noise was terrific. Machine gun bullets cracked all round like a thousand whips. A War Correspondent, who was in a position to have a full view, described how one of the tanks was lit up like a blacksmith's fire by the quantity of bullets striking it.[241]

After half an hour of this the enemy fire died down and the tanks halted. Two tank officers had become casualties, one badly wounded and one missing. Nearly all the crew members had also been wounded. "The tanks started to move again," recalled Hickey.

Immediately there was a hurricane of machine gun fire, and again we took cover. The night was pitch-black, except for occasional flares. The infantry advancing in short rushes along the side of the road were being mown down like grass, and lay where they fell. At this moment a runner reported that the tanks were returning. "They haven't got orders to turn, have they?" the Colonel asked me in amazement. I was equally staggered, and replied, "Certainly not! I'll go at once and tell them to keep straight on." "Yes, you must," he answered, and standing erect, urged the infantry on. As I made a dive forward with my runner in a hailstorm of bullets, I heard a choking gasp and saw the Colonel fall heavily to the ground, two feet away from me. While we ran the few yards to the tanks my runner's pack stopped a bullet....

Getting the tanks to go forward again was no easy job. I began with the rear tank, and had to batter on the front with my stick to attract the attention of the officer inside. It was like trying to turn a car in a narrow road, and there was a good deal of manoeuvring and reversing and shouting.... Then all at once I found I was about to be jammed between the two tanks as they struggled to get turned round. Frantically I scrambled up the back of one of them.[242]

While Hickey scrambled for his life his runner, Gunner Stittle, went gone forward to straighten out the first tank. He found that its officer, Lieutenant Jeffries, had vanished while outside. All but two of the crew were wounded, and "H-24" was badly perforated by armour-piercing bullets. "I happened to be standing in front of the leading tank when along comes an Australian officer brandishing his revolver and threatening me with my life if the tanks so much as moved," wrote Stittle years later.

I explained who I was, but it made no difference. He said, "I put you in charge, and if these tanks move you will be shot." His point was that we were drawing the enemy fire. I often wonder if he ever returned to cover as, no sooner had he left me than it started to rain bullets all round, and turning one side of the tank in front of which I was standing into a glorified pepper-box.[243]

The attack was degenerating into disaster and there appeared to be no chance of retrieving victory. Hickey gave the order for his tanks to retire.

Again I had the same difficulty turning them. I felt rather like a wild animal tamer with huge beasts to control. In the dark the tank crews could not easily understand my directions nor hear my voice above the noise. Every time the tanks moved, the enemy machine guns simply went mad, and there was a terrific fusilade of bullets. The tanks had moved back about 150 yards when I found a revolver being brandished in my face.[244]

The revolver was held by an Australian officer leading the reserves. Hickey ordered his tanks to stop, and a conference was held in the middle of the road under heavy fire. It was obviously useless to push the reserves forward. These, marching in fours, stretched almost two miles along the road, first the 38th Battalion followed by the 40th and the 39th. Three more tanks accompanied them. This column had not escaped injury. The German airplane, "almost brushing the avenue, had dropped bombs along it, one bursting on a waggon following the 40th Battalion with Stokes mortar shells. Animals and drivers were here strewn over the roadway."[245]

It was decided that the infantry must withdraw first. In the tense silence the tanks sat motionless, well behind German lines, as the infantry slipped back along the Roman Road. "All the time we were on the *qui-vive* in case the enemy should surround us," wrote Hickey who stayed with his tanks. "Owing to the darkness, concerted action by the tanks would be impossible, and we should be in a predicament without infantry support.

"At last a runner reported: 'All clear!'

"A hail of bullets sped the departing tanks, as at 3:45 in the morning, they took leave of the enemy after spending five-and-a-half hours in his company."[246]

The 232nd Reserve Infantry Regiment, which held the road, little realized the extent of the defeat it had inflicted. The unit's War Diary merely comments: "About midnight [*sic*] the enemy attacked on the Roman Road. In the light of flares three tanks were detected, followed by infantry in close order. The 8th Company, by machine gun fire, caused the enemy great losses and compelled him to retire."[247] The Allied losses had been severe among the forward elements. The three tanks lost three officers and nineteen men; the 37th lost three officers and 103 men. Although the northern portion of Monash's night attack had gone well, the southern operation had been a complete failure. Only dawn would tell if this miscarriage would have dire consequences for the 13th Brigade now isolated on the Etinehem Spur on the north bank of the Somme.

Command Decisions

Saturday, August 10, had been a busy day for the generals. Sir Douglas Haig had that morning sent a staff officer to General Horne of the First Army with instructions to complete the planning already well in hand for an offensive in conjunction with the Second and Third armies. Shortly after, at 11:00, Marshal Foch arrived at Haig's headquarters in Wiry. "He wishes the advance to continue on the line Noyon-Ham-Peronne, and to try to get the bridgeheads on the Somme," wrote Sir Douglas. "I pointed out the difficulty of the undertaking unless the enemy is quite demoralized, and we can cross the Somme on his heels.... In Foch's opinion the fact that the French First Army's getting on without meeting with serious opposition shows the enemy is demoralized. I agree that some German divisions are demoralized, but not all yet."[248]

Against Foch's desire for continued frontal attacks, Haig proposed switching the offensive to the British Third Army farther north. Foch, however, was not interested; he was convinced that the enemy was so demoralized that the Amiens offensive should be pressed on. And so, in accordance with the Generalissimo's directives, Haig issued orders to the Fourth Army and the French First Army to continue the frontal attacks.

After lunch, Haig paid a rare visit to Canadian Corps Headquarters, now moved forward to some dugouts in a hill near Demuin. There he met with Currie and Rawlinson. The latter was emphatic that further attacks on his Fourth Army's front would only waste lives. When Haig explained that this was the wish of the supreme commander, "Rawly the Fox" exploded, and in the words of the British Official History "became almost insubordinate and replied, 'Are you commanding the British Army or is *Marechal* Foch?'" At this juncture a message arrived from the Cavalry Corps' General Kavanagh. It was timed 2:25 p.m., and claimed that enemy opposition was diminishing. Just how little it had diminished could have been described by the survivors of the Fort Garry Horse if they had been asked. The result of Kavanagh's message was to destroy the arguments put forward by Rawlinson and Currie. The offensive would continue.

Sir Douglas next ventured forward to visit various divisional headquarters. It was nearly 6:00 when he reached Le Quesnel to hear a very pessimistic report from General Lambert of the 32nd Division, who had just returned from visiting his brigades. Lambert stressed the facts — enemy resistance was stiffening, and the old Somme battlefield favoured the defence. Haig was convinced. Nevertheless, his earlier orders remained; the offensive was to continue tomorrow, Sunday, August 11th. Rawlinson reluctantly ordered Fourth Army "to press on to the Somme between Ham (exclusive) and Peronne and establish bridgeheads on the right bank of the river." The Cavalry Corps was to spearhead the Canadian advance. General Debeney's orders to the French First Army were similar and included unrealistic instructions for II Cavalry Corps to "seek the opportunity to advance in front of the infantry." As on previous days, zero hour was to be decided by the Canadian Corps. Currie chose 4:20 a.m. When these orders reached General Kavanagh at Cavalry Corps Headquarters he sent a staff officer posthaste to Rawlinson to protest his corps' role, stressing that "the enemy's resistance was now very strong and that the ground over which the proposed advance was to be made was quite impassable for cavalry in any large numbers."[249] It was ironic that Kavanagh's earlier message stressing the optimistic view was one of the main reasons for the orders he was now protesting.

THE GERMANS

The Germans had continued to bring up reinforcements throughout Saturday. Four fresh divisions had joined von der Marwitz's command — the 38th, the 121st, the 221st, and the Alpine Corps, All these were inserted facing the Canadian Corps, which had only two divisions in line — the 32nd Imperial and the 4th Canadian. These new German divisions had received little or no briefing, but they had been fortunate in being assigned an area that was in itself a major obstacle — the 1916 lines. They now occupied a three-mile swath of old trenches concealed by long grass and weeds. Despite this gift of fortune, the scenes encountered by the new-comers had been demoralizing. The 94th Infantry Regiment had arrived near Chalnes to discover troops "falling back in disorderly flight, among them drunken Bavarians, who shouted ... 'What do you war-prolongers want? If the enemy were only on the Rhine — then the war would be over.'"[250]

CHAPTER THIRTEEN
FOR GOD'S SAKE STOP

"We all saw it, we all shouted, 'For God's sake stop! Don't push us any farther, we'll get smashed. Take us out. We're still fresh, we'll fight better somewhere else."
Major M.A. Pope, The Canadian Engineers[251]

THE FRENCH FIRST AND THIRD ARMIES

As dawn broke on Sunday, August 11, a thick ground-mist covered the battlefield. The only formations to advance at 4:20, the chosen zero hour, were the divisions of the French First and Third armies. Their advance was made against moderate opposition, except on their northern flank beside the Canadians where the 126th Division was stopped cold by German fire. Along the rest of the front advances of one and a half miles were made by nightfall.

THE CANADIAN CORPS

Once again the spearhead of the offensive, the Canadian Corps, ran into the usual timetable problems. It soon became evident that the tanks detailed to assist the 32nd Division would never be able to make it forward in time. Therefore, zero hour was rescheduled first for 8:30 and finally for 9:30. A message to this effect failed to reach the French 126th Division on the right resulting in the complete failure of its attack on "Z Wood."

As the August sun warmed the land the mist evaporated and the day became hot and dusty. When the men of the 1st Dorsets, 5th/6th Royal Scots, and 2nd King's Own Yorkshire Light Infantry jumped off at 9:30 they found that everything had gone wrong. Z Wood on their right had not been taken by the French, and they were enfiladed on their approach; their own artillery was firing two hundred yards beyond the German machine guns; and a waist-high belt of wire thirty to fifty feet wide blocked their advance. Of the sixteen tanks supplied by the 4th and 5th Tank Battalions twelve were soon knocked out. The terrific fire that poured from the German line prevented the Tommies from achieving more than a short advance. By 11:00 the Dorsets had made it to within one hundred yards of the village of Damery. Elsewhere the advance was negligible.

Meanwhile Major-General Lambert had received a message from Currie. It instructed him not to press strongly if it would entail heavy casualties. These instructions had originated with Rawlinson. As a result, the 32nd Imperial Division dug in on its newly won one-thousand-yard strip of ground in front of Damery. The division had in the last two days made two very slight advances at the cost of 1,748 casualties.

On the 4th Canadian Division's front the attack never took place — because the enemy launched their own first. The German objective was the salient at Hallu. The attackers were men of the crack Alpine Corps (actually a division), which had arrived yesterday amid scenes of utmost confusion. These disciplined troops had been scandalized by the demoralization they had witnessed, but their own performance had not been affected. The Corps, easily identified by its dark green uniform, threw wave after wave at the beleaguered garrison made up of the 78th Winnipeg Grenadiers and the 50th Calgary Battalion.

Both Canadian battalions were savagely mauled by the waves of attackers in what turned out to be the fiercest fighting of the Battle of Amiens. The Canucks' defence was severely hampered by their own artillery, which fired upon their positions in the village. S.O.S. signals to the artillery failed to get through, but Major Linnell hung on and requested reinforcements. At 11:45 the reply was finally received from Battalion Headquarters: "We have no reinforcements. You must fight every foot, and if you are forced to retire you can fall back on the line of the railway." But Major Linnell never read this disheartening message. He had been killed at his post. Finally, after beating off the third counterattack by the green-clad enemy, the decimated companies were ordered to withdraw from the village to the railway embankment west of it. At this juncture the enemy in turn was driven from Hallu by Canadian artillery fire. Brigadier MacBrien's plan to retake the village was overruled by Rawlinson himself who felt it was not practical to hold on to such an exposed position. The battle for the Hallu salient had cost the 50th and 78th heavily, the Calgarians alone losing 252. The Alpine Corps had also suffered crippling losses, and two days later this elite division reported its strength as "at best barely 300 fighters of all ranks."[252]

During Sunday, all along the 4th Canadian Division's front, a series of small chaotic fights took place in long-abandoned trenches and over the pitted, weed-covered ground. Increasing artillery fire and concentrations of machine guns prevented either side from mounting any further large-scale attacks. The spearhead of the Amiens offensive had been imbedded in the old Somme battlefield.

THE AUSTRALIAN CORPS

The Australian Corps had a better day than the Canadians. At 4:00 a.m., soon after the ground-mist had materialized, the 1st Australian Division commenced its advance with the 8th Victorian Battalion leading on the right, and assorted companies from the 10th, 11th, and 12th battalions leading the 3rd Brigade on the left. Nine Mark Vs of the 2nd Tank Battalion had been made available, but the ground-mist slowed them down, and six were several minutes late, with the remaining three only appearing an hour after zero. Although none were put out of action by enemy fire, seven suffered mechanical breakdowns.

The advance swept forward in the south where the 1st Australian Division overran the Germans at their breakfasts. There was little organized resistance, the greatest problem being several isolated posts bypassed in the mist. By 6:00 a.m. the Diggers had taken Lihons and Auger Wood, and most objectives had been reached. The fog, however, had caused numerous gaps in the line and even greater gaps in communications. Many companies were virtually isolated. Around 5:30 a German scout plane had dared the mist, swooping low along the Australian line, firing flares to mark the new-found targets. Soon after, both Crepey and Auger Woods were deluged with gas shells. Suddenly out of the fog swarmed German infantry! Converging from the north and from the rear were units of the newly arrived 5th Bavarian Division. Obviously, a large gap existed between the two Australian divisions. Three times the Bavarians attacked before being driven off for good.

North of Auger Wood *feldgrau* of the 38th Division were attacking the 11th Western Australians. At one point they broke through the Australian line, but with the help of trench mortars and the 10th South Australian Battalion the position was restored and consolidated. But the Germans had not given up; at 1:20 another serious attack was launched behind a barrage. After it was driven off the afternoon settled down to a deadly duel between infiltrating Germans and the entrenched Australians — the reverse of what had been happening for the last three days. Nevertheless Lihons Hill and northward was firmly held by the Diggers who were now in fact five hundred yards ahead of the Canadian left flank.

The 2nd Australian Division also advanced, but against very light opposition. At 5:00 a.m., an hour after commencing, the four leading battalions reported themselves in position with a defensive flank thrown back on their left to the 3rd Australian Division just west of Proyart. Despite constant sniping, these Aussies were able to settle down and enjoy a relatively quiet day along with the 3rd Australian Division, which was licking its wounds from last night's fiasco.

North of the Somme there was little action although the 5th Division troops who had taken part in the successful portion of the previous night's cutting-out operation made some disconcerting discoveries. First, the 50th South Australians discovered that they had not pushed far enough south. They were *not* in possession of the entire Etinehem peninsula; Germans still clung to the lower slopes that plunged down to the Somme. Secondly, they discovered that the 10th Brigade had failed in its share of the attack, and that they themselves were badly enfiladed by the Germans on the south side of the Somme. This was indeed a switch from the three previous days. A defensive flank had to be formed by two companies. The 51st provided one. The 131st Illinois, now bleary-eyed, hungry men who had forgotten such luxuries as sleep, supplied the other.

Meanwhile, at daybreak the company of the 51st, waiting astride the roads from Etinehem, had launched its attack into the village. It was disappointingly anti-climactic; instead of the "300 Huns" they had been promised only one badly frightened *feldgrau* was discovered. The enemy, it turned out, had utilized a partially destroyed footbridge to evacuate to the southern side of the Somme. The Germans' local commander had, in his own words, decided against "playing a futile Leonidas stunt."[253] There would be no German Thermopylae at Etinehem.

There was a final surprise for the Diggers facing Bray. Field-grey columns could be seen filing into that silent town from the east. Only then was it realized that Bray had been abandoned during last night's "tank panic." An Australian barrage soon sent the new occupants back out, but this, everyone knew, was only temporary.

By afternoon the Australian front had grown deceptively quiet. But the day's fighting was not yet over; the 3rd Division still had last night's humiliating defeat to avenge. At 7:30 that evening the division commenced another operation to pinch off the German garrison in the spur on the southern bank of the Somme northeast of Mericourt. Two standing barrages, parallel and a few yards apart, would stretch from the Australian line in a northeasterly direction straight to the Somme. Down this corridor would march the 41st Queensland Battalion following a creeping barrage. Each company was to stop after an interval and prepare to meet the Germans who would surely be retreating towards them.

The plan was more impressive than the reality. When 7:30 came — still broad daylight — the barrages began. They were so thin and feeble, however, that they served only to alert the Germans who were preparing to evacuate. A smoke barrage did, however, screen the companies of the 41st when they commenced their advance. Vickers machine-gun fire and the assistance of trench mortars made up in part for the feeble barrages. Consequently, at 9:15 at a loss of only seventy-four casualties, the 41st had rounded up almost four hundred prisoners. As it turned out, this little operation was the final blow of the Amiens offensive.

THE AIR OFFENSIVE

Throughout Sunday, the 11th of August, the air offensive continued above the battlefield, although with much lower intensity. The static nature of most of the day's isolated ground battles had made strafing less practical and more costly. The Royal Air Force's bomber offensive had also changed in character. It had become obvious to all except the Supreme Commander that the Amiens offensive had run down, and there would be little chance of pinning the German Second Army against the River Somme. Secondly, it was equally obvious that RAF attempts to hit the bridges had been a total failure. These operations were now suspended, and railway stations became the new target — a belated attempt to disrupt the arrival of reinforcements. Railyards at Perrone and Cambrai were twice bombed with several hits being registered. However, German fighters disrupted a third attack on Equancourt station and two of the bombers were shot down.

On Sunday, Lothar von Richthofen led the Flying Circus up without Loewenhardt, whose body still lay unclaimed in a field near Chaulnes.

Although von Richthofen shot down his 38th victim, it was in a losing cause as the Circus lost three. That night it was decided to merge the once supreme Flying Circus with several other depleted units and condense the whole into one *Staffel.*

THE DECISION-MAKERS

All that day, there had been developing a kind of passive resistance to the wishes of the Supreme Commander, Marshal Foch. The front-line soldier realized that the situation had changed and he had become more cautious, more deliberate. Some of those who commanded also understood. "I was sitting in a field, on a kitchen chair, having my hair cut when along came General Currie," recalled Brigadier J.A. Clark (7th Canadian Brigade) who spoke frankly to his Corps Commander. "We could be taken out of this line and put in somewhere where we could effect a surprise as we did on the 8th of August. We're in wonderful shape to continue the fighting, but to fight here will break the spirit or our men, to be asked to drive themselves against these defences."

"I agree," replied Currie, "and I'm telling you confidentially that I have just recommended to the Higher Command that we should not be asked to go on here."[254]

But Sir Douglas Haig had already begun to resist Foch's enthusiasm. During the morning he had visited Australian Headquarters at Bertangles where General Julian Byng of the Third Army also arrived by appointment. Haig instructed Byng to prepare his Third Army for an immediate offensive to outflank the enemy in the north. Next, Haig visited III Corps Headquarters two miles farther north at Villers-Bocage. From here it was on to visit the five Australian divisions and finally Ralwinson at his Fourth Army Headquarters at Villers-Bretonneux. After his visit with "Rawly the Fox," Sir Douglas returned to his train where Foch himself was scheduled to arrive at 10:00 that night.

After Haig's visit, Rawlinson called a conference of all Corps Commanders. The facts were simple enough: The Germans had been reinforced; they now occupied a particularly strong position; the country that lay ahead was difficult for infantry and impossible for tanks and cavalry; the enemy had decided to defend himself in his present position; sixteen Allied divisions (thirteen infantry and three cavalry) had engaged twenty-four German divisions;[255] the troops were now exhausted; tanks and crews were severely depleted; heavy artillery support had been impossible to

Day Three —
August 10

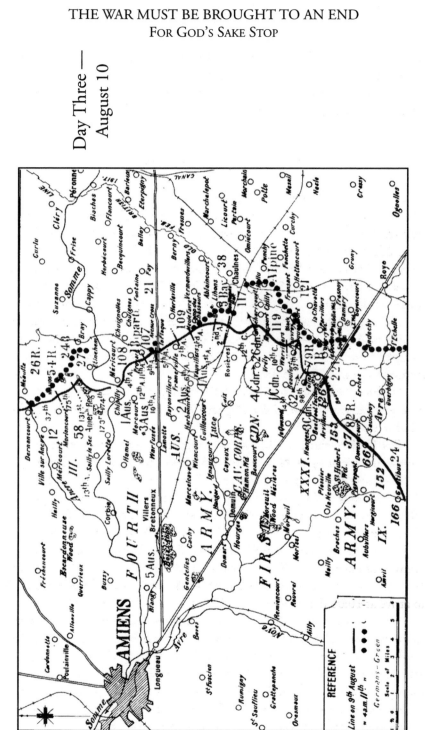

Sir James Edmond, Military Operations France and Belgium, 1918. London,
HM Stationary Office, 1947, sketch 7.

maintain because of transportation problems. It all made only one decision possible: the Amiens offensive must be discontinued — "for the moment."

The French too had halted their operations, although ostensibly for different reasons. The Battle of Montdidier, as their part in the offensive is now known, was "temporarily" halted to reorganize the First Army. Resumption of the attack was postponed to the 13th, then the 15th, 16th, and finally to "*une date ulterieure.*"

Late that night the Supreme Commander arrived at Haig's train. Foch still had hopes of the Fourth Army reaching the Somme, but these he now downplayed. The fiery Generalissimo instead begged that a new offensive be launched as soon as possible on each flank. This Haig had already initiated by his instructions to Byng of the Third Army. The Battle of Amiens had unofficially come to an end.

THE GERMANS

Meanwhile, the German General Staff had reached an even more momentous decision. Although German wireless was at that moment ridiculing "the nervous anxiety of the Entente leadership to maintain the initiative and to intercept the dreaded new German attack," their leaders were meeting to discuss Germany's imminent collapse. The Kaiser had been summoned to Avesnes to hear Ludendorff's summation. "I had no hope of finding a strategic expedient whereby to turn the situation to our advantage," wrote Ludendorff later. "On the contrary ... leadership now assumed, as I then stated, the character of an irresponsible game of chance, a thing I have always considered fatal. The fate of the German people was for me too high a stake. The war must be ended."[256]

After this bombshell the Kaiser and the Crown Prince ventured the suggestion that possibly too much had been asked of the troops. This Ludendorff dismissed; "the collapse of the Second Army on the 8th August could not be accounted for by the divisions being overtired."[257] He then offered his resignation, but this was immediately rejected by Hindenburg.

Now after two years in "cloud cuckoo land," the Kaiser found himself called upon to make the critical decision. He appeared calm, according to Major Niemann, his liaison officer to OHL, but his features were taut, his brow was deeply furrowed, and his eyes burned with emotion. Kaiser Wilhelm II paused, then announced his historic decision. "I see we must balance the books, we are at the limit of our powers. The war must be brought to an end."[258]

CHAPTER FOURTEEN
THE BALANCE COMES TO REST

"I drew the conclusion that the balance had finally come to rest on the side of the Entente."
Ludendorff[259]

The effects of the Battle of Amiens on the morale of the German General Staff had been the decisive result of the clash; but what had been the actual physical effects upon the Second and Eighteenth armies? Total German casualties are difficult to estimate because many units were unable to keep records during those cataclysmic days. The most reliable figure appears to be that calculated by Brigadier Edmonds, the British official historian, who estimated German casualties at over 75,000. Although this figure is not astounding when compared to battles like the Somme or Verdun, it is high for a four-day battle. But the statistic which is most indicative of the state of the German Army is the number who surrendered — 29,873.

Losses in materiel had also been enormous. The first day alone had cost the German Army over 400 guns, and the final total was 499 — 240 by the Fourth Army and 259 taken by the two French armies (First and Third). Uncounted numbers of machine guns and mortars had been captured — probably over 2,000 of the former and 4,000 mortars. An incredible array of booty now lay in Allied hands, ranging from entire railway trains and storage dumps to a box containing 450 brand new Iron Crosses. Losses in men and equipment had been so severe as to eventually force the disbanding of three German divisions — the 108th, 109th, and 43rd Reserve.

Allied casualties had been heavy, but by Great War standards, not severe. The British official historian calculated the total loss to the Fourth Army as 22,202 (omitting casualties suffered by the Tank Corps and the Royal Air Force). Of these casualties, the Canadian Corps suffered by far the highest number — 9,074, followed by III Corps with 6,250, the Australians with 5,991, and the Cavalry Corps with 887 casualties — and over 1,800 horses. Losses incurred by the two French Armies totaled 24,343, with the First Army bearing the brunt (13,982).

The battlefield east of Amiens was also littered with the blackened remains of burnt-out tanks — Mark Vs, Mark V*s, and Whippets. The losses inflicted upon the British Tank Corps had been severe. A total of 688 tanks had been in action during the four days of battle. Of these, 480 were handed over to the salvage crews who moved up to clear the recent fields of battle. This loss amounted to a stunning 70 percent of the force employed. Nearly all of the remaining 208 vehicles were badly in need of overhaul.

This enormous tank wastage was felt by the British throughout the last three months of the war. By August 12 there were only 210 tanks not requiring overhaul. This small number included one battalion of forty-two Mark Vs just out from England and two battalions each of forty-one old Mark IVs. One other tank battalion arrived later in the year, but it was too untrained ever to go into action. Because the machines and crews lost there could never be replaced, the Battle of Amiens was to be the last concentrated use of tanks in the Great War.

The actual performance of the tanks at Amiens has not been publicized as much as has their effect on morale. Amiens revealed that both the Mark V and the Whippet were too slow for mobile warfare. In open country in broad daylight, they became merely excellent targets. On August 8, 20 percent of the tanks employed were destroyed; on the second day 30 percent; on the third day 50 percent were knocked out. Infantry losses did not mount accordingly. The Canadian Corps, which provided the spearhead of the offensive, actually lost less each succeeding day. To protect the tank after August 8 there was no fog, no darkness, and no surprise. From being the hunter on the first day, the tank had become the hunted by day two. Tactics would have to be developed by the infantry, by the artillery employing smoke, by the air forces in close support, and by the tankmen themselves to solve this grave new problem. In the three months that remained till the end of the war, few developments were made to protect the now-vulnerable tank. It had helped to break the stalemate of trench war — the role first envisioned for the tank — but in open warfare it had proven to be woefully vulnerable to artillery. Nevertheless, its reputation had been made, and till the war's end the tank exerted a psychological effect out of all proportion to its strategic or even tactical effects.

The German General Staff in its demoralized state seized upon the "massed employment of tanks" as the excuse for the defeat of their Second and Eighteenth armies at Amiens and Montdidier. In fact, the tanks had not been massed, but had been scattered primarily along the Fourth Army front to assist the infantry. The fog, moreover, had in many cases prevented the tanks from coming to grips with the Germans till after the infantry had subdued them. The fog had also served to protect the tanks from field guns sited to defend against them. The succeeding days showed how vulnerable the tanks were to this direct artillery fire. Nevertheless, the German High Command continued to use the tank as the primary excuse for their defeat.

This rationalization produced two unexpected consequences. Crediting the tanks for the Allied victory pushed into an unwelcome spotlight Ludendorff's earlier scorn for the weapon and OHL's failure to produce a tank force of its own. OHL hastily reclassified tanks into the "urgent" class of war production; but this move was much too late to be effective. However, this turnabout served to undermine even further the *feldgraus'* faith in their remote leaders.

The second consequence was more devastating. If tanks were an acceptable excuse for the High Command, then they were certainly justification for failures by those of humbler rank. Regimental officers soon accepted the idea that a tank attack absolved them from responsibility for the loss of any position entrusted to them. Their men went one step further and deduced that the mere presence of tanks excused them from resisting. As the British tank expert, J.F.C. Fuller pointed out, most captured German officers now explained their capture as inevitable. "The tanks had arrived, there was nothing to be done,"[260] became the standard rationalization.

In vain did officers like General von der Marwitz try to combat this justification of panic: "It passes all comprehension," states his order of August 25,

> that inconceivable rumours have been spread about
> behind the front during the last few days by people who
> have lost their nerve. People with anxious temperaments

see everywhere squadrons of tanks, masses of cavalry, and dense lines of enemy infantry. It is, in fact, high time that our old battle-tried soldiers spoke seriously to these cowards and weaklings, and told them of the deeds that are achieved in the front line. Tanks are no bogey for the front line troops who have artillery in close support. For instance, a battery-sergeant-major with his gun destroyed 4 tanks; one battery destroyed 14; and a single division in one day 40. In another instance, a smart corporal climbed onto a tank and put the crew out of action with his revolver, firing through an aperture. A lance-corporal was successful in putting a tank out of action with a hand grenade.[261]

"The Automatic Boiler," however, argued in vain. Popular consent had already confirmed the tank to be "*Deutsch's Tod*" — "The Death of Germany."

Having seen, two years earlier, the tank's dramatic effects on morale, why had the Germans failed to develop their own? Prematurely employed in small numbers by the British during the closing phases of the 1916 Somme blood bath, the tank had not proven decisive, but its promise had been obvious. Germany certainly possessed the industrial skills required to copy and improve upon the tank. Fuller has suggested that Germany's failure to develop the tank was based on the Prussian disdain for a war of materiel, and in evidence quoted OHL accounts of their great March offensive: "The use of 300 British tanks at Cambrai (1917) was a battle of materiel.... The German High Command decided, from the very outset, not to fight a battle of materiel."[262] Did OHL deliberately pursue a policy of "cannon-fodder" before "materiel"? Was this why OHL consistently maintained an order of battle totalling some 250 infantry divisions including many men of doubtful and even unfit quality? The Germans had been innovative enough to introduce poison gas warfare as early as April 1915. Was the real reason simply that OHL could not "lower itself" to adopting an invention of the bumbling British?

The far-reaching consequences of this German conviction that the tank was *Deutsch's Tod* can be seen in the years following the First World War. The German General Staff, despite the limitations imposed by the Treaty of Versailles, made the development of tanks one of their first priorities. The eventual results are evident in Hitler's early successes, attained, in large measure, by his mobile *panzer* divisions. The *panzers* were not employed according to the tactics of the Battle of Amiens, but according to the theories of Col. J.F.C. Fuller and Captain Liddell-Hart, two of Britain's most advanced military theorists.

Britain, on the other hand, ignored its own leading thinkers, and entered the Second World War equipped with primitive tanks employing 1918 tactics — with disastrous consequences. One reason for this blindness might be found in the British reaction to the Germans' rationale for their 1918 defeat — a rationale that denigrated the courage and fighting qualities of the victors. "Since the war the Germans, to save their self-esteem as soldiers, have attributed their defeat to the massed attack of tanks," the British Official History protested. "Actually the infantry with machine guns was the instrument of success; but its vital assistant was the artillery."[263] Thus the British — possibly overly sensitive concerning their own performance during those last months of 1918 — seem to have over-reacted to the German excuse by playing down the role of the tank in the victory.

One must not forget that armoured forces of two other types were used during the Battle of Amiens. On the Australian front the 17th Armoured Car Battalion had raced about the roads behind the enemy, shooting up his transport and bases, and harassing both fugitives and reinforcements. This practically unknown unit of sixteen vehicles had exerted a tremendous psychological influence on the enemy and probably caused more casualties than had the entire Cavalry Corps. When the war ended the 17th had in their six months of existence fought ten major battles and inflicted thousands of casualties upon the enemy at a cost to themselves of only five men killed and seven cars destroyed. This is not to say that the armoured car did not have its limitations; it was confined to roads, lacked fire-power, and was inadequately armoured. But despite these limitations the armoured cars had produced results far outweighing their negligible cost.

The second oddball "armoured" unit was the Canadian Independent Force. Brutinel's "armour" was supplied by the two Canadian Motor Machine Gun Brigades. Their lightly armoured, open-top trucks were simply a means of moving machine guns about in force. They did not rush behind the enemy lines, nor were they equipped for it, but they did provide a tremendous fire-power for French and Canadians alike along the Amiens-Roye Road where enemy resistance was most determined. This mixed force, which included cyclists and truck-mounted mortars, exerted a very real influence on the course of the battle over the next several days, unlike the armoured cars that had shot their bolt by evening of the first day. Their secondary task of ferrying infantry forward to the front line presaged the role of the modern Armoured Personnel Carrier.

The success of these two virtually unknown units in three different roles illustrates vividly the lack of innovative minds among the ranks of First World War generals. If such primitive machines could achieve so much at so little cost, what might have been the results if some of the effort in manpower, labour, and money squandered on the cavalry had been utilized to build larger and better-equipped motorized units? Although they proved more innovative than OHL, most Allied leaders failed to grasp the potential of the internal combustion engine, the machine gun, and armour. The 17th Armoured Car Battalion was not even formed until April of 1918, and was only "a concession to the enthusiasm of a handful of grimy-fingered experts."[264] The Motor Machine Guns, on the other hand, had been formed almost at the beginning of the war by eccentric Canadians. The batteries had been expanded into brigades and had been usefully employed by Currie, but despite their outstanding success during the enemy's March offensives and again at Amiens, they were not copied by any other army.

Most Allied generals, rather than grapple with the future, had looked to the past for the answer to the problem of mobility. They had retained their admiration for the poetry-in-motion beauty of the cavalry long after the machine gun had written *finis* to its chapter in history. The performance of the cavalry, after years of waiting in the wings for the right moment, was an utter flop. Despite the unquestioned courage of several units, its scant successes were gained during the first afternoon while the enemy was at the height of his confusion. It is indeed a tragic irony that when the moment for action came, a handful of armoured cars achieved more than the entire Cavalry Corps, two divisions jealously hoarded and maintained throughout four desperate years for the sole purpose of providing the knockout blow.

At first glance the air offensive fought during the Battle of Amiens appears to have been inconclusive. Unlike the ground operations, this breakdown of plans began at the word "Go." On the first morning the mist that proved so effective an ally to the infantry totally disrupted the RAF's operations. The intended opening move had been to bomb the enemy aerodromes and thus severely handicap his subsequent performance. Virtually nothing was achieved on the first morning, and the attempt was not repeated.

On the other hand, August 8 was one of the most successful days of the war for the ground support squadrons. Before the battle the pilots had for the first time been carefully briefed on the offensive and on the geography of the battlefield. This innovation became standard practice once the day's results were in. Contact-patrol work — keeping in touch with the leading infantry formations — were successful throughout the first day. Thereafter a scarcity of flares on the part of the infantry reduced the contact drastically. The Tank Support Force was successful up to a point although visual signalling between tank and plane proved a dead loss. The glaring need was for some form of defence against anti-tank guns, both by indicating their position and by putting them out of action from the air. There was no shortage of lessons for the future.

RAF casualties were heavy, with over 70 percent belonging to the squadrons attacking the Somme bridges. This was due to three factors. First, the Germans were able to reinforce their fighter strength from other sectors much faster than had been expected. The earliest of these new-comers arrived in time to attack the bombers on the first afternoon. A second factor was the location of the German aerodromes, often within sight of the Somme bridges. This meant that German planes could spend most of the day in the sky where the main air battles were taking place. Because the bombers had to come in low to have any chance of hitting their targets, it was unnecessary for the German fighters to gain altitude before engaging. In consequence, only a few minutes' warning was needed to get the German fighters airborne and in position to defend the bridges. The third factor in the equation was the decision to arm the RAF fighters with bombs. Because of this extra weight they suffered heavy losses and were unable to protect the bombers.

The question arises, "Was there any value in bombing the Somme bridges?" Certainly on the first day the enemy did appear to be in full retreat, and the opportunity to cut him off by destroying the bridges was tempting. But the gamble had already been lost by the failure that morning to destroy the German aerodromes. As for actually destroying the bridges, even in the best possible conditions it would require exceptional luck just to hit a bridge by dropping bombs at it, and only a direct hit on an unsupported stretch of bridge would inflict appreciable damage with the 112-pound bombs then in use. Between Bray and Pithon there were *fourteen* permanent bridges over the Somme. In addition there were numerous footbridges and temporary military bridges. Obviously, what at first glance appeared to be a golden opportunity was in fact an impossibility.

By the second day events on the ground showed that the pursuit was over. The air offensive had become a matter of preventing reinforcements from arriving rather than trapping fugitives. The location of nearly all the reinforcing divisions was well known to Allied intelligence, as was the route each had to follow. Nevertheless, the futile attempts to hit the bridges continued while enemy reinforcements poured in. It was not till the fourth day that the major bombing effort was shifted to the rail centres, where it was hoped to catch troops detraining. But the move came days too late. This reckless gamble to bomb the bridges had resulted in some of the heaviest RAF casualties of the war, but had produced no gain whatever.

Despite the total failure of bombing during the Battle of Amiens, its proponents somehow managed to justify the use of bombers against small targets. "Pin-point bombing" has been a mirage followed by air forces ever since — and with almost negligible results. Pin-point bombing successes from Amiens to Desert Storm have been few and far between. Only two jump readily to mind: the Japanese performance in sinking H.M.S. *Prince of Wales* and *Repulse* off Malaya in 1942, and the RAF's destruction of the Ruhr Dams using specially designed bombs in May, 1943. The few other bombing "successes" have tended to be of the propaganda variety involving "saturation bombing" rather than the ballyhooed "pin-point" accuracy.

Despite its obvious failure, the bridge-bombing campaign brought the Allies one unexpected benefit. The Germans were so alarmed by these attempts to cut off the Second Army that they resolved at all costs to prevent the destruction of the bridges. Abandoning their guerrilla tactic of fighting only when they held the advantage, German pilots on August 8 and thereafter threw themselves wholeheartedly into defending the bridges, showing a real contempt for death. They had, in fact, adopted the despised British air tactics at the worst possible moment. German air loses became catastrophic after August 8. Within days only eleven of the fifty gaudily coloured planes of the famous Flying Circus were left. Although Lothar von Richthofen scored two more victories on Monday, August 12, he was shot down the next day. He survived, but it was his last flight of the war. He was succeeded by Hermann Göring. The Flying Circus, *Jagdstaffeln* No. 1, which for two years had been the heart and the brain of the German Air Service, had been fought to destruction. It was withdrawn from action to be restocked with young pilots, but in the few weeks left to it, the Flying Circus failed to recover its glory, expended during the Battle of Amiens.

The fate of the Flying Circus became the norm for the German Air Service. The destruction started with their desperate attempt to save the Somme bridges — which in all probability could not have been destroyed in any event. The German Air Service suffered irrecoverable losses, and likely would have been totally destroyed had it not been for the timely arrival of a remarkable new engine. The Fokker D VII was soon re-equipped with the BMW, an engine of great technical superiority. "Without this magnificent weapon the tenacious and successful resistance offered in the final months of the war would have been impossible," wrote Göring's biographer.[265]

How did the Battle of Amiens affect the Allied soldier? The spectacular success of the first day certainly raised morale both in the front line and at home, but the failures that followed pointed to some glaring weaknesses. The Tank Corps, the Canadians, and the Australians had fought magnificently. But the tank force had been all but expended, and would never again be *the* vital factor. Of almost as great importance was the knowledge that the enemy had at last learned to deal with tanks by using their field artillery in an anti-tank role — a glimpse of what the future would hold. For the Canadians the Battle of Amiens was one of their costliest operations, yet their morale soared and they would spearhead every major British operation till the war ended. The Australians, on the other hand, had been tired when the battle began, and now they were exhausted. Within a month the first Australian battalion mutinied. The 59th Victorian Battalion, described by the enemy on August 8 as "very slow to advance,"[266] refused to go into the line twenty-five days later on September 2. This was the first of a series of mutinies that swept the Australian Corps that month. "Although almost the entire complement of seven battalions 'mutinied' in the strict sense of the term, no man was put to death," acknowledged an Australian historian.[267] Due to lack of enlistments at home and the earlier stretching of the corps to five divisions, the battalions had become seriously depleted, as had their famous spirit.

The fact that British and French troops had failed in many cases to show the initiative expected of them indicated serious morale problems as well. Although both Tommies and *poilus* recovered in later days and fought very well in some of the last battles of the war, Amiens showed how close they were to disintegration. The sight of hordes of beaten Germans willingly surrendering helped in part to restore the confidence that many had lost long ago. "Suddenly I was aware of a great weight being lifted from me," wrote the young artilleryman, P.J. Campbell years later.

> The nightmare was over, the nightmare that had begun in the spring and lasted all through the long mid-summer months. I had woken up from my evil dream.... This was the end. Not the end of fear or of danger, only the end of a

nightmare ... the fear of defeat, of disgrace, of running away, of failure. That was worse than the fear of death, that was what had unnerved me.... I knew that it was over. Whatever happened in the future I should never suffer the same fear again, I could feel that the weight had been lifted, I wanted to sing.[268]

The first day — "the black day of the German Army," in Ludendorff's famous expression — had been an incredible success with its eight-mile advance and huge disparity in casualties. The day had been marred only by the failure of III Corps to keep pace with the Australians and Canadians. This was in large measure due to the attack by the Wurttembergers on Tuesday, August 6. This attack had knocked III Corps' plans off schedule and had destroyed any possibility of surprise on the 8th. And it must be understood that, above all else, it was surprise that had made possible such stunning results.

Several years later General Sir Arthur Currie commented: "The success of the Australians and Canadians on August 8th was so startling ... that in my opinion G.H.Q. had no definite ideas what to do. The object of the Battle of Amiens was the old Amiens outer defence line.... I do not know how long Haig thought it would take us to reach that line, but I do know that neither he nor anyone else expected us to reach it as we did by night of August 8. I also know that senior staff officers hurried up from G.H.Q. to see me and to ask what I thought should be done. They indicated quite plainly that the success had gone far beyond expectations, and that no one seemed to know what to do. I replied in the Canadian vernacular: 'The going seems good: let's go on!'"[269]

But the "going" turned out to be poorer than expected. Why? There were many reasons for the apparent failure to follow through the stunning achievement of the first day. Rawlinson and every Allied leader feared the German counterattack that had inevitably followed any advance. In this natural expectation, generals and privates alike failed to appreciate the demoralized state of their foe on August 8. Consequently, regardless of the original instructions to push on, the advance halted on the Blue Line while defensive positions were prepared. No attempt was made to advance during the hours of darkness and no reconnaissance was made till next morning.

The first day was a classic "set-piece battle" with every stage carefully orchestrated, but there were no precise plans beyond the Blue Line. The fact that this line was reached before the first day was done meant a sudden switch to a war of movement — a type of war almost forgotten in four years of trench fighting. When the opportunity came to shift the offensive into high gear, it idled in neutral for hours before beginning once again in low gear. Supply and communications problems had become too much for armies relying on roads and telephones. During the battle only two commanders moved their headquarters forward to maintain close touch with their commands. Field Marshal Haig, his headquarters aboard a train, moved up behind the front on one occasion. Arthur Currie advanced the Canadian Corps Headquarters twice during the battle. In all other cases lines of communication were simply stretched further and thinner with each advance. Given these communications problems, the decision made by General Montgomery on the first night to countermand orders already being acted upon was the critical factor that shattered any chance of co-ordination in the days that followed. His withdrawal of the 32nd Division from Currie's command after the troops had begun their march forward upset the ever-so-fragile timetable for Friday's attack. From that point on, all attempts at co-ordination failed, and with them vanished any chance of attacking before dawn, the ideal time to assault. On each of the succeeding days, advances did not get under way till well after daybreak, or even late afternoon. This not only gave the Germans precious hours to reinforce and prepare their defences, but it insured that Allied preparations would take place in full view. The resulting delays prevented the Allies from pushing through the 1916 trench lines before the enemy could bring up reinforcements. German divisions, which would probably have been destroyed piecemeal on open ground, were able to step into readily defensible positions immediately upon their arrival. Pursuit consequently degenerated into slogging — trench-warfare bereft of the normal communications and artillery support.

Another factor which prevented the Allies from gaining a triumph unprecedented in the war was their failure to provide adequate reserves. In this, the Germans were much more successful. After the original thirteen divisions of the British Fourth Army had been engaged only three more were available from reserve. Von der Marwitz, on the other hand, was supplied with eighteen additional divisions. This resulted in some strange statistics when it is remembered that military theory dictates that the attacker should have a large preponderance in numbers. The Canadian Corps, for instance, employed only five divisions (including the 32nd Imperial) against a total of fifteen German divisions — and completely routed four of them. The Allies' lack of an accessible reserve also suggests how modest were the expectations of Foch and Haig.

Another reason for the failure of the last three days lies in the form of the attack itself. Frontal attacks tend to consolidate resistance unless the enemy is totally destroyed or unless a mobile force is rushed through to place itself in the enemy's rear. On August 8 both of these requirements had been achieved, but without any follow-up action being taken. The enemy was allowed to consolidate in the 1916 lines, and Allied mobile forces either failed to penetrate the gap, as in the case of the Cavalry Corps, or withdrew, as did the 17th Armoured Car (because of the nature of their tiny force). Of the tank force, a lone Whippet, Lieutenant Arnold's "Musical Box," took advantage of the situation to carry out the penetration envisioned by planners.

The Battle of Amiens had been planned with a limited objective in mind — freeing the Paris-Amiens railway. The initial shattering effect upon the enemy had not been anticipated by Allied commanders, many of whom did not recognize it until too late. Some, it is true, began to see possibilities only dreamed of before, and their goals became grander — and vaguer. But the local German commanders had already sized up the situation and were moving to plug the great hole. Allied commanders appear to have reached the peak of their confidence at the same time that the enemy had regained control of the situation. Beyond the Blue Line every Allied decision had been made *after* the situation had changed. In the case of the French, the time-lags between reality, understanding, and reaction were even more protracted. Although ultimately the Amiens offensive extended for a distance of thirty-five miles along the Western Front, its last three days were really only a series of unco-ordinated attacks by individual divisions, brigades, and even battalions. It will be recalled that day one, which had brought huge results had cost Fourth Army approximately 8,500 casualties and the French 2,000. At the end of three more days of cobbled-together operations the Fourth Army casualty toll had risen by another 13,000 while the French had increased theirs by over 22,000 — all for rather limited gains. "It is well to remember," Liddell Hart reminds us, "that the problem of maintaining continuity of advance was never solved in the First World War."[270]

CHAPTER FIFTEEN
The Natural Sequel

"August 8 was the climax of the war, and what happened subsequently was the natural sequel."
Liddell Hart [271]

Although the Battle of Amiens had ground to a halt on Sunday, the senior Allied commanders were determined to renew it. This dedication to "flogging a dead horse" seems incredible in the light of the facts. On the night of Sunday, August 11, the last day of the offensive, Sir Douglas Haig sent for his senior liaison officer after Foch had departed. He ordered this officer, accompanied by two others, to proceed to the forward areas to obtain opinions of general officers commanding whether or not the offensive should be continued. The task appears to have been only partially completed, and no record was kept to show who was consulted. There is, however, no evidence to show that either Currie or Monash were interviewed. On the officers' return, Haig asked anxiously, "Now then, tell me: what do they think?" The liaison officer replied, "In all cases the officers consulted are against the Amiens operations being continued."[272]

Nevertheless, Haig issued orders to resume the attack on August 15. Currie, for one, was emphatically against the operation, and on the morning of Tuesday, August 13, sent a well-reasoned appreciation to Rawlinson. He concluded with the suggestion, that the Canadian Corps be taken out of this line: that the supply of tanks be replenished: then let us go and make an attack somewhere else where I believe we can do equally well if not better than we did here.... I believe if we made an attack on the Third Army Front in the direction of Bapaume and in conjunction with an attack by the French from their present line, we could force the Boche to evacuate the position he holds on this side of the Somme without ever attacking them.[273]

Rawlinson visited Currie that afternoon, and the same evening advised Haig that the proposed attack would be "very costly." The French First Army had already requested a postponement of the attack to replenish ammunition, so Haig invited Rawlinson to visit him the next day, Wednesday, to discuss Currie's objections. "He was opposed to attempting it," wrote Sir Douglas in his diary. "I accordingly ordered the date of this attack to be postponed but preparations to be continued with vigour combined with wire-cutting and counter battery work."[274] Sir Douglas had not given up on the Battle of Amiens yet.

When Marshal Foch was duly informed he immediately wired Haig that he "saw no necessity for delay."[275] Now it was Sir Douglas's turn to oppose the attack he himself had ordered. "I much regret that I cannot alter my orders to the two armies in question," he wired back.

The two met that afternoon at Sarcus, and a heated exchange followed. According to Haig's diary, "I spoke to Foch quite straightly and let him understand that I was responsible to my government and fellow citizens for the handling of the British Forces. Foch's attitude at once changed, and he said all he wanted was merely information of my intentions in order that he might co-ordinate the operations of other armies."[276] Foch's determination may have been weakened earlier that day when General Debeney of the French First Army reported that the planned attack "would certainly be difficult" and would leave French forces too weak to retain the ground to be taken. The eventual outcome of all these protests was the cancellation of the proposed attack for August 17. The Battle of Amiens was now *officially* finished.

In the meantime there had been a series of local attacks, often bloody and savage, that resulted in several more Victoria Crosses. The Australians took Proyart and the remainder of the Etinehem peninsula. The Canucks, after fierce fighting, took Damery, Parvillers, La Chavatte, and Fransart, thus pushing beyond the 1916 German lines. Then on the night of August

19/20 the Canadian Corps began to move out of the Amiens front to an unknown destination. Six days later they were hurled like a spear through the Hindenburg Line in the Battle of Arras.

Haig had in the meantime received another memorandum from the Chief of the Imperial General Staff, Sir Henry Wilson. This memorandum, like the one received on July 25, dealt with preparations for "the final offensive ... after 1 July, 1919." But Haig had begun to change his own views about an offensive next year; he now sensed the possibility of victory this autumn. When Winston Churchill, the Minister of Munitions, visited him on August 21, only ten days after the Battle of Amiens, he promised Haig more tanks and large quantities of ammunition for next June. Sir Douglas replied, "We ought to do our utmost to get a decision this autumn. We are engaged in a 'wearing out battle', and we are outlasting and beating the enemy. If we allow the enemy a period of quiet, he will recover, and the 'wearing out' process must be recommenced." According to Haig's diary, Churchill then stated that the General Staff back in London "calculated that the decisive period of the war cannot arrive until next July."[277] In fact, the "decisive period" had already passed — ten days before, on August 8, 1918.

If Sir Douglas Haig had just begun to sense the decisive nature of the Battle of Amiens, his German counterpart, Ludendorff, had already accepted it as fact. Nevertheless, face-saving was in full swing. General von Wrisberg, speaking to the Reichstag, brushed off "the black day of the German Army" by saying, "The attack on August 8 between Avre and the Ancre was not unexpected by our leaders. When, nevertheless, the English succeeded in achieving a great success the reasons are to be sought in the massed employment of tanks and surprise under the protection of fog." The myth of invincible German soldiers and their wise leaders persisted. Tanks were responsible for the defeat. But Germans were told not to worry about this weapon in future. "We are adequately armed against them. Anti-tank defence is nowadays more a question of nerve than materiel."[278]

The German press accepted this official nonsense without question. The *Essen Allgemeine Zeitung* wrote that the disaster was merely a strategic withdrawal. "Thanks to our leaders and the bravery of our soldiers, all the enemy's plans have been frustrated and the Army Command now, as before, retains its freedom of action."[279]

AMIENS:
DAWN OF VICTORY

The defeat at Amiens had only a marginal effect upon the German in the street, due partially to the propaganda campaign launched to cover it, and due in part to his preoccupation with the food shortage. For the ordinary *feldgrau* the defeat also meant very little — there had been defeats in the past. Nothing had changed: Some units still stood firm — disciplined and steady to the end; others were less reliable; while some were on the verge of mutiny. But this had been the case *before* "the black day." The decisive impact of the Battle of Amiens had taken place in the minds and hearts of the German General Staff. August 8 had brutally thrust reality into the leaders' faces, and in their despair they had given up. There was no talk of a new "Hagen" with its promise of victory. There was no attempt to adopt any alternative strategy. Despite the urgings of General von Lossberg and others, Ludendorff and OHL refused to consider an evacuation of France — which might have saved the German Army, and would certainly have created a new climate for diplomacy to end the war.

The duo who had made themselves masters of Germany by pushing aside the Kaiser and his more moderate advisors now blamed the German people for the collapse which they visualized for the first time. Ludendorff lamented, "In Berlin they only felt their own impotence in face of the enemy's spirit; they lost the hope of victory, and drifted. The desire for peace became stronger than the will to fight for victory."[280] But, he stressed, this was not his fault. "There is no question that the terrible disappointments towards the end of the war had worn me out, but my nerves never gave way under the strain."[281]

The senior titan, von Hindenburg, wrote to his wife that it would not be his fault if Germany lost the war; "That fault would lie with the homeland which had not succeeded in imparting the necessary spiritual strength to the fighting front." Impending starvation was no excuse for Germans, Hindenburg declared.[282]

Despite these disclaimers, both of Germany's colossi had cracked and then crumbled. Ludendorff had cracked on July 18 when the French counterattack shattered his Marne offensive. August 8, "the black day," had seen him crumble. Hindenburg's spirit lasted a few days longer, partly because by nature he was less temperamental, and partly because he had been kept in the dark about the true severity of the disaster. Although Hindenburg was idolized by the people and trusted by the Kaiser and the government, the Field Marshal had in fact become a figurehead. Ludendorff had begun to treat the Chief of the General Staff much as he treated the Kaiser, allowing him no part in the day-to-day decisions.

Ludendorff convened a conference at Spa, Belgium, on August 13 —

ironically enough in the *Hôtel Britannique* — to drop his bombshell and blame the nation for a lack of "moral endurance." In attendance were the Chancellor, the Secretary of State, and Hindenburg, who "took a more optimistic view of the military situation than I did."[283] The next morning the Kaiser arrived to be told that Germany was no longer able to force the enemy to sue for peace. Therefore, admitted Ludendorff, "the termination of the war would have to be brought about by diplomacy."[284] The Secretary of State, von Hintze, was thereupon instructed to open peace negotiations, if possible, through the Queen of the Netherlands.

OHL had planned large-scale bombing operations employing incendiaries of a new design against London and Paris. This deliberate "frightfulness" was now abandoned — on "humanitarian grounds" according to the German government, but there is no doubt that fear of retribution after defeat was the mainspring of their decision. As it turned out, the "frightfulness" was only being postponed — twenty-three years, in the case of London, whose citizens were to endure almost constant terror-bombing throughout the Second World War.

In the years following the Great War, the legend was planted, nurtured, and grew to fruition, that Germany had not been defeated in the field. A proud and unbowed German Army had been betrayed, "stabbed in the back" — so the legend goes — by democratic politicians. This absolute nonsense was embraced with open arms by a German people who wished that it was true. All guilt was thus removed from the soldiers, the citizens, and their leaders, and placed on the heads of a handful of democrats who, in fact, had taken no part in the collapse, but had been given the thankless task of suing for peace. With this grand lie, the German General Staff saved itself, and in the process provided Adolf Hitler with a path to power, and mankind with an even more terrible war to follow.

Throughout the First World War, Allied commanders had, by and large, made sensible strategic plans — long-range projects with significant goals to be achieved. But they had attempted to carry out these schemes employing faulty tactics. Most, lacking the imagination to devise new methods, had doggedly wasted their men's lives by repeating the same futile tactics in attack after attack. Consequently, every Allied offensive had failed without achieving its strategic goal. Amiens had pointed some senior officers in new directions. But not all. In 1926, eight years after "The War to End War" had ended, Sir Douglas Haig, the accidental victor, showed what he had learned of modern warfare by writing:

I believe that the value of the horse and the opportunity of the horse in the future are likely to be as great as ever. Aeroplanes and tanks are only accessories to the men and the horse, and I feel sure that as time goes on you will find just as much use for the horse — the well-bred horse — as you have ever done in the past.[286]

The German High Command had proven to be more flexible and open to innovation. Their operations were often tactically brilliant; but even the most successful German offensives had been launched without obtainable strategic goals in mind. Therefore, despite winning many battles, the Germans too had failed to make strategic gains.

The Battle of Amiens was only a slight variation on this theme. By the time the battle took place, the British had learned from the enemy's offensives much that they should have learned earlier. As a result, the planning to the Blue Line was impeccable; the Allies had improved tactically. However, beyond the Blue Line Allied tactics broke down and once again they failed to achieve their strategic goal. This failure can be traced to three major tactical errors: (1) their choice of a battlefield in which success would force the enemy back into the formidable 1916 defences; (2) their reliance upon cavalry, particularly on such a battlefield; and (3) their failure to provide an adequate reserve to exploit the initial success.

The Germans also reacted typically. Although stunned by the blow, they moved quickly — almost automatically — to retrieve the tactical situation. But shock and a glimpse of reality destroyed their nebulous "strategic plans," and left them incapable of devising any practical new strategy. The true value of the Allies' flawed victory at Amiens was its shock effect upon the German military leaders, Hindenburg, and in particular, Ludendorff. Throughout the four years of bloody and indecisive warfare they had supervised the duo had declared that only total military victory could achieve Germany's aims. Isolated from their people's mundane world of starvation, death, and despair, the two titans had, like the Kaiser, escaped to their own "cloud cuckoo land" — one filled with dreams of victory. As recently as four weeks before the Battle of Amiens, Ludendorff had told von Hintze (who was now suing for peace), "I hope to make the enemy ready for peace with my next stroke." Now, less than a month later, in place of total victory, the titans had accepted crushing defeat.

The Great War dragged on for another thirteen weeks after "the black day." During that time Germany and her armed forces disintegrated to the point of collapse. The slaughter was prolonged by OHL's stubborn and unrealistic expectations. Ludendorff, for one, actually assumed that any diplomatic settlement must allow Germany to retain Belgium and parts of Russia. Thus the slaughter continued, while these failed messiahs sought a way of saving face. The cost of their naïve pride was ghastly. Throughout those last ninety-five days from Amiens till the Armistice, both sides suffered a fearful toll in dead and wounded. For example, "Foch's Pets," the Canadian Corps, was employed repeatedly as the spearhead of the Allied attacks — at Arras, the Canal du Nord, Cambrai, and Valenciennes. During those final weeks the Canadians suffered 42,628 casualties — almost 20 percent of their total for the entire four years of war. As at Amiens, they inflicted four times that number of casualties upon their enemy. It is cruelly ironic that for both sides the greatest suffering occurred *after* the decision to sue for peace had been made. At last, on November 11, 1918, the four-year nightmare ended. But the first rays of peace had already appeared at dawn that Thursday morning, August 8. The Battle of Amiens truly was the dawn of victory.

NOTES

1   Authors' emphasis.
2   Quoted by Brigadier-General Sir James E. Edmonds, *Military Operations France and Belgium 1918.* Vol. IV, *History of the Great War,* London, 1947, p. 13. [Hereinafter referred to as "*B.O.H.*" (British Official History).]
3   Major-General E.K.G. Sixsmith, *British Generalship in the Twentieth Century,* London, 1970, p. 141.
4   John Terraine, *To Win a War: 1918 The Year of Victory,* London, 1978, pp. 60-61.
5   *B.O.H.,* p. 13.
6   Robert Blake (ed.), *The Private Papers of Douglas Haig 1914-1919,* London, 1952, p. 316.
7   Blake, p. 156.
8   Major-General E.K.G. Sixsmith, *British Generalship in the Twentieth Century,* London, 1970, p. 141.
9   Peter Firkins, *The Australians in Nine Wars,* London, 1971, p. 145.
10 C.E.W. Bean, *The Official History of Australia in the War of 1914-1918,* vol. VI *The A.I.F. in France,* Sydney, 1942, p. 464. [Hereinafter referred to as "*O.H.A.*" (Official History of Australia).]
11 *O.H.A.* p. 470.
12 The assembly of the First American Army did not in fact occur until August 30, seventy-three days before the war ended.
13 *Report of the Ministry Overseas Military Forces of Canada 1918,* London, n.d., p. 129. [Hereinafter referred to as "R.o.M." (Report of the Ministry).]

14 All figures are taken from Colonel G.W.L. Nicholson's *Canadian Expeditionary Force 1914-1919, The Official History ot the Canadian Army in the First World War*, Ottawa, 1962, pp. 391-393. [Hereinafter referred to as "*C.E.F.*" (Canadian Expeditionary Force).]

15 *R.o.M.*, p. 132.

16 P.J. Campbell, *The Ebb and Flow of Battle*, London, 1977, p. 50-51.

17 *The Private Papers of Douglas Haig*, (p. 291) quotes figures for March 3, 1918, showing one British soldier per thousand in prison, with nine Australians per thousand, and 1.6 per thousand from the remainder of the Empire.

18 R.H. Mortam quoted by George A. Panichas (ed.), *Promise of Greatness*, New York, 1968, p. 210.

19 Blake, p. 319.

20 Blake, p. 290.

21 C.E. Montague, *Disenchantment*, London, 1940, p. 63.

22 Campbell, p. 32.

23 Campbell, p. 52.

24 Montague, p. 179.

25 Panichas, pp. 92-93.

26 Blake, p. 315.

27 H.A. Jones, *The War in the Air: The Official History of the War*, vol. VI, Oxford, 1937, p. 444.

28 Captain Cyril Falls, *The First World War*, Toronto, 1959, p. 371.

29 Captain B.H. Liddell Hart, *The Tanks: The History of the Royal Tank Regiment*, vol. I, New York, 1959, p. 545.

30 *R.o.M.*, p. 128.

31 John Swettenham, *McNaughton*, vol. I, Toronto, 1968, pp. 134-5.

32 Roland Hill quoted in *Canada in the Great World War*, Toronto, United Publishers, 1920, pp. 133-4.

33 From the Canadian Broadcasting Corporation's *Flanders Fields*, written and produced by J. Frank Willis and edited by Frank Lalor, Toronto, 1964, No. 14, p. 4. [Hereinafter referred to as "CBC".]

34 *O.H.A.*, p. 518.

35 *B.O.H.*, p. 22.

36 CBC, No. 14, p. 5.

37 CBC, No. 14, p. 6.

38 État-Major de l'Armée, Service Historique, *Les Armées Françaises dans la Grande Guerre*, Paris, 1922-1938, Tomme VII, vol. 1, p. 149. [Hereinafter referred to as "*F.O.H.*" (French Official History).]

39 R.H. Williams, *The Gallant Company*, Sydney, 1933, p. 209.

40 Williams, p. 211.
41 *O.H.A.*, p. 511.
42 *O.H.A.*, pp. 513-14.
43 War Diary, 4th C.M.R., August 4, 1918.
44 *O.H.A.*, p. 521.
45 *F.O.H.*, Tomme VII, vol. 1, p. 156.
46 Swettenham, p. 140.
47 H.M. Urquhart, *The History of the 16th Battalion*, Toronto, 1932, p. 267. [Hereinafter referred to as "16th Battalion".]
48 James H. Pedley, *Only This: A War In Retrospect*, Ottawa, 1927, p. 333.
49 Blake, p. 321.
50 *F.O.H.*, Tomme VII, vol. 1, p. 156.
51 Pedley, pp. 336-7.
52 Captain D.H. Hickey, *Rolling Into Action*, London, 1936, p. 221.
53 J.F.B. Livesay, *Canada's Hundred Days*, Toronto, 1919, pp. 22-23.
54 *O.H.A.*, p. 525.
55 *O.H.A.*, pp. 523-4.
56 Swettenham, p. 141.
57 Williams, p. 215.
58 Will R. Bird, *Ghosts Have Warm Hands*, Toronto, 1968, p. 141.
59 W.W. Murray, *The History of the 2nd Canadian Battalion*, Ottawa, 1947, p. 259.
60 Swettenham, p. 143.
61 Quoted in *O.H.A.* p. 528.
62 Bird, p. 142.
63 Falls, p. 374.
64 Correlli Barnett, *The Swordbearers: Supreme Command in the First World War*, New York, 1964, p. 342.
65 Barnett, p. 355.
66 Walter Goerlitz, *The German General Staff*, New York, 1952, p. 148.
67 Goerlitz, p. 181.
68 Barnett, p. 342.
69 Barnett, pp. 343-4.
70 Erich von Ludendorff, *My War Memories*, London, 1919, vol. 2, p. 674.
71 Barnett, p. 345. Mertz von Quirnheim continued as a member of various German staffs until 1944, when he was shot by firing squad for his part in the July 20 attempt to assassinate Adolf Hitler.

72 Virginia Cowles, *The Kaiser*, New York, 1963, p. 387.

73 Quoted by Cowles, p. 391.

74 Cowles, pp. 391-2.

75 Quoted from *Courier de l'Air* by Will Bird, *The Communication Trench*, Amherst, 1933, p. 292.

76 G.H. Lutz (ed.), *The Causes of the German Collapse in 1918*, (no city), 1969, pp. 180-1.

77 Lutz, p. 185.

78 Cowles, p. 391.

79 Lutz, p. 105.

80 Laurence Moyer, *Victory Must Be Ours*, New York, 1995, p. 270.

81 Moyer, p. 271.

82 Comrade Ledeboun speaking at the General Congress at the Workmen's and Soldier's Councils in Germany on 17 December, 1918. Quoted by Lutz, p. 23.

83 Lt. Col. Wetzell, quoted by Lutz, p. 23.

84 Lutz, p. 23.

85 Cowles, pp. 390-1.

86 *Times History of the War*, vol. XIX, p. 151.

87 Lutz, p. 140.

88 Quoted in *B.O.H.*, p. 140.

89 *O.H.A.*, p. 481.

90 Admiral von Müller quoted by Cowles, p. 390.

91 Quoted in *Times History of the War*, London, 1914-1920, vol. XIX, pp. 149-150.

92 J.F.C. Fuller, *Tanks in the Great War 1914-1918*, London, 1920, p. 241.

93 Orders issued to 7th Cavalry Division, 26 Sept., 1917, Quoted by Captain D.G. Browne, *The Tank in Action*, Edinburgh, 1920, p. 286.

94 Fuller, p. 263.

95 "Tank Corps Intelligence Summary" quoted by Browne, p. 291.

96 Ludendorff, vol. II, p. 321.

97 McWilliams & Steel, p. 141.

98 Barnett, pp. 346-7.

99 *B.O.H.*, p 38.

100 Monograph: "The Catastrophe of the 8th August 1918" (Oldenburg: Stalling.) pp. 19-20. This is one of the series of German official monographs on the War.

101 Quoted by Barnett, p. 347.

102 Quoted by Lutz, p. 21.

103 Quoted in *O.H.A.*, p. 482.

104 Dr. August Herkenrath, *History of the 247th R.I.R,* quoted in O.H.A., p. 483.

105 Quoted by Lutz, p. 127.

106 Lutz, p. 127.

107 Lutz, p.121.

108 *The Times History of the War,* vol XIX, pp. 138-9.

109 *O.H.A.*, p. 607.

110 *O.H.A.* p. 608.

111 Quoted in *O.H.A.*, pp. 511-12.

112 *O.H.A.*, p. 607.

113 *B.O.H.*, p. 37.

114 *O.H.A.* p. 527.

115 Erich Ludendorff, *My War Memories,* vol. iv, London, 1919, p. 679.

116 Quoted by Thoumin, p. 493.

117 This outburst was commented on by many observers, Allied and German alike, although the *Australian Official History* states that III Corps' guns north of the Somme bungled their timing and opened up at 4:19, one minute early.

118 Livesay, p. 26.

119 "Dodo Wood" was sometimes referred to as "Rifle Wood" although there was another "Rifle Wood" beyond the Green Line.

120 *16th Battalion,* pp. 271-2.

121 *16th Battalion,* p. 273.

122 *16th Battalion,* pp. 277-8.

123 John Bernard Croak enlisted as "Croak" although his birth certificate records the spelling as "Croke."

124 John Swettenham, *Valiant Men,* Toronto, 1971, p. 109.

125 CBC, #14, p. 9.

126 Bryan Cooper, *Tank Battles of World War I,* London, 1974, p. 71.

127 CBC, #14, p. 16.

128 *O.H.A.,* p. 541.

129 Thoumin, p. 494.

130 *O.H.A.,* pp. 530-1.

131 Thoumin, pp. 494-5.

132 *O.H.A.,* p. 540.

133 *O.H.A.,* p. 534.

134 *O.H.A.,* p. 534.

135 *O.H.A.,* pp. 535-6.

136 *O.H.A.,* p. 538.

137 *O.H.A.*, p. 539.

138 *O.H.A.*, pp. 546-7.

139 *B.O.H.*, p. 79.

140 Falls, p. 375.

141 The French did not refer to the beginning of the attack as "Zero Hour" but as "H Hour."

142 Panichas, p. 231.

143 CBC, #14, p. 11.

144 Campbell, pp. 98-9.

145 Bird, p. 144.

146 Lt.-Col. C. Beresford Topp, *The 42nd Battalion, C.E.F. Royal Highlanders of Canada*, Montreal, 1931, p. 213. [Hereinafter referred to as "*42nd Battalion.*"]

147 Col. W.W. Murray, *History of the 2nd Canadian Battalion*, Ottawa, 1947, pp. 262-3.

148 Pedley, pp. 348-351.

149 *O.H.A.*, p. 550.

150 Williams, pp. 219-20.

151 Thoumin, pp. 496-7.

152 Fuller, p. 231.

153 *O.H.A.*, p. 559.

154 *O.H.A.*, p. 560.

155 *O.H.A.*, p. 567.

156 Sexton's real name was M.V. Buckley. No explanation is given in *O.H.A.* for the use of the name "Sexton".

157 *O.H.A.*, p. 570.

158 *O.H.A.*, pp. 572-3.

159 *O.H.A.*, p. 567.

160 *B.O.H.*, p. 82.

161 Calder, Major D.G. Scott (ed.) "The History of the 28th (Northwest) Battalion, C.E.F. (October, 1914-June, 1919)," unpublished manuscript held by the Moose Jaw Public Library, p. 203.

162 *O.H.A.*, p. 606.

163 Livesay, p. 22.

164 Thoumin, p. 496.

165 *42nd Battalion*, p. 214.

166 Canadian sources refer to the third objective as "The Blue-Dotted Line" while Australian records describe it simply as "The Blue Line." We have used the latter designation.

167 Bird, p. 147.

168 Bird, p. 147.

169 Lt.-Col. C.S. Grafton, *The Canadian "Emma Gees"*, London, Ontario, 1938, pp. 147-8.

170 Cooper, p. 232.

171 Cooper, p. 233.

172 Cooper, pp. 233-4.

173 *O.H.A.*, pp. 585-6.

174 *O.H.A.*, p. 588.

175 *O.H.A.*, pp. 588-9.

176 *O.H.A.*, pp. 589-90.

177 *O.H.A.*, p. 593.

178 Quoted in Captain B.H. Liddell Hart's *The Tanks: The History of the Royal Tank Regiment*, vol. I, New York, Praeger, 1952, p. 183.

179 Ibid.

180 Livesay, p.28.

181 Jones, p. 441.

182 John Terraine, *Ordeal of Victory*, Philadelphia, 1963, p. 457.

183 Urquhart (*Currie*), p. 237.

184 Bird, p. 147.

185 Campbell, p. 101.

186 Williams, p. 222.

187 *C.E.F.* p. 410.

188 Commandant M Dialle., *La Bataille de Montdidier*, Paris, 1924. p. 102.

189 Because many units did not keep a daily casualty count, there are few accurate figures for Allied casualties on 8 August. The Australian casualty estimate is from the Bean's Official History (p. 600, fn). Cavalry and III Corps' estimates are by the *British Official History* (p. 84, fn.).

190 Swettenham, p. 145.

191 Montague, p. 198.

192 *B.O.H.*, p. 75.

193 Quoted in *B.O.H.*, p. 85.

194 *B.O.H.*, pp. 88-9.

195 *B.O.H.*, p. 89.

196 *B.O.H.*, p. 90.

197 Ludendorff, p. 331.

198 Quoted in *O.H.A.*, p. 614.

199 Quoted in *Times History of the War* vol. XIX, p. 162.

200 Cowles, p. 392.

201 Brown, pp. 358-9.

202 *O.H.A.*, p. 601.

203 Quoted by Barnett, p. 355.

204 *B.O.H.*, p. 114.

205 Pedley, p. 356.

206 H.C. Singer and A.A. Peebles, *History of the Thirty-First Battalion, C.E.F.* (no City), (no date), p. 363.

207 Captain S.G. Bennett, *The 4th Canadian Mounted Rifles 1914-1919*, Toronto, 1926, pp. 120-1.

208 *O.H.A.*, p. 621.

209 *O.H.A.*, p. 629.

210 *O.H.A.*, p. 634.

211 *O.H.A.*, p. 638.

212 F.L. Huidekoper, *The History of the 33rd Division A.E.F.* vol. ii, Springfield, 1921, p. 421.

213 Maj. Gen. Sir Archibald Montgomery, *The Story of the Fourth Army*, London, 1919. p. 56.

214 *B.O.H.*, p. 111 fn.

215 *B.O.H.*, p. 113.

216 *B.O.H.*, p. 115.

217 *B.O.H.*, p. 116.

218 Dialle, p. 197.

219 C.B. Purdom, (ed.) *Everyman at War*, London, 1930, pp. 362-3.

220 Jones, pp. 449-50.

221 *B.O.H.*, p. 118.

222 Barnett, p. 354.

223 *O.H.A.*, p. 642 fn.

224 *B.O.H.*, p. 93.

225 *O.H.A.*, p. 684.

226 Quoted in *B.O.H.*, p. 122.

227 *B.O.H.*, p. 122.

228 *O.H.A.*, p. 658.

229 James L. McWilliams and R. James Steel, *The Suicide Battalion*, Edmonton, 1978, p. 155.

230 *O.H.A.*, p. 666.

231 *History of the 21st Bavarian Infantry Regiment*, quoted in *O.H.A.*, p. 667.

232 *History of the 19th Bavarian Infantry Regiment*, quoted in *O.H.A.*, p. 667.

233 Bill Lambert DFC, *Combat Report*, 1975, pp. 232-5.

234 Quoted by Peter Kilduff, *The Red Baron Combat Wing*, London, 1997, pp. 229-30.

235 Hickey, p. 233.

236 Hickey, p. 235.

237 *O.H.A.*, p. 685.

238 Quoted in *O.H.A.*, p. 697.

239 Quoted in *O.H.A.*, p. 697.

240 Hickey, p. 238.

241 Hickey, pp. 239-40.

242 Hickey, p. 242.

243 Hickey, p.248.

244 Hickey, pp. 246-7.

245 *O.H.A.*, p. 691.

246 Hickey, p. 249.

247 Quoted in *O.H.A.*, p. 692. Not only had the time been reported incorrectly, but even the date had been recorded incorrectly as "the 9th-10th of August."

248 Terraine, p. 459.

249 *C.E.F.*, p. 417.

250 Quoted by *B.O.H.*, p. 139.

251 CBC, "Flanders' Fields" #14, p. 19.

252 Quoted in *B.O.H.*, p. 146.

253 Quoted in *O.H.A.*, p. 698.

254 CBC, p. 19.

255 This figure was in error. The true number of German divisions involved was twenty-two.

256 Barnett, p. 354.

257 Quoted in *B.O.H.*, p. 140.

258 Barnett, pp. 354-5.

259 Quoted in *B.O.H.*, p. 162.

260 Fuller, p. 240.

261 Quoted by Montgomery, p. 69.

262 Fuller, p. 236.

263 *B.O.H.*, pp. 156-7.

264 *O.H.A.* p. 616.

265 Jones, p. 445.

266 *O.H.A.*, p. 611.

267 Patsy Adam-Smith, *The Anzacs*, London, 1978, p. 38.

268 Campbell, pp. 102-3.

269 Urquhart, *Currie*, p. 237.

270 Liddell Hart, p. 549.

271 Liddell Hart, p. 549.

272 Urquhart, *Currie*, pp. 239-40.

273 Ibid.

274 Urquhart, *Currie*, p. 241.

275 Terraine, p. 450.

276 Urquhart, *Currie*, p. 242.

277 Blake, p. 324.

278 Fuller, p. 240.

279 *Times History of the War*, vol. xix, p. 150.

280 Ludendorff, vol. 1, p. 6.

281 Ludendorff, vol. 1, p. 27.

282 Walter Goerlitz, *History of the German General Staff*, New York, 1952, p. 197.

283 Ludendorff, vol. II, p. 335.

284 Ludendorff, vol. II, p. 334.

285 Brigadier Edmonds, the Official British Historian, in a conversation with Sir Basil Liddell-Hart, commented, "I have to write of Haig with my tongue in my cheek. One can't tell the truth. He really was above the — or rather, below the average in stupidity." Quoted by John Laffin, *British Butchers and Bunglers of World War One*, Godalming, 1998, p. 161.

286 Quoted by John Laffin, *British Butchers and Bunglers of World War One*, Godalming, 1998, p. 168.

ORDER OF BATTLE

Fourth Army
(General Sir Henry Rawlinson, GVCO, KCB, KCMG)
Battle of Amiens, August 8, 1918

III Corps
(L/General Sir R.H.K. Butler, KCMG, CB)

12th Division

35th Infantry Bde:
7th Battalion, Norfolk Regiment
9th Battalion, Essex Regiment
1/1st Battalion, Cambridgeshire Regiment

36th Infantry Bde:
9th Battalion, Royal Fusiliers
7th Battalion, Royal Sussex Regiment
5th Battalion, Royal Berkshire Regiment

37th Infantry Bde:
6th Battalion, The Queen's (Royal West Surrey Regiment)
6th Battalion, The Buffs (East Kent Regiment)
6th Battalion, The Queen's Own (Royal West Kent Regiment)

18th Division (M/Gen R.P. Lee, CB)

53rd Infantry Bde:
10th Battalion, Essex Regiment
8th Battalion, Royal Berkshire Regiment
7th Battalion, The Queen's Own (Royal West Kent Regiment)

54th Infantry Bde:
11th Battalion, Royal Fusiliers
2nd Battalion, Bedfordshire Regiment
6th Battalion, Northamptonshire Regiment

55th Infantry Bde:
7th Battalion, The Queen's (Royal West Surrey Regiment)
7th Battalion, The Buffs (East Kent Regiment)
8th Battalion, East Surrey Regiment.

47th Division (Territorial) (M/Gen Sir G.F. Gorringe, KCB, CMD, DSO)

140th Infantry Bde:
1/15th Battalion, London Regiment
1/17th Battalion, London Regiment
1/21st Battalion, London Regiment

141st Infantry Bde:
1/18th Battalion, London Regiment
1/19th Battalion, London Regiment
1/20th Battalion, London Regiment

142nd Infantry Bde:
1/22nd Battalion, London Regiment
1/23rd Battalion, London Regiment
1/24th Battalion, London Regiment

58th Division (Territorial) (M/Gen F.W. Ramsay, CMG, DSO)

173rd Infantry Bde:
2/2nd Battalion, London Regiment

3rd Battalion, London Regiment
2/4th Battalion, London Regiment

174th Infantry Bde:
6th Battalion, London Regiment
7th Battalion, London Regiment
8th Battalion, London Regiment

175th Infantry Bde:
9th Battalion, London Regiment
2/10th Battalion, London Regiment
12th Battalion, London Regiment

Attached American Division — 33rd (Illinois) (M/Gen George Bell)

65th Infantry Bde:
129th Regiment (3rd Illinois)
1st Battalion
2nd Battalion
3rd Battalion
130 Regiment (4th Illinois)
1st Battalion
2nd Battalion
3rd Battalion

66th Infantry Bde:
131st Regiment (1st Illinois)
1st Battalion
2nd Battalion
3rd Battalion
132nd Regiment (2nd Illinois)
1st Battalion
2nd Battalion
3rd Battalion

AMIENS:
DAWN OF VICTORY
Australian Corps
(L/Gen Sir J. Monash, KCB)

1st Australian Division (M/Gen T.W. Glasgow, CB, CMG, DSO)

1st Infantry Bde:
1st (New South Wales) Battalion
2nd (New South Wales) Battalion
3rd (New South Wales) Battalion
4th (New South Wales) Battalion

2nd Infantry Bde:
5th (Victoria) Battalion
6th (Victoria) Battalion
7th (Victoria) Battalion
8th (Victoria) Battalion

3rd Infantry Bde:
9th (Queensland) Battalion
10th (Southern Australia) Battalion
11th (Western Australia) Battalion
12th (Tasmania) Battalion

2nd Australian Division (M/Gen C. Rosenthal, CB, CMG, DSO)

5th Infantry Bde:
17th (New South Wales) Battalion
18th (New South Wales) Battalion
19th (New South Wales) Battalion
20th (New South Wales) Battalion

6th Infantry Bde:
21st (Victoria) Battalion
22nd (Victoria) Battalion
23rd (Victoria) Battalion
24th (Victoria) Battalion

7th Infantry Bde:
25th (Queensland) Battalion

26th (Queensland) Battalion
27th (Southern Australia) Battalion
28th (Western Australia) Battalion

3rd Australian Division (M/Gen J. Gellibrand, CB, DSO)

9th Infantry Bde:
33rd (New South Wales) Battalion
34th (New South Wales) Battalion
35th (New South Wales) Battalion
36th (New South Wales) Battalion

10th Infantry Bde:
37th (Victoria) Battalion
38th (Victoria) Battalion
39th (Victoria) Battalion
40th (Tasmania) Battalion

11th Infantry Bde:
41st (Queensland) Battalion
42nd (Queensland) Battalion
43rd (Southern Australia) Battalion
44th (Western Australia) Battalion

4th Australian Division (M/Gen E.G. Sinclair-Maclagan, CB, DSO)

4th Infantry Bde:
13th (New South Wales) Battalion
14th (Victoria) Battalion
15th (Queensland and Tasmania) Battalion
16th (Western Australia and Southern Australia) Battalion

12th Infantry Bde:
45th (New South Wales) Battalion
46th (Victoria) Battalion
48th (Southern Australia and Western Australia) Battalion

13th Infantry Bde:
49th (Queensland) Battalion
50th (Southern Australia) Battalion
51st (Western Australia) Battalion

5th Australian Division (M/Gen Sir J. Talbot-Hobbs, KCB, VD)

8th Infantry Bde:
29th (Victoria) Battalion
30th (New South Wales) Battalion
31st (Queensland and Victoria) Battalion
32nd (Southern Australia and Western Australia) Battalion

14th Infantry Bde:
53rd (New South Wales) Battalion
54th (New South Wales) Battalion
55th (New South Wales) Battalion
56th (New South Wales) Battalion

15th Infantry Bde:
57th (Victoria) Battalion
58th (Victoria) Battalion
59th (Victoria) Battalion
60th (Victoria) Battalion

Corps Cavalry
13th (Victoria) Regiment, Australian Light Horse

Attached British Division — 17th Division (M/Gen P.R. Robertson, CB, CMG)

50th Infantry Bde:
10th Battalion, Prince of Wales's Own (West Yorkshire Regiment)
7th Battalion, East Yorkshire Regiment
7th Battalion, Dorsetshire Regiment

51st Infantry Bde:
7th Battalion, Lincolnshire Regiment
7th Battalion, Border Regiment
10th Battalion, Sherwood Foresters

52nd Infantry Bde:
10th Battalion, Lancashire Fusiliers
9th Battalion, Duke of Wellington's Regiment
12th Battalion, Manchester Regiment

Canadian Corps
(L/Gen Sir A.W. Currie, KCB, KCMG)

1st Canadian Division (M/Gen A.C. Macdonell, CB, CMG, DSO)

1st Infantry Bde:
1st (Western Ontario) Battalion
2nd (Eastern Ontario) Battalion
3rd (Toronto Regiment) Battalion
4th (Central Ontario) Battalion

2nd Infantry Bde:
5th (Western Cavalry) Battalion
7th (1st British Columbia Regiment) Battalion
8th (90th Rifles) Battalion
10th (Canadians) Battalion

3rd Infantry Bde:
13th (Royal Highlanders of Canada) Battalion
14th (Royal Montreal Regiment) Battalion
15th (48th Highlanders of Canada) Battalion
16th (The Canadian Scottish) Battalion

2nd Canadian Division (M/Gen Sir H.E. Burstall, KCB)

4th Infantry Bde:
18th (Western Ontario) Battalion

19th (Central Ontario) Battalion
20th (Central Ontario) Battalion
21st (Eastern Ontario) Battalion.

5th Infantry Bde:
22nd (French Canadian) Battalion
24th (Victoria Rifles of Canada) Battalion
25th (Nova Scotia Rifles) Battalion
26th (New Brunswick) Battalion

6th Infantry Bde:
27th (City of Winnipeg) Battalion
28th (Northwest) Battalion
29th (Vancouver) Battalion
31st (Alberta) Battalion

3rd Canadian Division (M/Gen L.J. Lipsett, CMG, DSO)

7th Infantry Bde:
Princess Patricia's Canadian Light Infantry
The Royal Canadian Regiment
42nd (Royal Highlanders of Canada) Battalion
49th (Edmonton Regiment) Battalion

8th Infantry Bde:
1st Canadian Mounted Rifles
2nd Canadian Mounted Rifles
4th Canadian Mounted Rifles
5th Canadian Mounted Rifles
 (The above all dismounted and formed as infantry battalions)

9th Infantry Bde:
43rd (Cameron Highlanders of Canada) Battalion
52nd (New Ontario) Battalion
58th (Central Ontario) Battalion
116th (Ontario County) Battalion

4th Canadian Division (M/Gen Sir D. Watson, KCB, CMG)

10th Infantry Bde:
44th (New Brunswick) Battalion*
46th (South Saskatchewan) Battalion
47th (Western Ontario) Battalion
50th (Calgary) Battalion
*This unit was the 44th (Manitoba) Battalion until redesignated New Brunswick just prior to the Amiens Battle.

11th Infantry Bde:
54th (Central Ontario) Battalion
75th (Mississauga) Battalion
87th (Canadian Grenadier Guards) Battalion
102nd (Central Ontario) Battalion

12th Infantry Bde:
38th (Ottawa) Battalion
72nd (Seaforth Highlanders of Canada) Battalion
78th (Winnipeg Grenadiers) Battalion
85th (Nova Scotia Highlanders) Battalion

Corps Cavalry

Canadian Light Horse

Motorized Machine Guns

1st Canadian Motor Machine Gun Brigade (L/Col W. K. Walker, DSO, MC)
"A" and "B" Motor Machine Gun Batteries
Borden's Motor Machine Gun Battery
18th Canadian Machine Gun Company

2nd Canadian Motor Machine Gun Brigade (L/Col H. F. V. Meurling, DSO, MC)
Eaton Motor Machine Gun Battery
Yukon Motor Machine Gun Battery

17th Canadian Machine Gun Company
19th Canadian Machine Gun Company
(The above brigades made up part of the Canadian Independent
Force under the general command of B/Gen R. Brutinel, CMG,
DSO. The Canadian Corps Cyclist Battalion (Major A. E.
Humphrey, DSO) and two sections of heavy trench mortars
which could be fired from trucks formed the remainder of the
Canadian Independent Force.)

Attached British Division — 32nd Division (M/Gen T. S. Lambert, CB,
CMG)

14th Infantry Bde:
5/6 Battalion, Royal Scots
1st Battalion, Dorsetshire Regiment
15th Battalion, Highland Light Infantry

96th Infantry Bde:
15th Battalion, Lancashire Fusiliers
16th Battalion, Lancashire Fusiliers
2nd Battalion, Manchester Regiment

97th Infantry Bde:
1/5th Battalion, Border Regiment
2nd Battalion, King's Own Yorkshire Light Infantry
10th Battalion, Argyll and Southerland Highlanders

Canadian Cavalry Brigade (B/Gen R. Paterson, DSO) attached to British
3rd Cavalry Division, Cavalry Corps.

Royal Canadian Dragoons
Lord Strathcona's Horse
Fort Gary Horse
"A" and "B" Batteries, Royal Canadian Horse Artillery

ORDER OF BATTLE

Tank Corps

Attached to III Corps:

10th Tank Battalion

Attached to Australian Corps:

5th Tank Brigade (B/Gen A. Courage, DSO, MC)
2nd Tank Battalion
8th Tank Battalion
13th Tank Battalion
15th Tank Battalion
17th Armoured Car Battalion

Attached to Canadian Corps:

4th Tank Brigade (B/Gen E. B. Hankey, DSO)
1st Tank Battalion
4th Tank Battalion
5th Tank Battalion
14th Tank Battalion

Attached to Cavalry Corps

3rd Tank (Whippets) **Brigade** (B/Gen J. Hardress-Lloyd, DSO)
3rd Tank Battalion
6th Tank Battalion

GLOSSARY

A/	Acting
AAG	Assistant Adjutant-General
AA	Anti-Aircraft
AA & QMG	Assistant Adjutant and Quartermaster General
Adjt.	Adjutant
ADMS	Assistant Director of Medical Services
AEF	American Expeditionary Force
AG	Adjutant-General
AHQ	Army Headquarters
AIF	Australian Imperial Force
ANZAC	Australian and New Zealand Army Corp
Arty.	Artillery
ASC	Army Service Corps
Aux	Auxiliary
Bde	Brigade
BEF	British Expeditionary Force
BGGS	Brigadier-General, General Staff
BGS	Brigadier, General Staff
BM	Brigade Major
Bn	Battalion
B/Gen or Brig.Gen.	Brigadier-General
B.O.H	British Official History
BSM	Battery Sergeant-Major

Bty	Battery
CAMC	Canadian Army Medical Corps
Canuck	Canadian soldier
Capt.	Captain
CBSO	Counter Battery Staff Officer
CCS	Casualty Clearing Station
Cdn	Canadian
CE	Canadian Engineers
CEF	Canadian Expeditionary Force
CFA	Canadian Field Artillery
CGS	Chief of the General Staff
CIGS	Chief of the Imperial General Staff
C-in-C	Commander-in-Chief
CMGC	Canadian Machine Gun Corps
CMMG	Canadian Motor Machine Gun
CMR	Canadian Mounted Rifles
CO	Commanding Officer
Coal boxes	Large calibre German artillery shell
Col.	Colonel
Cpl.	Corporal
CRA	Commanding Royal Artillery
CRE	Commanding Royal Engineer
DA & QMG	Deputy Adjutant and Quartermaster General
DCM	Distinguished Conduct Medal
Digger	Australian soldier
Div.	Division
DMI	Director Military Intelligence
DMS	Director of Medical Services
Doughboy	American soldier
D.S.O	Companion of the Distinguished Service Order
Estaminet	(French) A small cafe
feldgrau	German soldier: after the colour of his uniform
FGH	Fort Garry Horse
FOH	French Official History
FOO	Forward Observation Officer
Gen.	General
GHQ	General Headquarters

GO	General Order
GOC	General Officer Commanding
GOH	German Official History
GS	General Service
GSO I, II, and III	General Staff Officer, Ist, 2nd or 3rd Grade
H.E.	High Explosive
How.	Howitzer (high angle artillery cannon)
HQ	Headquarters
Inf.	Infantry
L/Cpl.	Lance Corporal
Lewis gun	A light automatic rifle
Lieut. or Lt.	Lieutenant
L.of C.	Line (s) of Communication
L/Col or Lt.-Col.	Lieutenant-Colonel
L/Gen or Lt.-Gen.	Lieutenant-General
Maj.	Major
MC	Military Cross
MD	Military District
MG	Machine Gun
M/Gen or Maj.-Gen.	Major-General
MGGS	Major-General, General Staff
MGRA	Major-General, Royal Artillery
MiD	Mentioned in Despatches
Minnies	German mortar bombs (Minenwerfer)
MM	Military Medal
MMG	Motor Machine Gun
MO	Medical Officer
NCO	Non-Commissioned Officer
OC	Officer Commanding
OHA	Official History of Australia
OHL	Oberste Heeresteitung (German Supreme Command)
OP	Observation Post
OR	Other Ranks
poilu	French Soldier (hairy one)
P.O.W.	Prisoner of War
PPCLI	Princess Patricia's Canadian Light Infantry
Pte.	Private

RA	Royal Artillery
RAF	Royal Air Force
RCD	Royal Canadian Dragoons
RCE	Royal Canadian Engineers
RCHA	Royal Canadian Horse Artillery
RCR	The Royal Canadian Regiment
RE	Royal Engineers
Regt.	Regiment
RFA	Royal Field Artillery
RFC	Royal Flying Corps
R.H.A.	Royal Horse Artillery
RHC	Royal Highlanders of Canada
RIR	(German) Reserve Infantry Regiment
RNAS	Royal Naval Air Service
RQMS.	Regimental Quartermaster Sergeant
RSM	Regimental Sergeant-Major
Rum Jars	German mortar bomb: Because of its shape
Sgt.	Sergeant
Stokes Gun	A British trench mortar
Sqn.	Squadron
VC	Victoria Cross
WD	War Diary
Whizz-Bang	Projectile from the German 77 mm field gun
WO	War Office
YMCA	Young Men's Christian Association

BIBLIOGRAPHY

Adam-Smith, Patsy. *The Anzacs*. London: Hamish Hamilton, 1978.

Allen, E.P.S. ("The Adjutant"). *The 116th Battalion in France*. Toronto: E.P.S. Allen, 1921.

Before and During the War. Illustrated Michelin Guides to the Battlefields 1914–1918. Clermont-Ferrand: Michelin & Cie, 1919.

Banks, Arthur. *A Military Atlas of the First World War*. London: Purnell, 1975.

Barclay, Brigadier C.N. *Armistice 1918*. New York: A.S. Barnes & Co., 1969.

Barnett, Corelli. *The Swordbearers: Supreme Command in the First World War*. New York: William Morrow & Co., 1964.

Bean, C.E.W. *The Official History of Australia in the War of 1914–1918, vol. VI, The A.I.F. in France*. Sydney: Angus and Robertson Ltd., 1942.

Beattie, Kim. *48th Highlanders of Canada 1891–1928*. Toronto: 48th Highlanders of Canada, 1932.

Bennett, Captain S.G. *The 4th Canadian Mounted Rifles 1914–1919*. Toronto: Murray, 1926.

Bird, Will R. *Ghosts Have Warm Hands*. Toronto: Clarke, Irwin & Co., 1968.

Bird, Will R. *The Communication Trench*. Amherst: Bird, 1933.

Bird, Will R. *Thirteen Years After*. Toronto: The Maclean Publishing Co., 1932.

Blake, Robert (ed). *The Private Papers of Douglas Haig 1914–1919*. London: Eyre and Spottiswoode, 1952.

Browne, Captain D.G. *The Tank in Action*. Edinburgh: Wm. Blackwood & Sons, 1920.

BIBLIOGRAPHY

Calder, Major D.G. Scott (ed). "The History of the 28th (Northwest) Battalion, (October, 1914–June, 1919)." Unpublished manuscript held at the National Archives of Canada, n.d.

Campbell, P.J. *The Ebb and Flow of Battle.* London: Hamish Hamilton, 1977.

Canada in the Great World War, vol. V. Toronto: United Publishers of Canada, 1920.

Chaballe, Colonel Joseph. *Histoire du 22e Bataillon canadien-francais Tome 1 1914–1919.* Montreal: Les Editions Chantecler Ltee., 1952.

Cooper, Bryan. *Tank Battles of World War I.* London: Ian Allen Ltd., 1974.

Corrigall, Major D.J. *The Twentieth Canadian Battalion (Central Ontario Regiment) Canadian Expeditionary Force in the Great War 1914–1918.* Toronto: privately published, 1935.

Cowles, Virginia. *The Kaiser.* New York: Harper & Row, 1963.

Cowley, Robert. *1918: Gamble for Victory.* New York: Macmillan, 1964.

Dancocks, Daniel G. *Gallant Canadians: The Story of the Tenth Canadian Infantry Battalion 1914–1919.* Calgary: The Calgary Highlanders Regimental Funds Foundation, 1990.

Dancocks, Daniel G. *Sir Arthur Currie: A Biography.* Toronto: Methuen, 1985.

Dialle, Commandant M. *La Bataille de Montdidier.* Paris: Beger-Levrault, 1924.

Dupuy, Trevor. *The Military Lives of Hindenberg and Ludendorff.* New York: Franklin Watts, 1970.

Duthie, William Smith & Charles Lyons Foster (eds). *Letter from the Front,* 2 vols. Toronto: The Canadian Bank of Commerce, 1920.

Edmonds, Brigadier-General Sir James E. *Military Operations France and Belgium 1918, vol. IV. of The Great War.* London: H.M. Stationery Office, 1947.

Falls, Captain Cyril. *The First World War.* Longmans: 1960.

Fetherstonhaugh, R.G. *The 13th Battalion Royal Highlanders of Canada 1914–1919.* 13th Battalion Royal Highlanders of Canada, 1925.

Fetherstonhaugh, R.G. *The 24th Battalion C.E.F. Victoria Rifles of Canada 1914–1919.* Montreal: Gazette Printing Co., 1930.

Fetherstonhaugh, R.G. *The Royal Canadian Regiment 1883–1933.* Montreal: Gazette Printing Co. 1936.

Fetherstonhaugh, R.G. *The Royal Montreal Regiment 14th Battalion C.E.F. 1914–1919.* Montreal: The Royal Montreal Regiment, 1927.

Firkin, Peter. *The Australian in Nine Wars.* London: Pan, 1971.

Fitzsimons, Bernard (ed). *Tanks and Weapons of World War One.* New York: Beekman House, 1973.

Fonck, Captain Rene. *Ace of Aces.* (ed. S.M. Ulanoff. trans. M.H. Sabin & S.M. Ulanoff) New York: Ace Books, 1967.

Fuller, J.F.C. *Tanks in the Great War 1914–1918*. London: John Murray, 1920.

Fussell, Paul. *The Great War of Modern Memory*. New York: Oxford University Press, 1975.

Gammage, Bill. *The Broken Years: Australian Soldiers in the Great War*. Canberra: Australian National University Press, 1974.

Goerlitz, Walter. *History of the German General Staff*. (trans. Brian Battershaw) New York: Praeger, 1952.

Goodspeed, D.J. *Ludendorff — Genius of World War I*. Toronto: Macmillan of Canada, 1966.

Goodspeed, D.J. *Battle Royal: A History of the Royal Regiment of Canada 1862–1962*. Toronto: The Royal Regiment of Canada, 1962.

Gould, L.M. *From B.C. to Baisieux: Being the Narrative History of the 102nd Canadian Infantry Battalion*. Victoria, Thos. R. Cusack Presses, 1919.

Grafton, Lieutenant-Colonel C.S. *The Canadian "Emma Gees."* London, Ontario: The Canadian Machine Gun Corps Assn., 1938.

Gray, Edwin A. *The Killing Time: The German U-Boats 1914–1918*. London: Pan, 1972.

Hayes, Lieutenant-Colonel Joseph. *The Eiglity-Fifth in France and Flanders*. Halifax: Royal Print & Litho Ltd., 1920.

Hodder-Williams, Ralph. *Princess Patricia's Canadian Light Infantry 1914–1919*. 2 vols. London: Hodder & Stoughton, 1923.

Huidekoper, F.L. *The History of the 33rd Division A.E.F.* 3 vols. Springfield, Illinois: State Historical Library, 1921.

Johnson, Group Captain J.E. *Full Circle*. New York: Ballantyne, 1964.

Johnston, Lieutenant-Colonel Chalmers. *The 2nd Canadian Mounted Rifles in France and Flanders*. Vernon: The Vernon News Printing and Publishing Co., n.d.

Jones, H.A. *The War in the Air. The Official History of the War*, vol. VI. Oxford: Clarendon Press, 1937.

Kilduff, Peter. *The Red Baron Combat Wing*. London: Arms & Armour Press, 1997.

Lambert, Bill DFC. *Combat Report*. London: Corgi Books, 1975.

Le Panorama DE LA GUERRE 1914–1918, Tome VI. Paris: Societe D'editions et de Publication Librairie Jules Tallandier, N.D.

Les Armes francaises dans la Grande Guerre, Tome VII, vol. 1. Paris: Imprimerie National, 1923.

Liddell Hart, Captain B.H. *History of the First World War*. London: Cassell, 1970.

Liddell Hart, Captain B.H. *The Tanks: The History of the Royal Tank Regiment*. New York: Praeger, 1959.

Livesay, J.F.B. *Canada's Hundred Days*. Toronto: Thomas Allen, 1919.

Lucas, Sir Charles (ed). *The Empire at War*, vols. I & III. London: Oxford University Press, 1921.

Ludendorff, Erich von. *My War Memories*, 2 vols. London: Hutchinson & Co. 1919.

Lutz, R.H. (ed). *The Cause of the German Collapse in 1918*. Archon Books, 1969.

McEvoy, Bernard and Captain A.H. Finlay. *History of the 72nd Canadian Infantry Battalion Seaforth Highlanders of Canada*. Vancouver: Cowan & Brookhouse, 1932.

McGowan, S. Douglas, Harry Heckbert, and Byron OLeary. *New Brunswick's "Fighting 26th": A History of the 26th New Brunswick Battalion C.E.F. 1914–1919*. Saint John: Neptune Publishing Co., 1994.

McWilliams, James L. and R. James Steel. *The Suicide Battalion*. Edmonton: Hurtig Publishers, 1978.

Money Barnes, Major R. *The British Army of 1914*. London: Seely Service & Co., 1968.

Montague, C.E. *Disenchantment*. London: Evergreen Books, 1940.

Morton, Desmond. *When Your Number's Up*. Toronto: Random House, 1993.

Moyer, Lawrence. *Victory Must Be Ours*. Hippocrene Books: New York, 1995.

Murray, Colonel W. W. *The History of the 2nd Canadian Battalion*. Ottawa: The Historical Committee 2nd Battalion C.E.F., 1947.

Nicholson, Colonel G.W.L. *Canadian Expeditionary Force 1914–1919*. Ottawa: Queen's Printer, 1962.

Nicholson, Colonel G.W.L. *Gunners of Canada vol. 1*. Toronto: McClelland and Stewart Ltd., 1967.

Panichas, George A. (ed). *Promise of Greatness*. New York: John Day Co., 1968.

Pedley, James H. *Only This: A War Retrospect*. Ottawa: Graphic Publishers, 1927.

Purdon, C.B. (ed). *Everyman at War*. London: J.M. Dent, 1930.

Report of the Ministry Overseas Military Forces of Canada 1918. London: Ministry Overseas Military Forces of Canada, n.d.

Robertson, Sir William. *Soldiers and Statesmen 1914–1918*. 3 vols. London: Cassell, 1926.

Roy, Reginald H. *For Conspicuos Bravery*. Vancouver: University of British Columbia Press, 1977.

Russenholt, E.S. *Six Thousand Canadian Men*. Winnipeg: 44th Battalion Assn., 1932.

Seton, Sir Bruce and John Grant. *The Pipes of War*. Glasgow: Maclehose, Jackson & Co., 1920.

Singer, H.C. and A.A. Peebles. *History of the Thirty-First Battalion C.E.F.* Calgary: privately published, 1939.

Sixsmith, Major-General E.K.G. *British Generalship in the Twentieth*

Century. London: Arms and Armour Press, 1970.

Stacey, Colonel C.P. (ed). *Military History for Canadian Students*. Ottawa: Queen's Printer, 1960.

Steel, R. James and Captain John A. Gill. *The Battery: The History of the 10th (St. Catharines) Field Battery, Royal Canadian Artillery*. St.Catharines: 10th Field Battery Assn., 1996.

Stem, Sir Albert G. *Tanks 1914–1918: The Log Book of a Pioneer*. London: Hodder & Stoughton, 1919.

Swettenham, John. *McNaughton, vol.* 1. Toronto: The Ryerson Press, 1968.

Swettenham, John. *To Seize the Victory*. Toronto: The Ryerson Press, 1965.

Swinton, Major-General Sir Ernest (ed). *Twenty Years After*. 3 vols. London: George Newnes Ltd., n.d.

Terraine, John. *Ordeal of Victory*. Philadelphia: J.P. Lippincott Co., 1963.

Terraine, John. *To Win a War: 1918, The Year of Victory*. London: Sidgwick & Jackson, 1978.

The Royal Armoured Tank Museum. (5 booklets). Bovington: Royal Armoured Corps, 1964.

Tank Corps Honours and Awards 1916–1919. Birmingham: Midland Medals, 1982.

Thoumin, General Richard. *The First World War*. (trans. Martin Kieffer) New York: Putnam, 1964.

Times History of the War. 22 vols. London: The Times, 1914–1920.

Topp, C.B. *The 42nd Battalion C.E.F. Royal Highlanders of Canada*. Montreal: Gazette Printing Co., 193 1.

Urquhart, Hugh M. *The History of the 16th Battalion (The Canadian Scottish)*. Toronto: Macmillan, 1932.

Urquhart, Hugh M. *Arthur Currie*. Toronto: J.M. Dent & Sons, 1950.

Williams, Captain S.H. *Stand To Your Horses*. Winnipeg: privately published, 1961.

Williams, R.H. *The Gallant Company*. Sydney: Angus & Robertson, 1933.

Willis, J. Frank, Frank Lalor (ed.). *Flanders Fields*. Toronto: Canadian Broadcasting Corporation, 1964.

Wilson, C. Murray (ed). *Fighting Tanks*. London: Seeley Service & Co., 1929.

Wise, S.F. *Canadian Airmen and the First World War. The Official History of the Royal Canadian Air Force* vol. 1. (no city) University of Toronto Press/Department of National Defence, 1980.

INDEX

INDEX

INDEX

INDEX

AMIENS:
Dawn of Victory

FRENCH

GERMAN

ARMIES

First 21, 23, 35, 51, 59, 76, 135, 157, 158,
  178, 185, 197, 218, 224, 226, 228,
  234, 247, 249, 256, 257, 258, 2569
Third 50–1, 225, 234, 257
Tenth 82

CORPS

II Cavalry 219, 247
X 23, 218
IX 158, 178, 218
XI 23
XXXI 23, 134, 157, 185, 192, 197, 217–8
XXXV 23, 193, 219

DIVISIONS

15th Colonial 158
37th 48, 134, 158, 185
42nd 23, 76, 134–5, 157, 158, 178, 185,
  192, 193, 218
46th 219
66th 134, 158
74th 48
126th 193, 218, 249
133rd 219
153rd 134, 178, 185, 188
169th 219

INFANTRY REGIMENTS

94th Infantry 109, 135, 138, 163
332nd Infantry 163

MISCELLANEOUS FRENCH
FORMATIONS

French Air Service 38, 48, 186, 191, 221
International Force 109, 139

ARMIES

Second 100–1, 186, 225, 253, 256, 257,
  259
Eighteenth 51, 224, 257, 259

DIVISIONS

1st Reserve 163
4th Bavarian 135
5th Bavarian 212, 221, 251
13th 99, 100, 102, 127, 146–7, 198, 221
14th Bavarian 98
21st 221
26th Reserve 101, 199, 242
27th Wurttemberg 58, 98, 101, 133–4,
  242, 266
38th 248, 252
41st 98, 99, 102, 103, 127, 198, 221
43rd Reserve 96, 98, 133, 221, 258
54th Reserve 98
79th Reserve 221
82nd Reserve 221, 222
107th 98
108th 98, 128, 258
109th 95–6, 98, 103, 199, 258
117th 96, 98, 103, 104, 113, 125, 143,
  198, 199, 222
121st 248
192nd 98, 164
221st 248
225th 98, 198, 221
243rd 98, 199

FOOT ARTILLERY REGIMENTS

13th 152–3
15th 145
27th 145, 146
58th 128, 146–7
79th 148

INDEX

The Authors' Acknowledgements

The authors wish to express their sincere thanks to the many, many individuals who assisted in producing *Amiens: Dawn of Victory*. Because the work was spread over twenty-two years, it is almost certain that we will have omitted names which merit inclusion in our acknowledgements. For any such omissions, we offer our most sincere apologies.

In 1978 we began the work of assembling material from three sources: War Diaries and other official documents, published works, and interviews or correspondence with veterans of the battle. After many failures to bring the story of Amiens into print our manuscript lay gathering dust in various basements and crawlspaces until 1998 when we once more pulled out the fading original and reworked it again and again. In the intervening decades only the official documents remained as they were. Many new sources had been published which we were able to utilize. Unfortunately, the veterans themselves were no more, but their memories had been preserved, and at long last their voices will be heard in the publication of this history.

Official documents and published sources have been acknowledged in the Notes and in the Bibliography. However, special mention should be made of three exceptional sources without which it would have been impossible to reconstruct the Battle of Amiens:

C.E.W. Bean's *The Official History of Australia in the War of 1914–1918*.
Brigadier J.E. Edmonds' *History of the Great War, Military Operations in France and Belgium*, commonly known as "The British Official History."
Col. G.W.L. Nicholson's *Canadian Expeditionary Force, 1914–1919*.

Special thanks are due to the following: Mrs. Bertha I. Tuxford of Victoria, B.C., for kind permission to quote from the unpublished memoirs of George S. Tuxford; and Fred Hazell of Langley, B.C., for permission to include photographs from his unpublished collection.

Although no effort has been spared to ensure that the facts in these pages are correct in every detail, the responsibility for error is ours alone. Every effort has been made to credit accurately all sources used in this book, but we shall welcome any information that will enable us to correct any errors or omissions.

J. McW. & R.J.S.

Of course, especially to be thanked are the following veterans of the Australian Imperial Forces and the Canadian Expeditionary Force who responded to our pleas for assistance between 1978 and 1980.

Wilfred Bedford (34th Bn., AIF) Strathfield, New South Wales
Harry Brice (Canadian Engineers, CEF) Riverhurst, Saskatchewan
Charlie Brown (10th Bn., CEF) Victoria, British Columbia
George Brown (Canadian Light Horse, CEF) Regina, Saskatchewan
John Gane (31st Bn., AIF) Toowoomba, Queensland
Spencer Giffin (85th Bn., CEF) Isaac's Harbour, Nova Scotia
Charles Gooch (75th Bn., CEF) St. Catharines, Ontario
Art Goodmurphy (28th Bn., CEF) Regina, Saskatchewan
Bert Hart (8th Bn., CEF) Victoria, British Columbia
Richard Herrod (28th Bn., CEF) Moose Jaw, Saskatchewan
Frank Hessie (25th Bn., CEF) Yarnmouth, Nova Scotia
Charles "Bubbles" Hughes (13th Bn., CEF) Thorold, Ontario
Ed Hunter (1st CMR, CEF) Moose Jaw, Saskatchewan
Bill Inglis (50th Bn., CEF) Victoria, British Columbia
Stewart Inglis (25th Bn., CEF) Fonthill, Ontario
G.B. Key (49th Bn., CEF) Victoria, British Columbia
Robert Lewis (25th Bn., CEF) Yarmouth, Nova Scotia
Alex MacLennan MC & Bar (16th Bn., CEF) Victoria, British Columbia
Jerred I. Mansfield (3rd MG Bn., CEF) Tillsonburg, Ontario
John Mitchell (34th Bn., AIF) Capalaba, Queensland
Stewart Murphy (15th Bn., CEF) Fredericton, New Brunswick
Gad Neal (46th Bn., CEF) Victoria, British Columbia
Charles Oke (50th Bn., CEF) McCreary, Manitoba
Tom Peck (2nd CMR, CEF) Nanaimo, British Columbia
Bob Price (54th Bn., CEF) St. Catharines, Ontario
Donald Scott-Calder (Canadian Cavalry MG Sqdn., CEF) Regina, Saskatchewan
Harry Sheppard (11th Battery, CFA, CEF) St. Catharines, Ontario
Art Spencer (31st Bn., CEF) Magrath, Alberta
Sam Storer (14th Bn., AIF) Swan Hill, Victoria
C.S. Torns (1st CMR, CEF) Winnipeg, Manitoba
C.H. "Slim" Wilsone (48th Bn., CEF) Gainsborough, Saskatchewan